Best Bike Rides
Philadelphia

Help Us Keep This Guide Up to Date

Every effort has been made by the author and editors to make this guide as accurate and useful as possible. However, many things can change after a guide is published—roads are detoured, phone numbers change, facilities come under new management, etc.

We would love to hear from you concerning your experiences with this guide and how you feel it could be improved and kept up to date. While we may not be able to respond to all comments and suggestions, we'll take them to heart and we'll also make certain to share them with the author. Please send your comments and suggestions to the following address:

Globe Pequot Press
Reader Response/Editorial Department
P.O. Box 480
Guilford, CT 06437

Or you may e-mail us at:
editorial@GlobePequot.com

Thanks for your input, and happy riding!

BEST BIKE RIDES® SERIES

Best Bike Rides
Philadelphia

Great Recreational Rides in the Metro Area

TOM HAMMELL and MARK PLOEGSTRA

FALCON GUIDES

GUILFORD, CONNECTICUT
HELENA, MONTANA

AN IMPRINT OF GLOBE PEQUOT PRESS

FALCONGUIDES®

FalconGuides is an imprint of Globe Pequot Press.
Falcon, FalconGuides, Outfit Your Mind, and Best Bike Rides are registered trademarks of Morris Book Publishing, LLC.

Maps by Trailhead Graphics Inc. © Morris Book Publishing, LLC
Photos by the authors

Text design: Sheryl Kober
Layout: Mary Ballachino
Project editor: Ellen Urban

Library of Congress Cataloging-in-Publication Data

Hammell, Tom.
Best bike rides Philadelphia : great recreational rides in the metro area / Tom Hammell and Mark Ploegstra. — 1st ed.
p. cm. — (Best bike rides)
Includes index.
ISBN 978-0-7627-7759-4
1. Cycling—Pennsylvania—Philadelphia Metropolitan Area—Guidebooks.
2. Philadelphia Metropolitan Area (Pa.)—Guidebooks. I. Ploegstra, Mark. II. Title.
GV1045.5.P42H36 2012
796.6'40974811—dc23

2012019190

Printed in the United States of America

10 9 8 7 6 5 4 3 2 1

The author and Globe Pequot Press assume no liability for accidents happening to, or injuries sustained by, readers who engage in the activities described in this book.

Contents

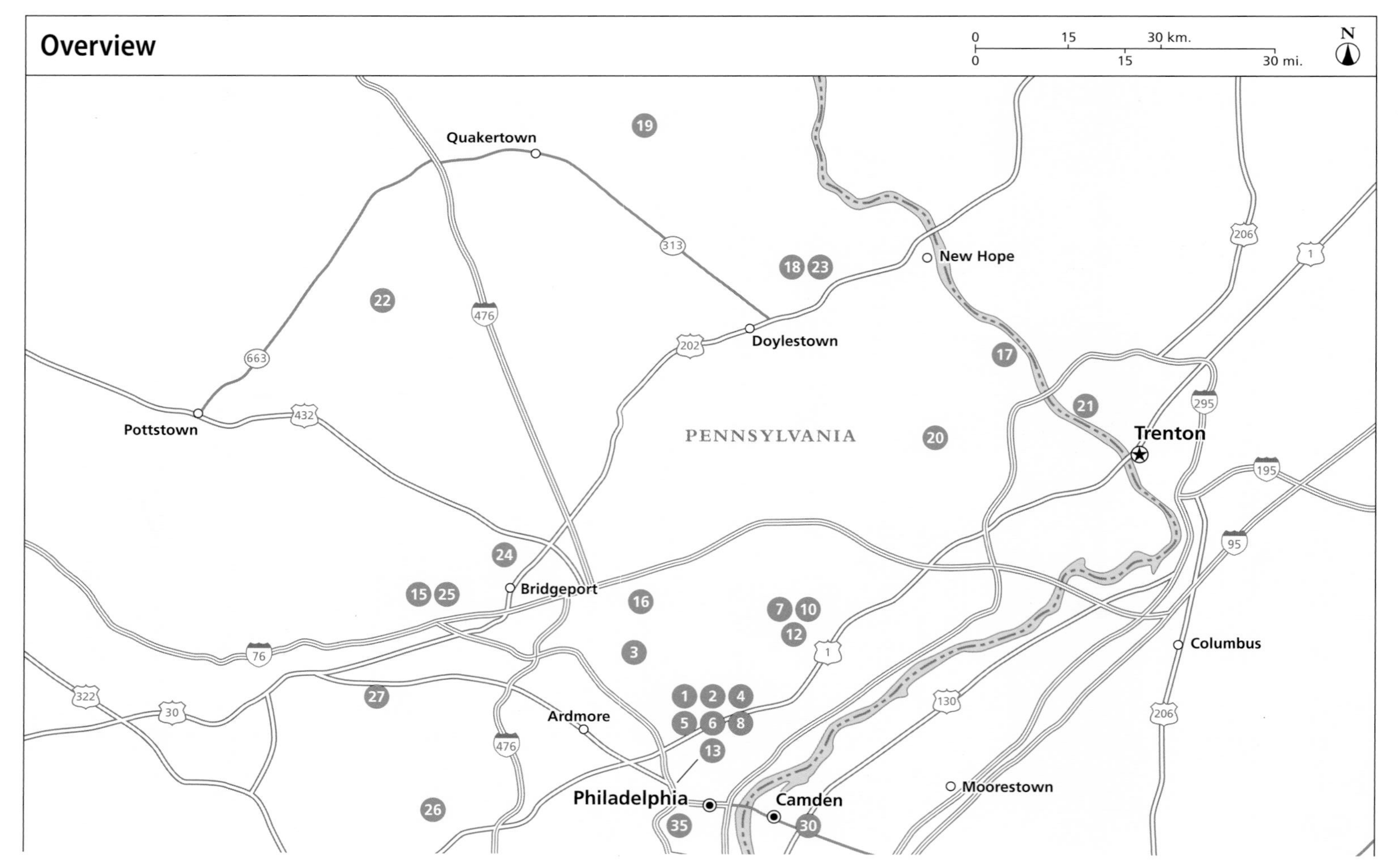
Overview
0
15
30 km.
0
15
30 mi.
N
Quakertown
Pottstown
New Hope
Doylestown
PENNSYLVANIA
Trenton
Bridgeport
Ardmore
Philadelphia
Camden
Moorestown
Columbus
476
313
663
432
202
206
1
295
195
95
76
322
30
130
19
22
18
23
17
21
20
24
15
25
16
3
7
10
12
1
2
4
5
6
8
13
27
26
35
30

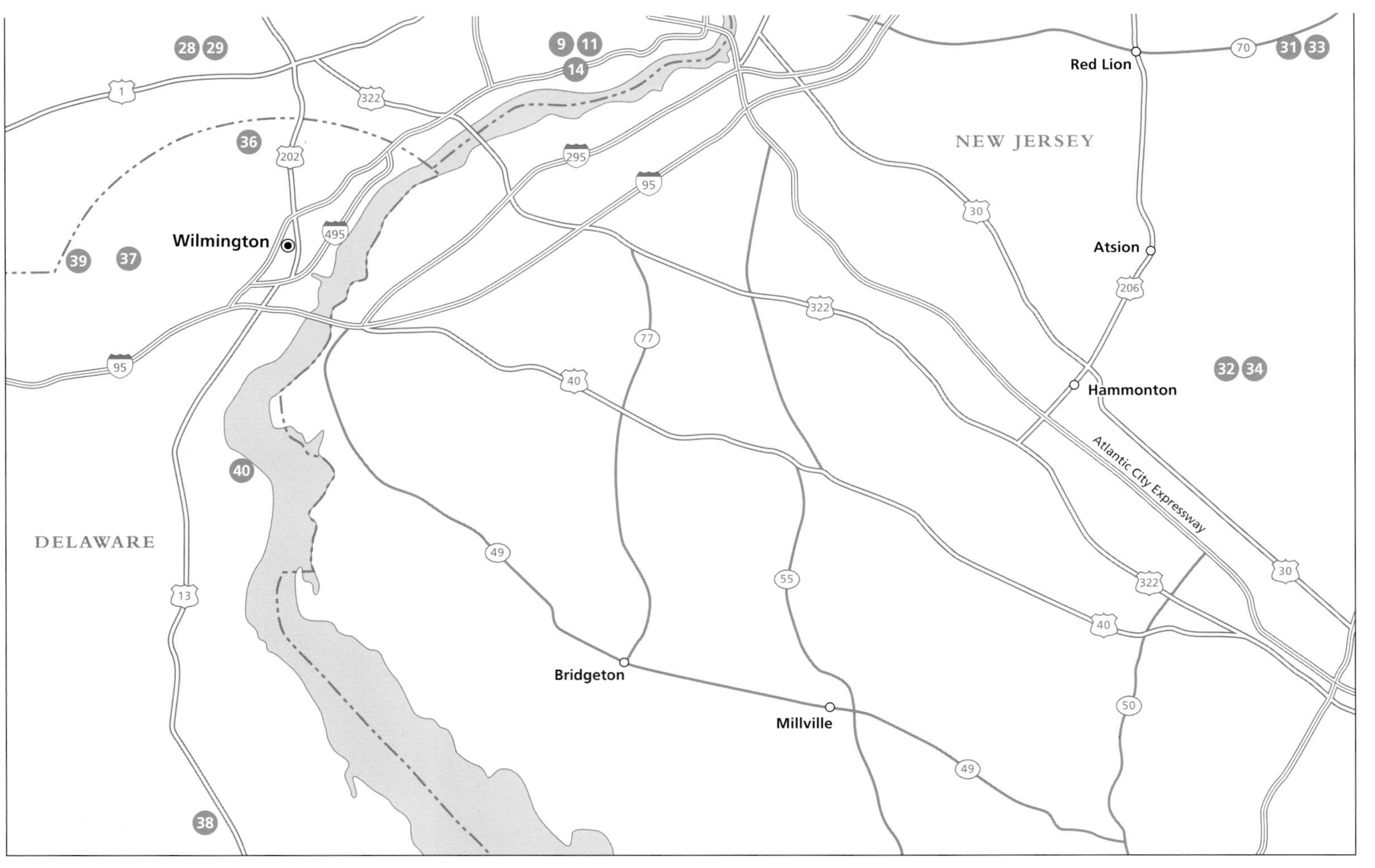
NEW JERSEY
DELAWARE
Red Lion
Atsion
Hammonton
Atlantic City Expressway
Wilmington
Bridgeton
Millville

Acknowledgments

Creating a book like this would be impossible without the support of many people who helped us along the way. Although it is impossible to thank everyone, we would like to acknowledge a few groups and people whose assistance made this book possible.

First we would like to thank the Bicycle Club of Philadelphia (BCP) for providing us invaluable information on roads to ride on, places to stop, and general knowledge of the city. Riding with BCP introduced us to a cross section of people who are passionate about biking Philadelphia, which was infectious and made our research fun.

We encountered many other fellow bikers in our travels who also gave us good advice about many of the routes. We don't know any of their names, but their companionship and support are some of the things that made biking a lot easier and enjoyable.

This book would also not be possible without the dedicated people at FalconGuides and Globe Pequot Press, who work hard to make the format and information in the book as clear and accurate as possible.

Tom would like to thank Laura, Cheryl, Jeff, and Chris for coming along on some of the rides and sometimes getting lost along the way. Tom would also like to thank Chris for teaching him the basics of mountain biking and showing him how much he has to learn (i.e., I'm still pretty bad at it). Lastly but most importantly Tom would like to thank his wife for allowing him the time to enjoy his passion for biking.

Mark would like to thank his mother and father for putting up with his hobby over the years, and Carl and Bud for being good sports when they came along on the rides.

One of the many beautiful murals you will see riding around the city

Introduction

Our country was founded in Philadelphia, a city with a rich and diverse history that gives it a special character. Philadelphia is the home of the cheesesteak, the Liberty Bell, and the Mummers, but it is much more than the sum of these things. The city is an interesting mix of a big city and a working-class town.

In one way Philadelphia has the feel of a big city with its vibrant business center, world-class museums, major league sports teams, great restaurants, and plenty of entertainment. In another way it feels like a city of neighborhoods like Manayunk, University City, Germantown, and many others. Each of these neighborhoods has a different character and its own unique history. To get to really know Philadelphia, you have to spend some time in its different neighborhoods.

Philadelphia is the city of brotherly love, which may be why people call each other "bro." It is one of the things that are distinctly "Philly." Oh yeah, that's right, the city has a nickname. Most people from Philadelphia call it Philly like it's their friend.

Hidden in and around this city are some great roads, trails, and bike paths that would take years to fully explore. Just behind the Art Museum is the Schuylkill River Trail. You can use this paved trail to take a quick 8-mile ride up one side and down the other of the Schuylkill River or follow it all the way out to Valley Forge. If you want to do some mountain biking, Wissahickon and Pennypack Parks are only a few miles from Center City. The city itself is very accessible by bike. A lot of streets like Spring Garden, Spruce, and Pine Streets have dedicated bike lanes; a number of other streets without bike lanes are very rideable. This makes it relatively easy to get around the city by bike.

If you are willing to head a little outside the city, you can find even more great places to ride. Head north or west and you will discover places like Fort Washington, Skippack, Doylestown, and Washington Crossing. In this area there are plenty of parks, quiet roads, and historic towns to explore. Head east into New Jersey and you will encounter the mysterious Pine Barrens with numerous trails, empty roads, and some interesting legends. Head south and you will be in the Brandywine area, where beautiful Longwood Gardens is located. Keep going a little farther and you will cross into Delaware and be surprised at the variety of rural roads and nice trails this small state has to offer.

All this endless variety makes biking in and near Philadelphia a lot of fun. The truth is that no matter what type of riding you like to do, this is an area that you can explore for a lifetime and never get bored.

About This Book

This book is for people looking to explore the area in and around Philadelphia by mountain, hybrid, or road bike. Most of the rides in the book are between 10 and 30 miles, although there are some rides that are a little shorter or longer. The rides were designed this way to cater to people who want to do more than a couple miles but aren't looking to take the time and effort to do 50 or 60 miles. A number of the rides, however, are close together so those who want to do longer rides can combine or modify rides to create new or longer routes.

All the rides in the book are appropriate for anyone who is healthy and has done some riding. Each ride includes a description of the length and terrain that will give you an idea of the difficulty of the ride. Before attempting longer and more difficult rides, it is a good idea to get some training under your belt by doing some of the shorter and easier rides.

This book also contains some brief words on bike safety, bike handling, and a list of resources for bike maps, bike clubs, and other things that will help you explore and enjoy bicycling around Philadelphia. Lastly, you'll find a small section on how to go beyond the rides in this book to further explore on your own.

ORGANIZATION

The bike rides in this book are grouped into four geographic areas:

- Center City—rides that are in or very close to the city itself
- Montgomery and Bucks Counties—rides that are in Montgomery and Bucks Counties that are mostly north of the city
- Delaware and Chester Counties—rides that are in Delaware and Chester Counties that are west or south of the city
- South Jersey and Delaware—close rides that are in South Jersey and Delaware

This grouping lets you choose a ride by the area you want to explore. Rides in the Center City section tend to be a little more urban and crowded. These rides are in or near the city center so the roads, paths, and trails will have more people on them and may require some urban riding skills. Rides outside of Philadelphia or in New Jersey or Delaware will tend to be on more rural parks or roads and will be less crowded, although parts of these rides may go through small city centers that may be a little crowded.

Turtle Rock Lighthouse

RIDE FORMAT

All the rides have the same format and information. Each ride has a number and name and a brief summary. Following that is a section that provides more details about the ride, including:

- Start: The location where the ride begins
- Length: The length in miles of the ride, including the type of ride (loop, out and back, or one way)
- Approximate riding time: An estimate of the time it will take to do the ride, including stops
- Best bike: Suggestions for the type of bike best suited to the ride's terrain

Virtual Rides

If you really want to prepare for the ride and make sure you don't get lost, you can do a quick virtual bike ride to check out the route. Go to Google Maps (maps.google.com) and type in the city and state where the ride is starting. You will be presented with a map of the area. If you click on the "Satellite" button on the map, you will see a satellite view of the area with the roads overlaid on the map. You can zoom in or out and move the map to view the roads of the ride. You can also use the street view to get an actual street-level view of a road that you may be riding on. This is a great feature that makes it easy to decide whether it is a good idea to ride a bike on a certain road.

The satellite and street-view images available for the area in and around Philadelphia are quite detailed, and you can really get a good idea of the type of roads you will be riding on. Sometimes you can even tell whether the road has a shoulder. The satellite and street-view images may be a few years old, so they don't show the current conditions. But since most roads don't change that often, the images are usually pretty accurate. The one thing that is hard to tell from the satellite view is the type of terrain and how hard a particular climb is. Other than that, the Google Map is the next best thing to doing the ride.

- Terrain and trail surface; The type of terrain you will encounter on the ride (flat, hilly, etc.) as well as the trail surface (paved, gravel, single track, etc.)
- Traffic and hazards: A description of the type of traffic, both car and pedestrian, you will encounter as well as any other things to look out for along the way
- Things to see: A list of some of the things you will see during the ride
- Getting there: A set of directions that will get you to the starting point

Then comes a detailed description of the ride, along with some of the things you will see along the way.

The next section, Miles and Directions, is a step-by-step description of the ride with mileage. And the last section, Ride Information, includes local attractions, restroom locations, and references to maps of the area.

Each ride is accompanied by a map of the route that shows an overview of the roads of the ride and the surrounding area. The route is clearly marked on the map, including symbols to mark the start and end of the ride and the miles at each turn. (See the map legend for a complete list of the symbols used.)

Some of the routes will contain alternate starting points that will let you turn a long ride into a shorter one or take the easy way around some tough hills.

PREPARING FOR A RIDE

The write-up for each ride should give you enough information to complete each ride as long as you take some time to prepare. If you are familiar with the area of the ride, then the Miles and Directions section should be all that you need to follow the route.

If you are unfamiliar with the area of the ride, you should spend some more time preparing for the ride. The map that is shown for each ride is a complete map of the route. This map is not a full street map but does show most of the major roads and should provide enough information to give you some points of reference.

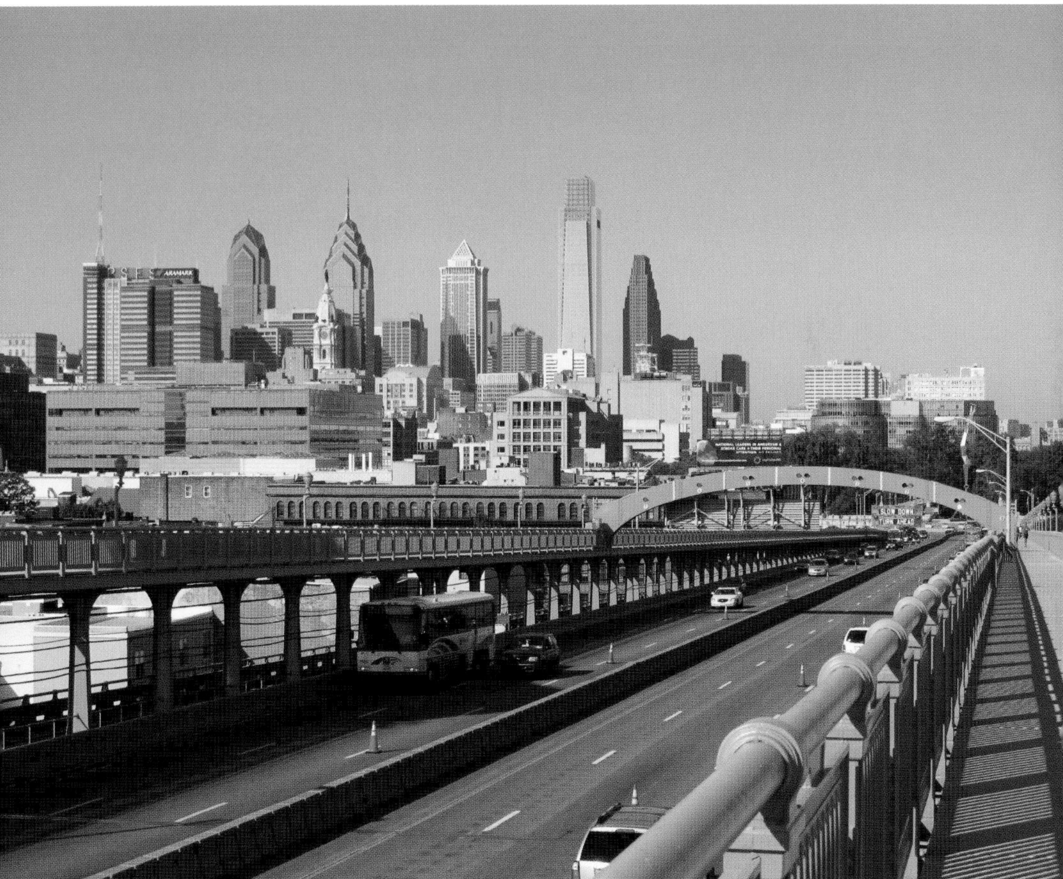

The city skyline from the bike path on the Ben Franklin Bridge

Bike rides always looks different when you're actually riding the route. Two-dimensional maps cannot fully communicate the actual bike route, so if you are riding in an area that you are not familiar with, it's a good idea to bring along other more detailed maps in case you get lost. A Hagstroms County Map is a good choice.

The route directions contain mileage for each turn on the ride. Although the actual miles you have on your bike computer may be slightly higher or lower, you should be able to use the route map and route directions to know when you have missed a turn. If you miss a turn, the best way to get back to the route is to backtrack until you find the missed turn or a previous turn. Of course, getting lost can be half the fun.

The key to having a good ride is to know the route and your abilities. Taking the time to study the route directions and map will make it much easier to follow the route when you do the ride. We recommend having the ride directions clipped on to the handle bars so you can easily get the information about the next turn. Some of the turns are bunched together and come up quickly so it's good to know the distance for the next two or three turns so you don't ride by them. You should also keep any maps in an easy to reach place in case you get lost or need to make a detour.

If you know your abilities on the bike, you will know the distance, terrain, and speed that you can handle and never do a ride that you will regret.

The important thing is to ride safely and have fun.

RIDE TERMS

In The Ride and Miles and Directions sections, we have tried to be consistent with the terms to describe the turns, roads, and traffic conditions. Below is a description of these terms.

- For turns besides the usual turn left or right, bear left or right, you will sometimes see acute or hard left or right to indicate that the turn is greater than 90 degrees. Turns will also be marked quick left or right to indicate that this turn is very close (usually within a quarter mile) of the last turn.
- For traffic the words light, moderate, and heavy or busy are used to describe the traffic conditions. Light traffic means that on the average you will encounter a car every 2 to 5 minutes. Moderate traffic means that you will encounter a car every minute or two, and there may be small periods of time when there will be a constant flow of cars. Heavy traffic means there will be a constant flow of cars. These estimates are subjective and can change over time as certain areas become more populated. It is good to be constantly on the lookout for traffic, even on roads that have almost no traffic.

The Rides

GETTING TO THE RIDES

If you are a resident of Philadelphia, then getting to the ride can just be a matter of stepping out the door and riding to the starting point. If you live in the outlying suburbs or the starting point is too far to ride to, then you either have to drive or take mass transit. SEPTA, Philadelphia's mass transit system, is very bike friendly and allows bicycles on its trains and buses except during morning and evening rush hours.

The following mass transit agencies serve the Greater Philadelphia area: SEPTA (Southeastern Pennsylvania Transportation Authority), septa.org; PATCO (Port Authority Transit Corporation), ridepatco.org; and NJ Transit, njtransit .com. You can find the bicycle policies for each agency by searching for "bicycle" on its website. Folding bicycles are allowed on all transit at all times, provided that the bicycle is folded.

Regional and Light Rail

- Non-folding bicycles are allowed on the NJ Transit River Line and Atlantic City Line at all times. Otherwise, plan not to use rail services during weekday rush times.
- Bring elastic bungee cords with you so that you can tie down your bike if necessary. Elastic cords with ball ends work the best.
- Generally speaking, most people board the train in the middle, so the ends of the train have the most room for bicycles.
- NJ Transit River Line cars are equipped with hanging racks. For other rail services, you might be directed to board at a wheelchair-accessible entrance and store the bike in a wheelchair-accessible space on the train.
- NJ Transit Atlantic City Line is the only transit line in the Philadelphia area that is equipped with restrooms, and most train stations are just platforms without any restrooms. If possible, take care of business before arriving at the station.

Buses and Trolleys

- Non-folding bicycles cannot be brought onto any bus or trolley.
- Buses are generally equipped with bike racks, which can be used at all times. You might be required to remove accessories from the bike before loading the bike into the rack.

One of the many bike lanes in the city

Driving into Philadelphia has the normal hassles associated with most major cities, traffic and parking. Traffic usually isn't too bad as long as you are not traveling at rush hour. You should also check the local news for any events in the city that may close roads so you can take alternate routes.

Parking in Philadelphia is actually easier than a lot of other big cities. There are of course a number of parking garages around the city, but there is also a lot of free parking to be had. Your best places to park for free are the parking lot behind the Art Museum (two-hour limit) or Sedgely Road in Fairmount Park, which has plenty of free parking along the road. There are also a number of other parking lots and street parking in other parts of Fairmount Park.

WHAT TO BRING WITH YOU

Taking a few things with you on your ride will help you take care of any problems along the way. To take care of most mechanical problems you may have on your ride, you should carry a spare tube, tire levers, and bike pump as well as a multitool that fits all the screws and nuts on the bike. Water and food are good to have with you especially if you are going to be in rural areas without a lot of stores. Last, it's also always good to have a couple of small antibacterial wipes and adhesive bandages with you in case you fall. If all else fails, you should have a cell phone to call for help.

YOUR MILEAGE WILL VARY

Every effort has been made to make the mileage for the rides as accurate as possible. The distance between each turn should be accurate to better than a tenth of a mile, and the overall ride distance should be within 1 percent. The mileage that you will see on your bicycle computer will most likely be a little higher or lower. This is caused by a couple of factors.

First, most bicycle computers are not as well calibrated as a car's odometer. To calibrate the odometer on your bicycle computer, you have to accurately measure the circumference of the front wheel to a millimeter or small fraction of an inch and enter this number into the bicycle computer. If this number is off just a little bit, it can make a big difference in how accurate the odometer is. For example, say that your calibration of your odometer is off by just 0.5 percent. This means that each mile you ride you will be off by 0.05 mile. This may not sound like a lot, but after 10 miles your odometer will be off by 0.5 mile, by 20 miles off by a mile, and by 40 miles off by 2 miles.

The other main factor that contributes to your mileage being off is that you will probably not do the ride exactly as it is mapped out. You may reset your odometer in the parking lot before the mileage for the ride starts. You may have to turn around to get a dropped water bottle. At the rest stops you may walk or ride your bike a tenth of a mile or so. If you miss a turn, you have to double back. All these little things add a tenth of a mile here or there and before long you are a mile or two off.

As long as you understand the difference between the mileage you see on your bicycle computer and the mileage in the Miles and Directions section, you should have no problem using it, along with the road signs and landmarks described in the ride description, to find your way along the route without getting lost.

GOING BEYOND THE RIDES

The rides in this book have been designed to help show you the best places to ride in and around Philadelphia, but there are many more rides to be found. Some rides in this book are close to or partially overlap another ride. If you are interested in longer rides, you should be able to combine short rides to make longer ones or combine pieces of two or three rides to make a new ride.

To go beyond the rides in this book, you are going to need to do some exploring on your own, which can be a lot of fun.

Using Google Maps, MapMyRide.com, or some of the other resources listed in the back of the book, you can find new trails and roads to ride. To create a new ride, you should have some kind of goal in mind, like exploring the covered bridges in Bucks County. Once you have a goal, you can search for the roads and trails to help you create a ride that will meet your goal. While you are planning your ride, you should be able to answer the following questions.

- Where should I start the ride?
- How long do I want the ride to be?
- How hilly will the ride be?
- What types of roads/trails will I be riding?
- Where can I stop for food and drink?

Planning a ride can be a lot of work and it can take a couple hours to work out all the details. Planning gets easier the more you do it and the more familiar you become with the area you want to ride in. You may not be able to fully plan a ride before you actually do it because of lack of information. At some point you will have to stop planning and do the actual ride. No matter how much planning you do before riding in an unknown area, it will always be different than expected, but this is the fun of doing new rides.

Expanding the area you ride in and exploring new routes breaks the monotony of doing the same rides over and over again. Exploring is infectious;

once you get started it's hard to stop, and it's even more fun if you can find some people who will join you for the journey.

SOME WORDS ABOUT BIKE SAFETY

Bike riding, like any other sport, comes with its own set of problems and safety risks. These risks can be greatly reduced by following some simple rules and using some common sense.

- **Be visible.** The most important safety rule is to always be visible. When riding a bike, you will be riding among cars, other bikes, and sometimes pedestrians. Accidents happen when people don't see what's coming. Besides wearing bright colors and reflective material, make sure when you are riding that you can be seen from all angles. Never shadow a car around a corner or weave in, out, or around parked or moving cars.
- **Signal your intentions.** Besides being visible it's important that other people on the road know where you are going and when you are going to make a turn. This includes the usual hand signals for left and right turns as well as signals for stopping and changing lanes. We prefer to signal left turns with the left arm pointed left and right turns with the right arm pointed right. We don't like using the left arm pointed up at the elbow to signal right turns because it confuses some people. Clearly signaling your intentions will help you earn some respect from other motorists and also let the other riders on the ride know where you are going. It's also not a bad idea to yell out "Right turn," "Left turn," or "Stopping" as some riders tend to look around at intersections and may miss the hand signals.
- **Ride predictably.** When riding, especially in traffic, it is important to be predictable so other vehicles on the road know where you are going. Try to ride in a straight line in the same part of the road as much as possible. Do not weave in and out even when riding around parked cars. As the road gets wider or narrower, anticipate the change and slowly drift in or out.
- **Anticipate and call out hazards.** When riding on any road or trail, you will have to navigate around potholes, bumps, tree limbs, and other hazards. Try to constantly scan ahead for hazards so you don't have to make any sudden moves. Call out and point to the hazards as you go by them so other bikers in the group are aware of them and can adjust their line accordingly to avoid them.
- **Wear a helmet.** A helmet is the most important piece of safety gear to wear while riding. If you ride enough miles, eventually you will take

Riding toward the Art Museum on MLK Drive, which is closed to cars on the weekends

a fall, and when you do you have a much better chance of getting up and riding away if you have a helmet on. It's also a good idea to wear glasses to keep the rocks, bugs, and other debris out of your eyes. We also highly recommend having a mirror on your helmet, glasses, or handlebars. A mirror gives you a way to see behind you quickly without having to turn your head.

- **Know and obey the law.** Every state has a set of laws that apply to bicyclists. It's good to be familiar with the law and try to abide by it. See the Resources section for a link to the bike laws. For the most part bicyclists must follow the same laws as cars and must obey all traffic signs and signals.
- **Beware of other bikers.** The most dangerous thing on the road is not cars but other bikers or people on the road or trail. Far more people on bikes get hurt by riding into each other than get hurt by getting hit by a car. When riding on a crowded trail, a split second's inattention can lead

to bumping wheels or running into someone and then down everybody goes. Avoid this by riding in an orderly manner and continually keeping an eye out for other bikes or people in your path.

- **Don't do stupid things.** A lot of bike accidents are caused by people doing stupid things. I have seen bikers run red lights, make sudden illegal turns, weave around people on a bike path, and many other stupid things. Use some common sense and think about what you are doing and we will all be safer.

RIDING IN TRAFFIC

Every effort has been made to design the rides in this book to use the quietest roads and trails possible, but there will be times, especially when riding in the city, when traffic can't be avoided. During these times there are a few things that you can do to reduce your risk of getting in an accident.

Riding in traffic is an art that is learned over time. Novice riders can be easily overwhelmed by traffic and make bad decisions. By using some common sense and some best practices, you can greatly reduce your chances of being in an accident.

- **Ride defensively.** When riding in traffic, it is best to assume that no car can see you and that if they do then they are trying to hit you. This is a very paranoid attitude, but paranoids are sometimes right. This attitude will help you anticipate problems before they occur and have a plan to get out of any bad situation.
- **Communicate with the traffic.** As you are riding, make sure you are communicating your intentions to the cars around you. This not only includes signaling turns and lane changes but also moving to the right when you see them coming up from behind you, waving them around you when you are stopped and thanking them for letting you make a left. Do not use the one-finger wave to express your displeasure with someone's driving skills. As good as this feels, it almost always makes the situation worse.
- **Share the road.** Sharing the road works both ways. Just as cars should be courteous to bikers on the road, bikers need to be polite to cars on a busy road by staying as far to the right as is safe, riding in a single file, and letting cars pass when possible.
- **Don't hog the road.** When riding in a group, never ride more than two abreast. If you see a car coming from behind, get into single file so the car can easily pass the group. This will show the cars that you are trying to be courteous.

- **Learn to take the lane.** There will be times when you need to block a lane of traffic to safely negotiate an intersection. This is especially true when making a left-hand turn. The idea is to stay in the middle of the lane so that you are visible to the traffic that you are traveling with as well as oncoming and cross traffic. To take a lane, first make sure it is clear then signal the move with a hand signal and slowly move into the middle of the lane. Stay in the middle of the lane so no cars can get around you. Once you negotiate the intersection, slowly move back to the right to let cars pass you again.
- **Beware of parked cars.** When riding by parked cars, try to keep a door's width away. This may annoy some drivers trying to get past you, but it will prevent you from being taken out by somebody opening a car door without looking.
- **Maintain eye contact.** While riding in traffic, make sure you can see the eyes of anyone in a car that may cross your path. If you can see their eyes, then they can probably see you and are less likely to hit you.
- **Focus on riding.** It is easy to get distracted when riding in traffic, especially if you are riding through the center of a town. If you are looking at the sights or watching people on the street, you are not focusing on how best to get through the traffic, and a moment's distraction can get you in trouble.

If you use and stick to these practices as you ride in traffic, they will become second nature and automatic over time. As you continue to ride in traffic, it will get easier and you will soon become comfortable and know how to handle any situation that occurs.

Map Legend

Transportation

Interstate/Divided Highway	55
Featured U.S. Highway	41
U.S. Highway	14
Featured State, County, or Local Road	CR 583
State Highway	20
County/Local Road	CR 583
Featured Bike Route	
Bike Route	

Hydrology

- Lake/Reservoir/Major River
- River/Creek
- Marsh

Land Use

- Large State Park/Large Wildlife Area
- State Line

Symbols

Trailhead (Start)	10
Mileage Marker	17.1
Small Park	
Visitor Center	
Wildlife Area	
Historical Site	
Point of Interest/Structure	
Museum	
Park Office	
City	
Town	
Bridge	
Airport	
University/College	
Direction Arrow	

Ride No.	Ride Name	Best City Rides	Best Rural Rides	Best Mountain Bike Rides	Best Hill Rides	Best Rides with Kids	Best Scenic Rides	Best Rides from Public Transit
1	Center City Tour	●						●
2	Falls Bridge					●		
3	Forbidden Drive			●			●	
4	Battleship *New Jersey*	●						●
5	The Manayunk Wall				●			
6	Schuylkill River Trail Ride						●	
7	Bryn Athyn Cathedral						●	
8	Fairmount Park	●						
9	Airport Loop	●						

10	Pennypack Park						●	
11	John Heinz Ride			●				
12	Center City Connector	●						
13	Ambler Ramble	●						
14	Cobbs Creek Ride	●						
15	Valley Forge Ride					●		
16	Fort Washington		●					
17	Washington Crossing Ride		●					
18	Doylestown				●			
19	Lake Nockamixon						●	
20	Tyler State Park						●	

Ride No.	Ride Name	Best City Rides	Best Rural Rides	Best Mountain Bike Rides	Best Hill Rides	Best Rides with Kids	Best Scenic Rides	Best Rides from Public Transit
21	D&R Canal Towpath Trail		●	●				
22	Green Lane				●			
23	Bucks County Covered Bridges						●	
24	Farm to Farm Ride						●	
25	Perkiomen Trail Ride						●	
26	Ridley Creek State Park				●			
27	Devon Ramble							
28	Longwood Gardens		●					
29	Brandywine South		●					

30	Cooper River Park Ride					●		
31	Brendan Byrne State Forest			●				
32	Wharton State Forest			●				
33	Nixon's General Store Ride		●					
34	Batsto Village		●					
35	Philadelphia to Atlantic City							●
36	Smith's Bridge		●					
37	Newark Ramble		●					
38	Blackbird Loop						●	
39	White Clay Creek State Park			●				
40	Crossing Delaware Ride		●					

The city skyline from Belmont Plateau. See Ride 8.

Center City Philadelphia

The heart of the city of Philadelphia is called Center City, and it is roughly bounded by the Delaware River in the east, the Schuylkill River in the west, Spring Garden Street to the north, and South Street in the south. This irregularly shaped area contains the main skyline of the city along with most of its famous landmarks, including the Art Museum and Independence Hall to name a few.

Like the heart of most major cities, this is a crowded and congested area where sometimes bikes and cars are at odds with each other. Despite the congestion of Center City, this is a very bikeable area. The Bicycle Coalition of Greater Philadelphia along with a number of other dedicated individuals have worked hard to make the city an easy place to get around on a bike. Their efforts have paid off because Philadelphia has twice as many bike commuters per capita as any other big city in the United States. So with some urban riding skills and knowledge of the roads, it is easy to ride and explore this part of the city.

Center City has an amazing variety of places to ride. If you want a simple short ride, you can ride along the Schuylkill River Trail by the Art Museum. If you want to explore some of the history of the city, you can take to the roads and head down to Old City and Independence Mall. Want to see an aquarium or WWII battleship? Just ride over the Ben Franklin Bridge into New Jersey. If mountain biking is what you want, head just outside of the official boundaries of Center City to Forbidden Drive, where you can ride a wide gravel path along the Wissahickon Creek or branch off onto the many first-class single-track trails in this part of Fairmount Park.

If you go beyond the confines of Center City to some of the outlying neighborhoods, you will find even more great places to ride. You can explore the quiet confines of Pennypack Park or visit a beautiful historic cathedral, or, if you want to challenge yourself, you can try to scale the famous Manayunk Wall. No matter what kind of ride you are looking for, you will most certainly find something in and around Center City to enjoy.

Independence Hall

Center City Tour

The city of Philadelphia is busy and crowded, but that doesn't mean you can't make your way around it by bike. In fact Philadelphia is relatively easy to get around. There are a lot of bike lanes and paths that can get you in and around most parts of the city as long as you don't mind doing a little urban riding. This ride will take you from the Art Museum to Penn's Landing and back; along the way you get to see some of the city's neighborhoods and historic sights.

Start: Italian Fountain behind the Art Museum

Length: 10.2-mile loop

Approximate riding time: 1.5 hours

Best bike: Road or hybrid bike

Terrain and trail surface: Flat to rolling as you ride on the pavement of city streets. As with any city you will find some potholes and rough roads along the way. There will also be a couple short stretches of cobblestone roads, which can be a little bumpy.

Traffic and hazards: This ride will be on the streets of Philadelphia so you will be doing some urban riding. Most of the streets you will be riding on will have dedicated bike lanes, but you will still have to be cautious of the traffic and pedestrians along the route.

Things to see: Art Museum, Rittenhouse Square, Independence Hall, Penn's Landing, Old Swedes' Church, Edgar Allan Poe's house

Getting there: By car: From I-95 take I-676 west to the Benjamin Franklin Parkway exit (22nd Street, Museum area) on the right side. At the end of the exit ramp, turn right onto 22nd Street and get into the far left lane. The Benjamin Franklin Parkway is a boulevard with two outer lanes and two inner lanes. Turn left onto the outer lanes of the parkway. The Museum will be in front of you on the hill. Stay in the outer lanes and go past the Museum to Kelly Drive, then make a left at the light onto Waterworks Drive. The Italian Fountain is at the far end of the parking lot close to the Museum. GPS: N39 58.04 / W75 10.98
By train: Take the train to the 30th Street Station then cross the Schuylkill River on Market Street and take Schuylkill River Trail north to the Art Museum.

THE RIDE

There are a number of ways to tour the sights of Philadelphia. You can take one of the many walking, Segway, boat, or bus tours. If you take a walking tour, you can only go as far as your feet will take you. A bus tour will allow you to cover more ground but will limit where you can stop and explore. That's why a bike is a good way to tour the city. It allows you to cover more distance than you could on foot but still lets you stop whenever you see something interesting. Although one ride can't cover all the sights in Philadelphia, this route should take you past the more popular sites.

To start the ride, get on the Schuylkill River Trail, which is on the back side of the parking lot by the river, and head toward the museum. The trail can be crowded at times with runners, skaters, and other bikers, so be careful as you go around the curves. The Schuylkill River Trail ends at a circle. Right before the circle you will make a left onto Locust Street and ride through some residential neighborhoods before encountering Rittenhouse Square. Rittenhouse Square is one of the five open-space parks planned by William Penn and has become one of the more desirable sections of the city to live in. The park is surrounded by high-rise residences, luxury apartments, and some very nice restaurants. After riding through the square find Locust Street and continue east. Then make a right on 17th Street and take that to Pine Street, a one-way street with a bike lane heading east to the Delaware River. Spruce Street also has a dedicated bike lane, but this is a one-way street that heads west. These are the best streets for traversing the city, especially the busier sections. In a crowded city like Philadelphia, the bike lanes will be occasionally blocked by double parking, construction, etc. So you will still have to use your urban riding skills to coexist with cars, especially at intersections where cars can turn into your path.

When you cross Broad Street, look to your left and you will see Philadelphia's City Hall. With almost 700 rooms, it is the largest municipal building in the United States. On the Hall tower is a statue of William Penn, which sits above the only observation deck in the city.

At 5th Street you will head north toward Independence Mall. After you cross Walnut Street, the road turns to cobblestone. It's a little rough but rideable. It can be a bit congested by the Independence Mall so be careful. Once you cross Chestnut Street there will be a bike lane again, but you may choose to cross over to the other side of the street here and explore the mall itself. Independence Mall is bounded east and west by 5th and 6th Streets and north and south by Arch and Chestnut Streets. There is a bathroom and water fountain on the northwest corner of 5th and Chestnut. If you stand on the mall and look south, you will see Independence Hall, to the north you will see the Constitution Center and on the mall itself is Liberty Bell Center where you can see the Liberty Bell.

Looking north on Broad Street at City Hall

Once you are done exploring the mall you will head south on 6th Street and back to Pine, which will take you most of the way to the Delaware River. When you make the right on to Spruce Street, you will encounter another cobblestone road that is hard to ride, even on a mountain bike, so use the sidewalk until you reach Columbus Boulevard.

Columbus Boulevard will take you along the waterfront, which is a little gritty and industrial, but the bike lane makes riding with traffic easy. In a little over 1.7 miles you will see Old Swedes' Church on your right. This is the oldest church in Pennsylvania and the second oldest church in the country. The current church was built around 1698 and is a beautiful historic building in a nice garden setting that still holds Sunday services.

Urban Riding Tips

Riding in an urban environment carries some special challenges for bikers. Watching out for cars, pedestrians, and other hazards can be a daunting task for a person who is not familiar with urban riding. The main problem with urban riding is learning to be visible without getting in the way. There is a great website, bicyclesafe.com, that explains how to avoid a lot of the common hazards of riding in a city. Understanding these common hazards will help you make better decisions while riding the streets.

Another thing that will help improve your urban riding is understanding the do's and don'ts for each city as well as getting good information about what are the best streets to ride on and when is the best time to ride on them. For example, in the Philadelphia Bike Map for Center City they mark Chestnut Street as bike-friendly, but in truth it is too narrow and congested to ride safely. There is a combination bike/bus lane, but during the morning and evening commute there are too many buses and double-parked cars to ride this street safely. Pine Street is a better alternative for going east as is Spruce for going west if you are going to and from Center City from the Delaware or Schuylkill River. To get to or from the Art Museum from the Delaware River your best bet is Spring Garden.

As far as riding on sidewalks and park paths, this should be avoided because hitting a pedestrian can hurt as much as hitting a car. However, there are times when the sidewalk must be used because the street is just not safe to ride in. Use your best judgment here and make sure to slow down and yield to pedestrians.

Urban riding is a skill that takes time to learn, but with experience riding in a busy city will become second nature.

From the church you will head back up Columbus Boulevard to Penn's Landing. This is a popular gathering place on the waterfront especially when there is a festival or concert going on. At Penn's Landing you can visit the ships of the seaport museum, take a ride on the ferry over to the New Jersey Aquarium, or just enjoy the view.

From Penn's Landing you will take Columbus Boulevard to Spring Garden. The bike lane disappears for a few blocks, so you may want to ride on the wide sidewalk here since bikes and pedestrians can easily share it. Spring Garden will take you back to the Art Museum and your starting point. The street has a bike lane and is one of the more popular commuting routes for cyclists, so you will not be alone here. It is a busy street so just be on the lookout for cars pulling out on you or crossing the bike lane. If you look carefully you will see a number of nice murals along the road like the bike mural on your left at 2nd Street. The only other attraction worth noting here is Edgar Allan Poe's house on the corner of Spring Garden and 7th Street. Be careful at the intersection of Spring Garden and 23rd Street as this is a confusing intersection where five different roads meet.

Bike Shops

Breakaway Bikes, 1923 Chestnut St., Philadelphia 19103; (215) 568-6002 Breakaway Bikes is a great bike shop and training center. Joe and Glenn are great ambassadors of Philadelphia biking and are always happy to help you with all your biking needs.

MILES AND DIRECTIONS

0.0 Get on the Schuylkill River Trail and head back toward the Art Museum.

1.4 The Schuylkill River Trail ends; make a left, cross the railroad tracks to get on to Locust Avenue.

1.8 Locust Avenue runs into Rittenhouse Square. Cross the street and ride through the square and pick up Locust Street again on the other side.

2.1 Turn right onto 17th Street.

2.3 Turn left onto Pine Street; there is a bike lane to ride in here.

3.4 Turn left onto 5th Street.

3.7 Cross Chestnut Street. You can cross over 5th Street to Independence Mall here if you want to explore the area and see some of the sights.

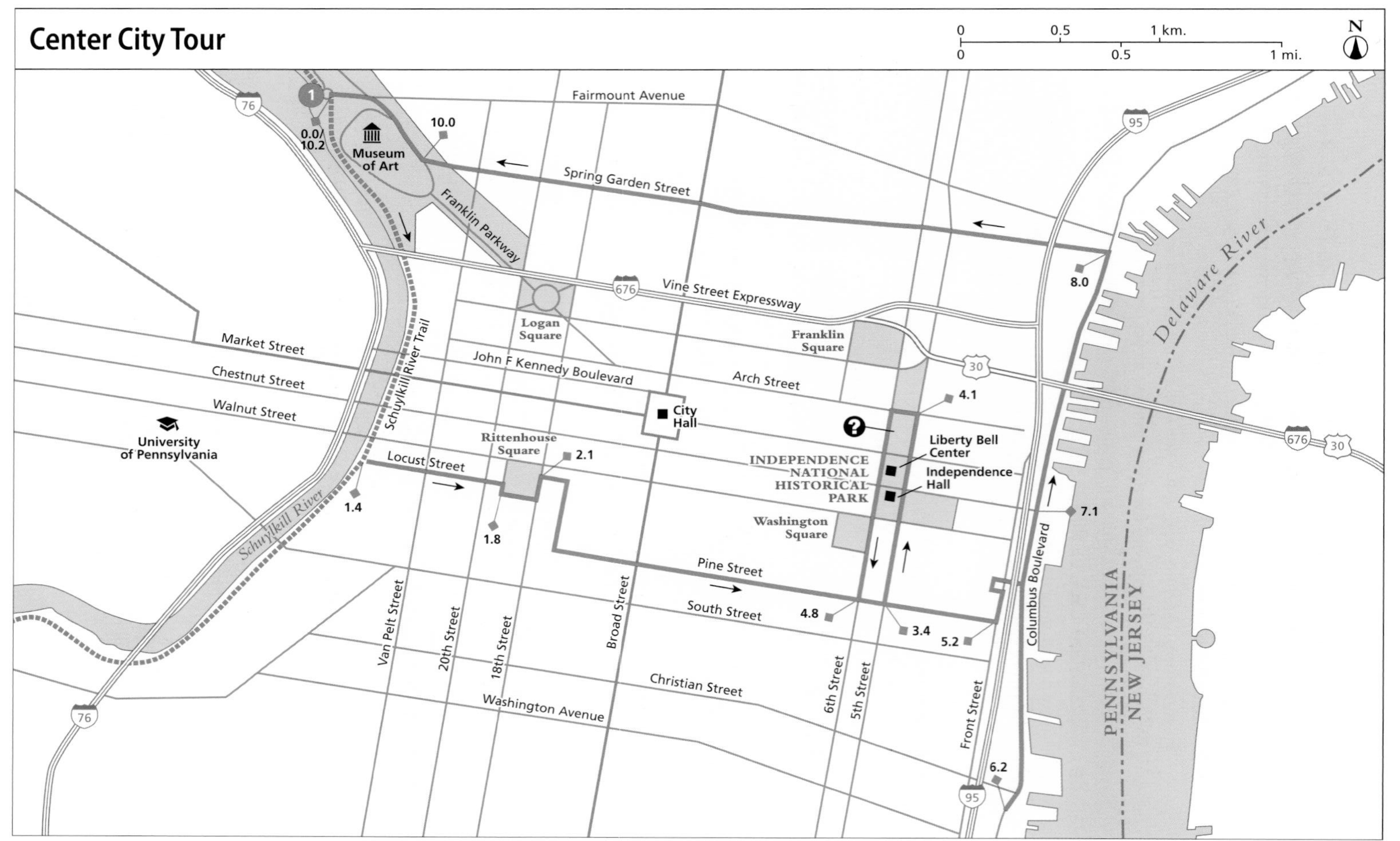

Center City Tour
0
0.5
1 km.
0
0.5
1 mi.
N
Fairmount Avenue
76
1
0.0/
10.2
Museum
of Art
10.0
Spring Garden Street
Franklin Parkway
95
8.0
Delaware River
Vine Street Expressway
676
Logan
Square
Franklin
Square
Market Street
Chestnut Street
Walnut Street
John F Kennedy Boulevard
Arch Street
30
4.1
City
Hall
Schuylkill River Trail
University
of Pennsylvania
Rittenhouse
Square
2.1
Locust Street
Liberty Bell
Center
INDEPENDENCE
NATIONAL
HISTORICAL
PARK
Independence
Hall
1.4
1.8
Washington
Square
7.1
Schuylkill River
Pine Street
Columbus Boulevard
South Street
4.8
3.4
5.2
Van Pelt Street
20th Street
18th Street
Broad Street
Christian Street
Washington Avenue
6th Street
5th Street
Front Street
PENNSYLVANIA
NEW JERSEY
6.2

4.1 Turn left at the top of the mall by Arch Street, then take the next left onto 6th Street. There is a bike lane here to ride in.

4.8 Turn left onto Pine Street.

5.2 Turn left onto Front Street.

5.3 Turn right onto Spruce Street. The cobblestone road here is very rough; use the wide sidewalk here to get to Columbus Boulevard.

5.5 Turn right onto Columbus Boulevard.

6.2 Stop at Old Swedes' Church where Columbus Boulevard meets Washington Street.

6.2 After exploring the church, head back up (north) on Columbus Boulevard.

7.1 Turn right just before the Walnut Street Bridge to enter Penn's Landing. Be careful of the cars pulling in here to park.

From 1901 until 1987, City Hall was the tallest building in Philadelphia. This was because of a gentlemen's agreement that limited the height of any building to the height of the William Penn statue atop City Hall. This agreement was broken during the building boom of the late 1980s when One Liberty Place was constructed.

7.1 After exploring Penn's Landing, get back to Columbus Boulevard and continue to head north. The bike lane is not well marked here so you may want to ride on the wide sidewalk.

8.0 Turn left onto Spring Garden Street.

10.0 Cross 23rd Street. Stay left where Spring Garden Street goes down into a tunnel. You can ride on the sidewalk here to avoid the traffic.

10.0 Make a right onto Kelly Drive and continue up the sidewalk until you can cross over at the light at 25th Street.

10.2 Ride up the path back to the parking lot behind the Art Museum where you started the ride.

RIDE INFORMATION

Events/Attractions

The Schuylkill River Trail is a multiuse trail that runs from Center City Philadelphia to Valley Forge and beyond. Detailed information about the different parts of the trail can be found at schuylkillrivertrail.com.

1

Local Attractions

If you're not familiar with the city of Philadelphia, check out the official visitors' site, visitphilly.com, for a lot of good information about things to see and do in the city as well as places to eat.

Restrooms

Mile 0.1: Corner of Kelly Drive and Waterworks Drive.
Mile 3.7: Corner of 5th Street and Chestnut Street.

Maps

Delorme Pennsylvania Atlas & Gazetteer: Page 86, D3

2

Falls Bridge

Just behind the Art Museum is the southern part of Fairmount Park and the Schuylkill River. This is one of the nicest parts of Philadelphia and the easiest place to take a bike ride. This ride will take you up the east side of the Schuylkill River and down the west side for a relaxing 8-mile ride that will show you some of the beautiful and historic sights of the city.

Start: Italian Fountain behind the Art Museum

Length: 8-mile loop

Approximate riding time: 1 hour

Best bike: Road or hybrid bike

Terrain and trail surface: Flat ride on a paved bike path

Traffic and hazards: There will be no car traffic to worry about, but the Schuylkill River Trail that you will be riding on can be crowded at times with other bikers, runners, and in-line skaters.

Things to see: Boathouse Row, Art Museum, Schuylkill River, Fairmount Park

Getting there: By car: From I-95 take I-676 west to the Benjamin Franklin Parkway exit (22nd Street, Museum area) on the right side. At the end of the exit ramp, turn right onto 22nd Street and get into the far left lane. The Benjamin Franklin Parkway is a boulevard with two outer lanes and two inner lanes. Turn left onto the outer lanes of the parkway. The Museum will be in front of you on the hill. Stay in the outer lanes and go past the Museum to Kelly Drive, then make a left at the light onto Waterworks Drive. The Italian Fountain is at the far end of the parking lot close to the Museum. GPS: N39 58.04 / W75 10.98
By train: Take the train to the 30th Street Station then cross the Schuylkill River on Market Street and take the Schuylkill River Trail north to the Art Museum.

THE RIDE

Fairmount Park is one of the largest and oldest municipally-operated park systems in the United States. The park encompasses over 9,000 acres and shows how government and citizens can work together to create useful public spaces. The bike path that is part of Fairmount Park makes it very easy to take a leisurely ride through this beautiful landscape.

To start the ride get on the Schuylkill River Trail, which is on the back side of the parking lot, and head away from the Museum toward Kelly Drive. When you get to the end of Waterworks Drive, the bike path will start following Kelly Drive. The buildings that you see on your left as you start up Kelly Drive are the fifteen houses of Boathouse Row and the Turtle Rock Lighthouse. These houses are between 100 and 150 years old and host rowing clubs and their boats. Each house is unique with its own history. You will have a good view of these houses from the river side on your way back.

A view of Boathouse Row from the other side of the Schuylkill River by the falls

As you continue the ride, you will be riding along the east side of the Schuylkill River. There is lots of nice scenery here along the river and a number of places to stop and relax. On a nice day a lot of people will be using the trail so it may be crowded.

After just under 4 miles you will come to Falls Bridge, which is where you will cross the river and start your way back. Make a left over the bridge and then a left right after you cross the bridge.

The Schuylkill River Trail on the west side of the Schuylkill River is usually less crowded than on the other side of the river. The trail is nice and wide but can be a little bumpy in spots because of the number of tree roots that are infringing on the trail, so keep your eyes open so you can avoid the bigger bumps. The trail parallels Martin Luther King Jr. (MLK) Drive. On Saturday and Sunday mornings between April and October, the upper part of MLK Drive is closed to car traffic from 6 a.m. to 5 p.m. The lower portion of MLK Drive from Eakins Oval, by the Art Museum, to Sweetbriar Drive is also closed but reopens to traffic at noon. This was started in 1995, by the City of Philadelphia, as a way to attract people to enjoy exercising and picnicking along the Schuylkill River and it has worked very well.

Riding on this part of the Schuylkill River Trail is a lot of fun when MLK Drive is closed and a lot of people take advantage of it. There are also a number of events planned during the closure, like charity runs/rides, rowing competitions, etc, which can make it even more entertaining.

Bike Shops

Trophy Bikes, 3131 Walnut St., Philadelphia 19104; (215) 222-2020 Trophy Bikes is a good bike shop in the university part of the city with good service and a nice selection of bikes.

Although there isn't anywhere to get food along the trail, you will see a few small parking lots along the trail that usually have portable toilets you can use. As you continue along, you will get some good views of the city skyline from the river. After you go under the Girard Bridge, you will see Boathouse Row again. This time you will get a good view of the river side of the houses. Just in front of the houses you will see a small waterfall, which is the Fairmount Dam. This dam was first constructed in 1822 to provide a spillway to be used to power pumps for the water system. The side effect of the construction of the dam was that it created several miles of tranquil water above the dam that was perfect for rowing.

After you pass the dam, the trail will become narrower and you will cross a bridge over to the other side of the river. The trail will eventually bring you to

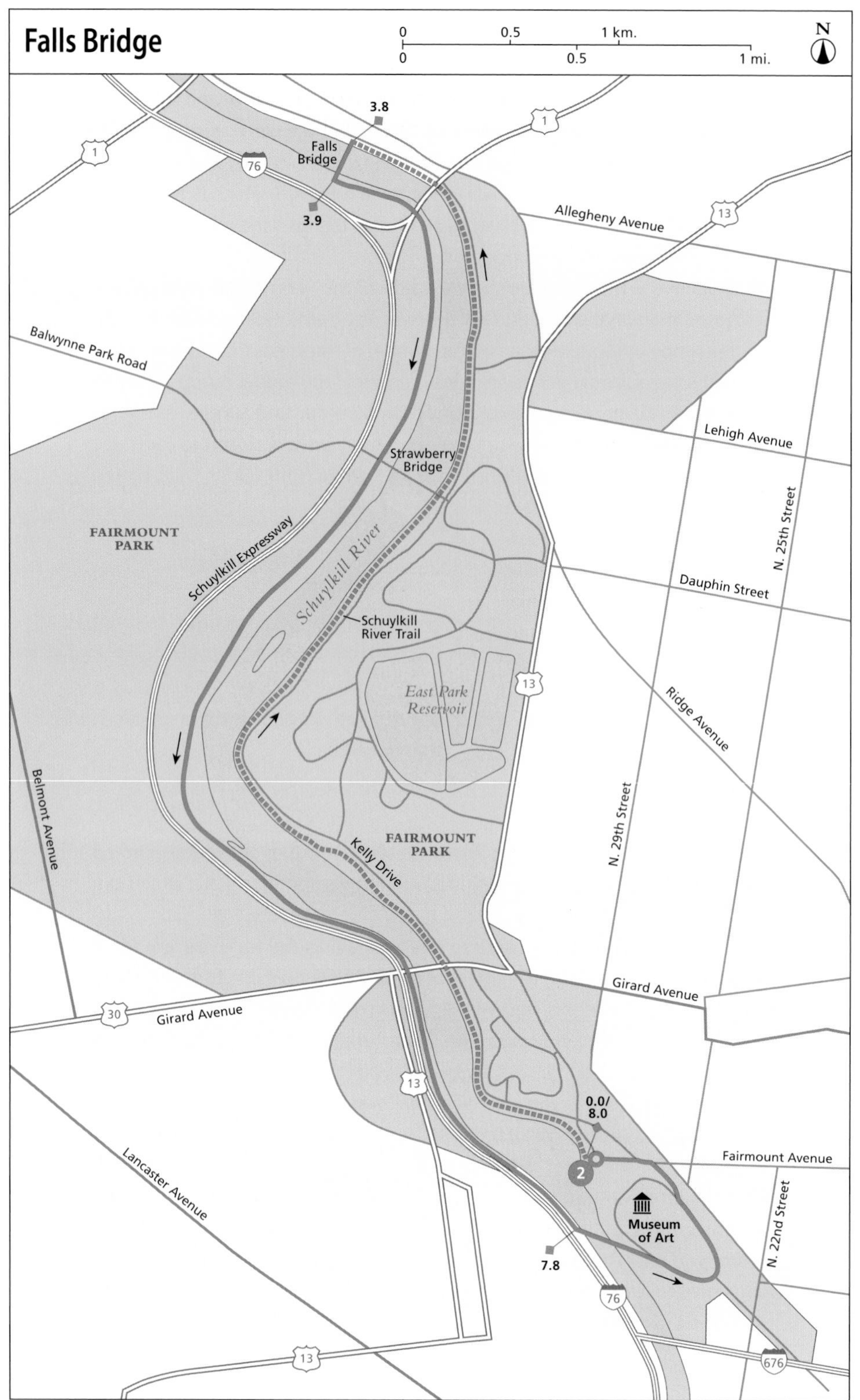
Falls Bridge
0
0.5
1 km.
0
0.5
1 mi.
N
3.8
Falls Bridge
3.9
1
76
1
13
Allegheny Avenue
Balwynne Park Road
Lehigh Avenue
Strawberry Bridge
N. 25th Street
FAIRMOUNT PARK
Schuylkill Expressway
Schuylkill River
Dauphin Street
Schuylkill River Trail
13
East Park Reservoir
Ridge Avenue
Belmont Avenue
N. 29th Street
FAIRMOUNT PARK
Kelly Drive
Girard Avenue
30
Girard Avenue
13
0.0/ 8.0
Fairmount Avenue
2
N. 22nd Street
Museum of Art
Lancaster Avenue
7.8
76
13
676

the front of the Art Museum and the stairs made famous by the movie *Rocky*. This area is almost always crowded with cars and people, so be careful here. If you continue around the museum along the path, it will bring you around to the back and return you to the Italian Fountain where you started your ride.

MILES AND DIRECTIONS

0.0 Start at the Italian Fountain behind the Art Museum. Follow the Schuylkill River Trail up Kelly Drive.

3.8 Make a left at Falls River Bridge and cross over the river.

3.9 Make a left after crossing the bridge back onto the Schuylkill River Trail and follow it along Martin Luther King Jr. Drive.

7.8 Cross back over the Schuylkill River and continue to follow the trail around the Art Museum.

8.0 Arrive back at the Italian Fountain.

Boathouse Row

Boathouse Row is a National Historic Landmark and one of the main centers of rowing in the United States. The construction of the Fairmount Dam in 1822 transformed the water above the dam from a tidal stream to a tranquil lake that was perfect for rowing in the summertime and skating in the winter. As rowing became more popular, a number of rowing clubs formed and constructed simple wood frame buildings along the river by the dam. Rowing continued to grow in popularity, and Philadelphia hosted a number of regattas. In 1858 the Schuylkill Navy was formed by the rowing clubs as a governing body to help promote amateur rowing and prevent some of the shady practices and race fixing that had become common.

In 1859 the wooden boathouses were in a state of disrepair and an eyesore so they were condemned by the city. The Schuylkill Navy worked to get some new ordinances passed to allow construction of new boathouses. The new boathouses were constructed using brick and stone in a primarily Victorian Gothic style. These were much more aesthetically pleasing and became more than just places to store the boats. These new houses set the standard for what is today one of the more picturesque sites on the Schuylkill River.

RIDE INFORMATION

Events/Attractions

Martin Luther King Drive: Information about when Martin Luther King Drive is closed can be found on the Fairmount Park website at fairmountpark.org/mlk_closure.asp.

Boathouse Row: Information about the history of rowing and events at Boathouse Row can be found at the Schuylkill Navy of Philadelphia website at boathouserow.org.

Kelly Drive was named in honor of John B. Kelly Jr., a Philadelphia city councilman, Olympic rower, and the brother of Grace Kelly.

Restrooms

Portable toilets can be found in some of the parking lots along the trail.

Maps

Delorme Pennsylvania Atlas & Gazetteer: Page 86, D3

3

Forbidden Drive

Wissahickon Valley Park is a 7-mile-long forested alpine gorge cut by the Wissahickon Creek that is just outside of Center City Philadelphia. Its spectacular 1,800 acres are an incredible pocket of wilderness that contains over 50 miles of trails for hiking and mountain biking. One of the nicest ways to get an overview of the park is to ride along Forbidden Drive. This popular and beautiful trail along the Wissahickon Creek runs the length of the valley from Chestnut Hill all the way down to Lincoln Drive in Manayunk. This ride will take you along the trail and show you the sights along the way.

Start: Bells Mill parking area

Length: 10 miles out and back

Approximate riding time: 1.5 hours

Best bike: Hybrid or mountain bike

Terrain and trail surface: Relatively flat gravel path

Traffic and hazards: There will be no car traffic on Forbidden Drive, but this is a multiuse path so you have to keep your eye out for other bikers, joggers, pedestrians, and equestrians. If you want to ride on the single-track trails off Forbidden Drive, you will need a permit. See the Ride Information below on how to get a permit.

Things to see: Thomas Mill Road Covered Bridge, Valley Green Inn, Wissahickon Creek

Getting there: By car: From I-95 take I-676 west to I-476. Take I-476 north to exit 18A, Conshohocken. Make a right at the end of the exit onto Ridge Avenue and go east for 3.7 miles then make a left onto Bells Mill Road. The parking area is on the right 0.9 mile ahead. GPS: N40 04.70 / W75 13.64
By train: From the Market East Station take the SEPTA R8 Chestnut Hill line to Chestnut Hill West Station. From the Station turn left onto Germantown Avenue then turn left onto Bells Mill Road. The parking area is on the right 0.9 mile ahead.

THE RIDE

Forbidden Drive got its name in 1920 when cars were forbidden to ride along it. Since then people have been strolling along the Wissahickon Creek and enjoying its many sights. To start the ride, make a right out of the parking lot onto Bells Mill Road and head toward Forbidden Drive.

You will head down a hill and after 0.1 mile see the entrance to Forbidden Drive. Make a right here and head down the trail. Forbidden Drive is a wide, hard-packed gravel trail along Wissahickon Creek. This is basically a multiuse trail so you will be sharing this trail with hikers, runners, walkers, and other bikers. The trail does have a few ups and downs but nothing that would be considered a real climb.

After 0.6 mile you will pass the Thomas Mill Road Covered Bridge. This is a much photographed bridge that was built in 1855 and renovated in 1939 and

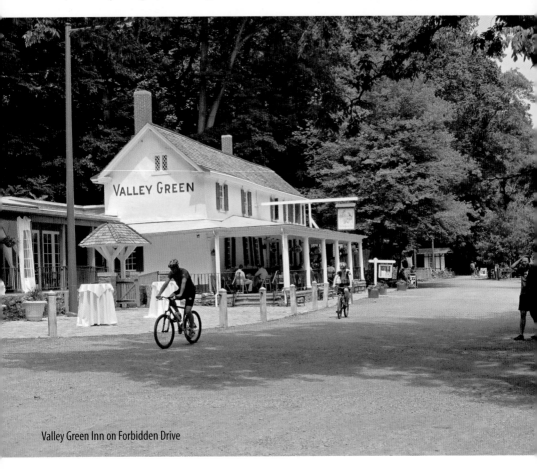

Valley Green Inn on Forbidden Drive

2000. The best view of the bridge is from the other side. If you cross over the bridge, you can also access some of the single-track trails on the north side of the Wissahickon Creek, but this requires a permit.

As you continue along Forbidden Drive, you will reach the Valley Green Inn after 2.1 miles. This beautiful old hotel is now a restaurant and snack bar. The restaurant has a small parking lot here so there is a small part of Forbidden Drive that is open to cars so that they can get from the side streets to the parking lot, so just be on the lookout for an occasional car here.

As you continue on there are no notable attractions along the way but a lot of nice scenery. Forbidden Drive is almost all tree covered; add to that its pathway along the creek, and you have a very comfortable place to ride even on a hot summer day or cold windy day.

At 5 miles you will get to the end of Forbidden Drive where it meets Lincoln Drive, which is the turnaround point for the ride. If you want a longer ride than described here, you can make a right at the bike path at the end of the parking lot and hook up with the Schuylkill River Trail at the intersection of Lincoln Drive and Kelly Drive.

Your ride back to the starting point will retrace the same path, but this is one of those trails that is a joy to repeat. In fact this is one of those places that changes during each season, so it is fun to come back to again and again.

Bike Shops

Cadence Cycling, 4323 Main St., Philadelphia 19127; (215) 508-4300 Cadence Cycling is a great bike shop for beginning cyclists, enthusiasts, and triathletes of all abilities. They provide all types of services including retail product, coaching, physiological testing, and general bike repair.

MILES AND DIRECTIONS

0.0 Make a right out of the parking lot onto Bells Mill Road and head toward Forbidden Drive.

0.1 Make right onto Forbidden Drive.

0.6 Pass the Thomas Mill Road Covered Bridge.

2.1 Pass Valley Green Inn.

5.0 Arrive at parking lot at end of Forbidden Drive by Lincoln Drive.

5.0 Turn around and retrace your route back to the starting point.

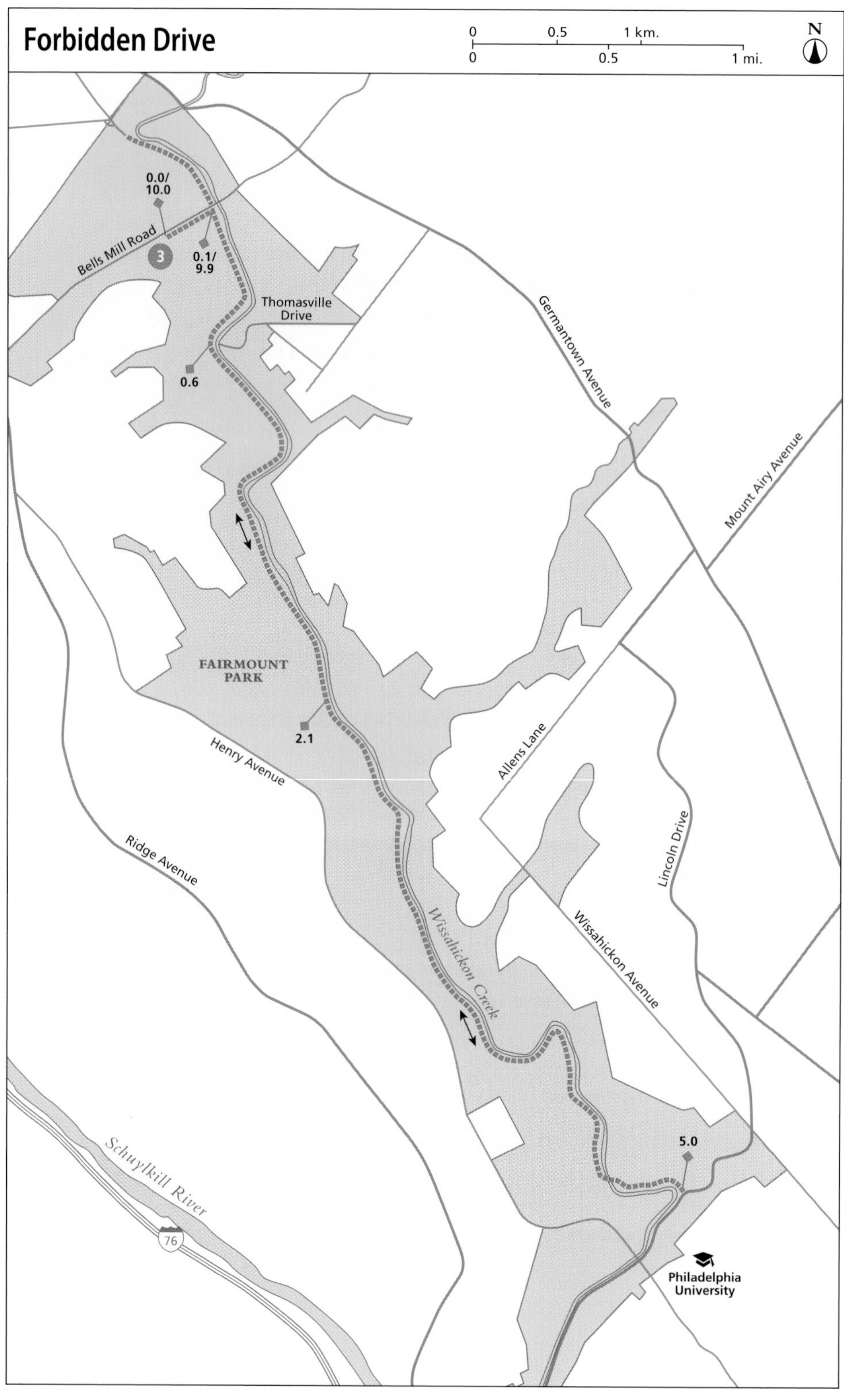

Forbidden Drive
0
0.5
1 km.
0
0.5
1 mi.
N
0.0/
10.0
0.1/
9.9
Bells Mill Road
3
Thomasville
Drive
0.6
Germantown Avenue
Mount Airy Avenue
FAIRMOUNT
PARK
2.1
Henry Avenue
Allens Lane
Lincoln Drive
Ridge Avenue
Wissahickon Creek
Wissahickon Avenue
5.0
Schuylkill River
76
Philadelphia
University

9.9 Make left onto Bells Mill Road.

10.0 Make a left back into the parking lot on Bells Mill Road.

RIDE INFORMATION

Events/Attractions

Fairmount Park: Information about Forbidden Drive and how to obtain a trail permit that will allow you to ride on the mountain biking trails in the park can be found on the Fairmount Park website, fairmountpark.org.

The Thomas Mill Road Covered Bridge is the only remaining covered bridge in Philadelphia and the only covered bridge in a major US city.

Restrooms

Mile 2.1: Valley Green Inn.

Maps

Delorme Pennsylvania Atlas & Gazetteer: Page 86, D3

Valley Green Inn

For well over 150 years, people have been enjoying the food and hospitality of the Valley Green Inn. The original hotel was built in 1850 by Edward Rinker at the same time the Wissahickon Turnpike (Lincoln Drive) was being completed. This allowed people into the valley by carriage and horseback to view the lovely scenery. A number of innkeepers followed Rinker until 1899, when the chief engineer of Fairmount Park recommended the building be demolished because it was in disrepair and the Park Commission, which owned the inn at this time, did not have the money needed for the renovation. Luckily a local committee came up with the funds for the restoration, which was completed in 1900. Additional restoration was done in 1937 and 2002 to allow the Valley Green Inn to continue to survive and become a timeless reminder of days gone past.

Battleship *New Jersey*

With its many restaurants, attractions, and special events, Penn's Landing, along the Delaware River, is one of the main public gathering areas in Philadelphia. This area is also one of the best places to get nice views of the city and riverfront. If you look across the river, you will see the Battleship New Jersey *next to the Aquarium. This ride will help you explore the waterfront from both sides of the river and will take you from Center City to the Battleship* New Jersey *and back. Along the way you get some good views of the river and learn a little of the history of the area.*

Start: Italian Fountain behind the Art Museum

Length: 10.1-mile loop

Approximate riding time: 1.5 hours

Best bike: Road or hybrid bike

Terrain and trail surface: Mostly flat ride on city streets. You will be riding over the Ben Franklin Bridge, which will require climbing up and over the bridge, but the climb over the bridge is relatively gentle.

Traffic and hazards: This ride will be on the streets of Philadelphia so you will be doing some urban riding. Most of the streets you will be riding on will have dedicated bike lanes, but you will still have to be cautious of the traffic and pedestrians along the route.

Things to see: Art Museum, Ben Franklin Bridge, Battleship *New Jersey*, Penn's Landing, Adventure Aquarium

Getting there: By car: From I-95 take I-676 west to the Benjamin Franklin Parkway exit (22nd Street, Museum area) on the right side. At the end of the exit ramp, turn right onto 22nd Street and get into the far left lane. The Benjamin Franklin Parkway is a boulevard with two outer lanes and two inner lanes. Turn left onto the outer lanes of the parkway. The museum will be in front of you on the hill. Stay in the outer lanes and go past the museum to Kelly Drive then make a left at the light onto Waterworks Drive. The Italian Fountain is at the far end of the parking lot close to the museum. GPS: N39 58.04 / W75 10.98
By train: Take the train to the 30th Street Station then cross the Schuylkill River on Market Street and take Schuylkill River Trail north to the Art Museum.

THE RIDE

To start the ride get on the bike path, which is on the back side of the parking lot, and head toward and past the museum as you make your way to Center City. You will take Schuylkill River Trail to where it ends at a turnaround circle. Before the circle you will make a left and go across the tracks to get onto Locust Street.

Locust Street will take you to Rittenhouse Square, which was named after David Rittenhouse, an astronomer, instrument maker, and leader of the Revolutionary era. This area is one of the more fashionable districts in the city. From here you will continue to make your way toward the river as you ride through residential and historic sections of the city. Eventually you will come to the end of Dock Street, where you will cross Columbus Boulevard to get to Penn's Landing.

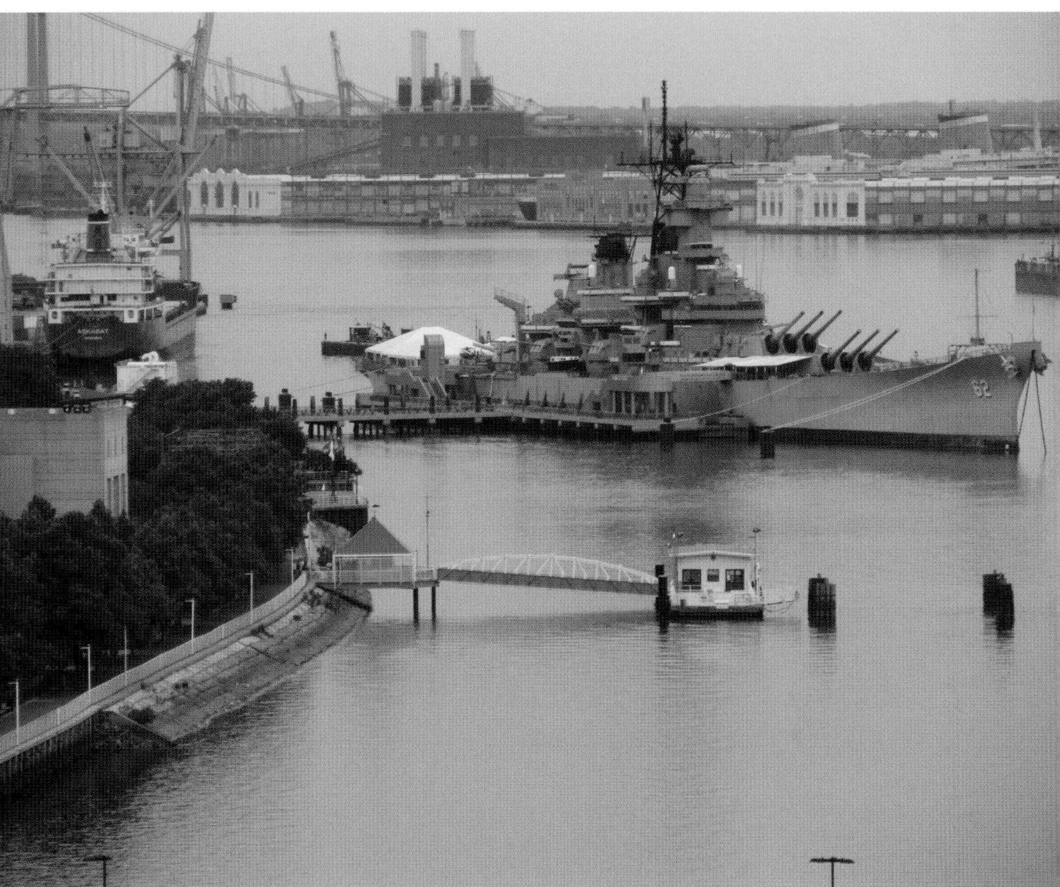

A view of the Battleship *New Jersey* from the Ben Franklin Bridge

The Battleship Museum

The Battleship *New Jersey* is the most decorated battleship our nation has. It also was one of the longest serving. Although it was decommissioned a number of times, the *New Jersey* kept being recalled back to serve the Navy and was used from 1943 in World War II all the way through 1991. The battleship was built in the Philadelphia shipyards in 1942. It was one of the last of the "fast battleships" and could deliver a lot of firepower with its nine 16-inch guns and twenty 5-inch guns. The *New Jersey* saw major action during World War II, including participation in the "Marianas Turkey Shoot," the landing at Iwo Jima, and numerous other events. Although she was decommissioned in June 1948, she was quickly recommissioned in November 1950 and used in a number of battles during the Korean War.

After a brief retirement from 1957 to 1968, the *New Jersey* was recommissioned again to participate in the Vietnam War to help reduce the loss of aircraft as well as provide an increase in firepower to support the escalation of the war. Because of reasons of economy, the *New Jersey* only served one tour and was decommissioned again in December 1969. The *New Jersey*'s last reactivation was in 1982 and led to her participation in the Lebanese Civil War. She was decommissioned for the last time in February 1991 and has been preserved as a museum ship so people can experience the rich history this ship has seen.

There are a number of attractions at Penn's Landing such as the Independence Seaport Museum and the River Stage, which hosts outdoor concerts. The ice rink allows people to skate by the river from November through April. Just north and south of Penn's Landing are other piers that contain nightclubs and restaurants. In the summer there is almost always some festival or event here to enjoy. Even when there is no event there are usually still a lot of people by the waterfront.

When you are done exploring Penn's Landing, make your way toward the Independence Seaport Museum, where you will find the RiverLink Ferry that will take you across the river to Camden. The ferry only runs from May to October; if you are not doing this ride during this time, you will have to use the alternate route in the Miles and Directions to ride across the Ben Franklin Bridge.

The ferry will give you a nice ride across the river with clear views of the city. The ferry will dock near the aquarium. After you get off the ferry, head to the right along the path to see the battleship. If you have not done so before, it is worth taking a tour of the Battleship *New Jersey* to learn about its long and interesting history.

When you are done enjoying the waterfront around the battleship and aquarium, follow the path along the river toward the Ben Franklin Bridge. The path will end at Pearl Street, which you will follow alongside the bridge. After you cross 3rd Street, you will see a set of stairs on your left that will take you up to the south walkway of the bridge. A ramp on the stairs will let you walk your bike up to the walkway.

Once on the bridge you will have a gentle climb that will take you over the river and back into Philadelphia. On a clear day you will get some great views of the city, Penn's Landing, and the Camden waterfront so feel free to stop along the way to enjoy the view.

At the end of the bridge is Franklin Square, which is a large circle with multiple lanes of traffic. What you want to do here is to get to 5th Street, but the problem is that 5th Street is actually underneath this circle. There is a walkway at the end of the bridge that will allow you to walk under the bridge and get to the north side where 5th Street comes out from underground, but an easier way is to make a left at the end of the bridge and go through the parking lot, then cross Race Street and follow the sidewalk in front of the US Mint. By the entrance to the mint you will see an entrance to a tunnel where 5th Street goes underground. There is a bike lane here so just follow 5th to Spring Garden and that will get you back to the Art Museum. Where Spring Garden crosses 23rd Street it splits in two. The right lane goes down into a tunnel. You want to stay left here, aboveground, then cross Kelly Drive to the front of the Art Museum, where you can follow the sidewalk to the back side of the museum where you started the ride.

MILES AND DIRECTIONS

0.0 Get on the Schuylkill River Trail and head back toward the Art Museum.

1.4 The Schuylkill River Trail ends; make a left, crossing the railroad tracks to get onto Locust Avenue.

1.4 Turn right onto 24th Street.

1.6 Turn left onto Pine Street; there is a bike lane to ride in here.

3.2 If you don't want to take the ferry to the Battleship *New Jersey,* turn left onto 5th Street. Follow 5th Street past Independence Mall to the front of the US Mint, where you ride up the sidewalk to the bike lane on the Ben Franklin Bridge.

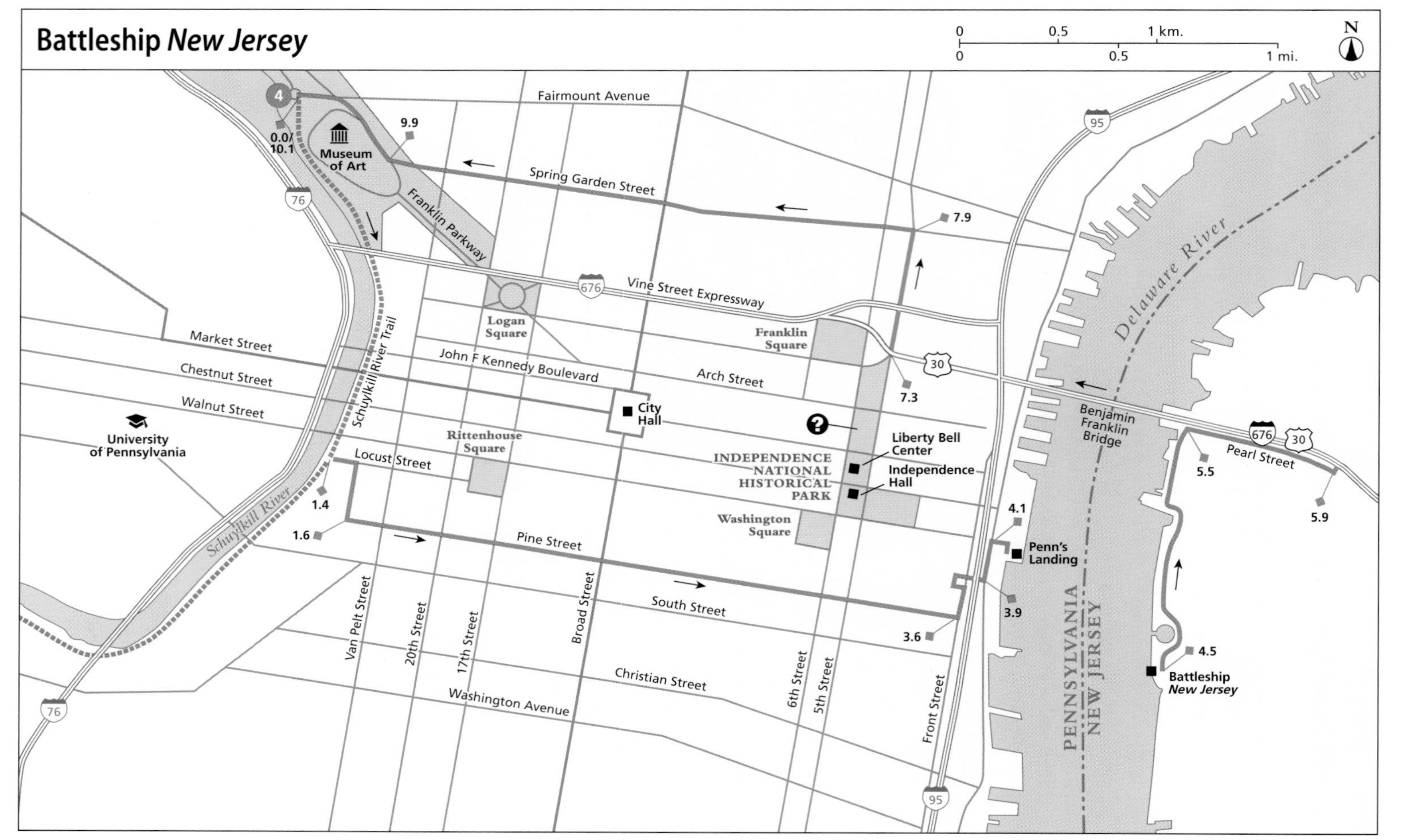
Battleship *New Jersey*
0
0.5
1 km.
0
0.5
1 mi.
N
Fairmount Avenue
4
0.0/
10.1
9.9
Museum
of Art
Spring Garden Street
76
Franklin Parkway
7.9
95
676
Vine Street Expressway
Logan
Square
Franklin
Square
Delaware River
Market Street
Schuylkill River Trail
John F Kennedy Boulevard
Arch Street
30
7.3
Chestnut Street
Walnut Street
City
Hall
Benjamin
Franklin
Bridge
676
30
University
of Pennsylvania
Rittenhouse
Square
Liberty Bell
Center
Pearl Street
5.5
Locust Street
INDEPENDENCE
NATIONAL
HISTORICAL
PARK
Independence
Hall
5.9
1.4
Schuylkill River
4.1
1.6
Washington
Square
Penn's
Landing
Pine Street
3.9
South Street
Van Pelt Street
20th Street
17th Street
Broad Street
3.6
PENNSYLVANIA
NEW JERSEY
4.5
Battleship
New Jersey
Christian Street
6th Street
5th Street
Front Street
Washington Avenue
76
95

3.6 Turn left onto Front Street.

3.7 Turn right onto Spruce Street. The cobblestone road here is very rough; use the wide sidewalk here to get to Columbus Boulevard.

3.9 Turn left onto Columbus Boulevard.

4.1 Turn right just before the Walnut Street Bridge to enter Penn's Landing. Be careful of the cars pulling in here to park. The ferry is to the right at the end of the pier.

4.1 After getting off the ferry, head to the right along the path toward the battleship.

4.5 Arrive at the Battleship *New Jersey.*

4.5 When finished exploring the Battleship *New Jersey,* head north along the path toward the Ben Franklin Bridge.

5.5 Where the path ends make a right onto Pearl Street.

5.9 Take the stairs on your left up to the bike path on the Ben Franklin Bridge and ride across the bridge. (If the south bike path is closed, you will have to use the stairway on the other side. To get there go back to 3rd and go under the bridge, then make a right at Elm followed by a right onto 5th. At the end of 5th, make a right onto Fulton. The stairway to the bridge is at the corner of Fulton and 4th.)

7.3 Once on the other side of the bridge, ride across the small parking lot on your left then follow the sidewalk to the front of the US Mint. (If you rode across the north side of the bridge, you can take the tunnel at the end of the path to get to the south side.)

7.4 At the front of the US Mint, follow the bike lane through the 5th Street tunnel.

7.9 Make left onto Spring Garden Street.

9.9 Cross 23rd Street. Stay left where Spring Garden Street goes down into a tunnel. You can ride on the sidewalk here to avoid the traffic.

Bike Shops

Breakaway Bikes, 1923 Chestnut St., Philadelphia 19103; (215) 568-6002
Breakaway Bikes is a great bike shop and training center. Joe and Glenn are great ambassadors of Philadelphia biking and are always happy to help you with all your biking needs.

9.9 Make a right onto Kelly Drive and continue up the sidewalk until you can cross over at the light at 25th Street.

10.1 Ride up the path back to the parking lot behind the Art Museum where you started the ride.

RIDE INFORMATION

Events/Attractions

Penn's Landing hosts a number of festivals and special events throughout the year. To get information about the many attractions and events here, check out the website at delawareriverwaterfrontcorp.com.

The Philadelphia Naval Shipyard was the first in the country. Although the Navy closed this facility in 1995, at its peak period, during World War II, it built 53 ships, repaired 574, and employed over 40,000 people.

The Battleship *New Jersey* is a wonderful museum on the Camden Waterfront showcasing the history of this great warship. For information about visiting the ship, check out the website at battleshipnewjersey.org.

Restrooms

Mile 4.3: Penn's Landing
Mile 4.7: Battleship *New Jersey*

Maps

Delorme Pennsylvania Atlas & Gazetteer: Page 86, D3

5

The Manayunk Wall

In bicycling terminology, a "wall" is a steep incline. In bicycle racing there is no more famous "wall" than the Manayunk Wall, part of the Philadelphia International Cycling Championship. In early June each year the pro riders visit this area to test their strength on this short but steep hill during a grueling 156-mile race. Although you might not be looking to race for a yellow jersey, you might want to test your legs on this hill as you explore the historic area of Manayunk.

Start: Italian Fountain behind the Art Museum

Length: 19-mile out-and-back

Approximate riding time: 2.5 hours

Best bike: Road or hybrid bike

Terrain and trail surface: Flat ride on a paved bike path and city streets with a few rolling hills and one steep but relatively short climb up the wall

Traffic and hazards: There will be no car traffic on the Schuylkill River Trail on your way to Manayunk, but the trail can be crowded at times with other bikers, runners, and inline skaters. When you get to Manayunk, you will be doing some urban riding in the streets, which can be crowded with traffic at times. If you are not comfortable riding in traffic, you can choose to ride through Manayunk on the Schuylkill River Trail as long as you have wider tires and don't mind a few rough spots including a small section of cobblestones.

Things to see: Boathouse Row, Art Museum, Schuylkill River, Fairmount Park, Main Street Manayunk

Getting there: By car: From I-95 take I-676 west to the Benjamin Franklin Parkway exit (22nd Street, Museum area) on the right side. At the end of the exit ramp, turn right onto 22nd Street and get into the far left lane. The Benjamin Franklin Parkway is a boulevard with two outer lanes and two inner lanes. Turn left onto the outer lanes of the parkway. The museum will be in front of you on the hill. Stay in the outer lanes and go past the museum to Kelly Drive, then make a left at the light onto Waterworks Drive. The Italian Fountain is at the far end of the parking lot close to the museum. GPS: N39 58.04 / W75 10.98

By train: Take the train to the 30th Street Station then cross the Schuylkill River on Market Street and take Schuylkill River Trail north to the Art Museum.

THE RIDE

Manayunk is a neighborhood in the northwest section of Philadelphia by the Schuylkill River. In the 19th century, this area was filled with textile mills and other factories powered by the water from the canals. Today most of the old factories have been turned into loft apartments as this has become a desirable place to live with good shopping. Due to the many bars and restaurants in this area, it is also a popular nightlife destination for college students and business commuters. This is a very culturally diverse area that is fun to explore.

The starting line of the Philadelphia International Championship race

This ride has two purposes: One, to show you the Manayunk Wall and give you a chance to conquer it, and two, to show you the first part of the Schuylkill River Trail that heads all the way out to Valley Forge. To start the ride, get on the bike path on the back side of the parking lot and head away from the museum toward Kelly Drive. When you get to the end of Waterworks Drive, the bike path will start following Kelly Drive. The famous Boathouse Row is on your left. These houses host rowing clubs and their boats. You will have a good view of these houses from the riverside on your way back.

As you continue along you will be riding along the east side of the Schuylkill River. On a nice day a lot of people will be using the trail so it may be crowded. Just keep an eye on the trail as you enjoy the scenery here along the river.

After just under 4 miles you will come to Falls Bridge. As you continue along the trail it will get narrower and become the width of a sidewalk. You are now where Kelly Drive, Ridge Avenue, and City Avenue meet; you will see a couple of overpasses and quickly come to the intersection of Lincoln Drive and Ridge Avenue, where you will make a left. There is no real bike path here so you will have to continue on the sidewalk for a little while until the Y where Main Street and Ridge Avenue split. From here you can start riding on the road. Main Street usually has some car traffic, but nobody is moving fast here. So as long as you stay to the right when you can and ride defensively, you can easily navigate this area. Those riding a hybrid bike and who don't mind a little bit of a bumpy ride can jump on the Schuylkill River Trail, which can be accessed by making a left at Lock Street. The Schuylkill River Trail will take you all the way to Nixon Street and bypass the traffic of Manayunk.

Bike Shops

Cadence Cycling, 4323 Main St., Philadelphia 19127; (215) 508-4300
Cadence Cycling is a great bike shop for beginning cyclists, enthusiasts, and triathletes of all abilities. They provide all types of service including retail product, coaching, physiological testing, and regular bicycle repairs

The climb up the famous Manayunk Wall will start when you make the right off Main Street onto Levering. The climb will start at an 8 percent grade and be 17 percent at its steepest point. It is a tough climb but it is only 0.5 mile, so with the right gears and a little determination you can make it. The hardest thing about the climb is narrow streets with parked cars on both sides which requires to you watch out for traffic while negotiating the hill. During the Philadelphia International Cycling Championship the pros have to climb this hill fourteen times. If you don't want to do the climb, you can just continue straight on Main

Street until the T, then make a right followed by a quick left onto Umbria to rejoin the route.

Umbria Street will take you through a small neighborhood then through a commercial section of town before you will make a few turns to get you back to the river.

The turnaround point for the ride is about a third of a mile after the right turn onto Nixon. This is where Schuylkill River Trail splits off from River Road. From here you can just retrace your way back the way you came.

When you get to Falls Bridge, you can make a right over the bridge then a left after crossing the river and follow the trail down Martin Luther King Drive back to the starting point. As you continue along you will get some good views of the city skyline from the river. After you go under the Girard Bridge, you will see Boathouse Row again. This time you will get a good view of the river side of the houses. Just in front of the house you will see a small waterfall which is the Fairmount Dam.

After you pass the dam, the trail will become narrower and you will cross a bridge over to the other side of the river. The path will eventually bring you to the front of the Art Museum. This area is almost always crowded with cars and people so be careful here. If you continue around the museum along the path it will bring you around to the back where you will return to the Italian Fountain where you started your ride.

MILES AND DIRECTIONS

0.0 Start at the Italian Fountain behind the Art Museum. Follow the Schuylkill River Trail up Kelly Drive.

3.8 Continue straight at Falls River Bridge and continue following the Schuylkill River Trail.

4.5 Turn left at the light at Ridge Avenue.

5.0 Bear left at the Y onto Main Street. This is where you will start riding on the road.

5.7 Pass Lock Street. This is where you can get back on the Schuylkill River Trail.

6.2 Turn right onto Levering Street to start the climb up the wall.

6.4 Road changes name to Lyceum Avenue.

6.7 Turn left onto Pechin Street.

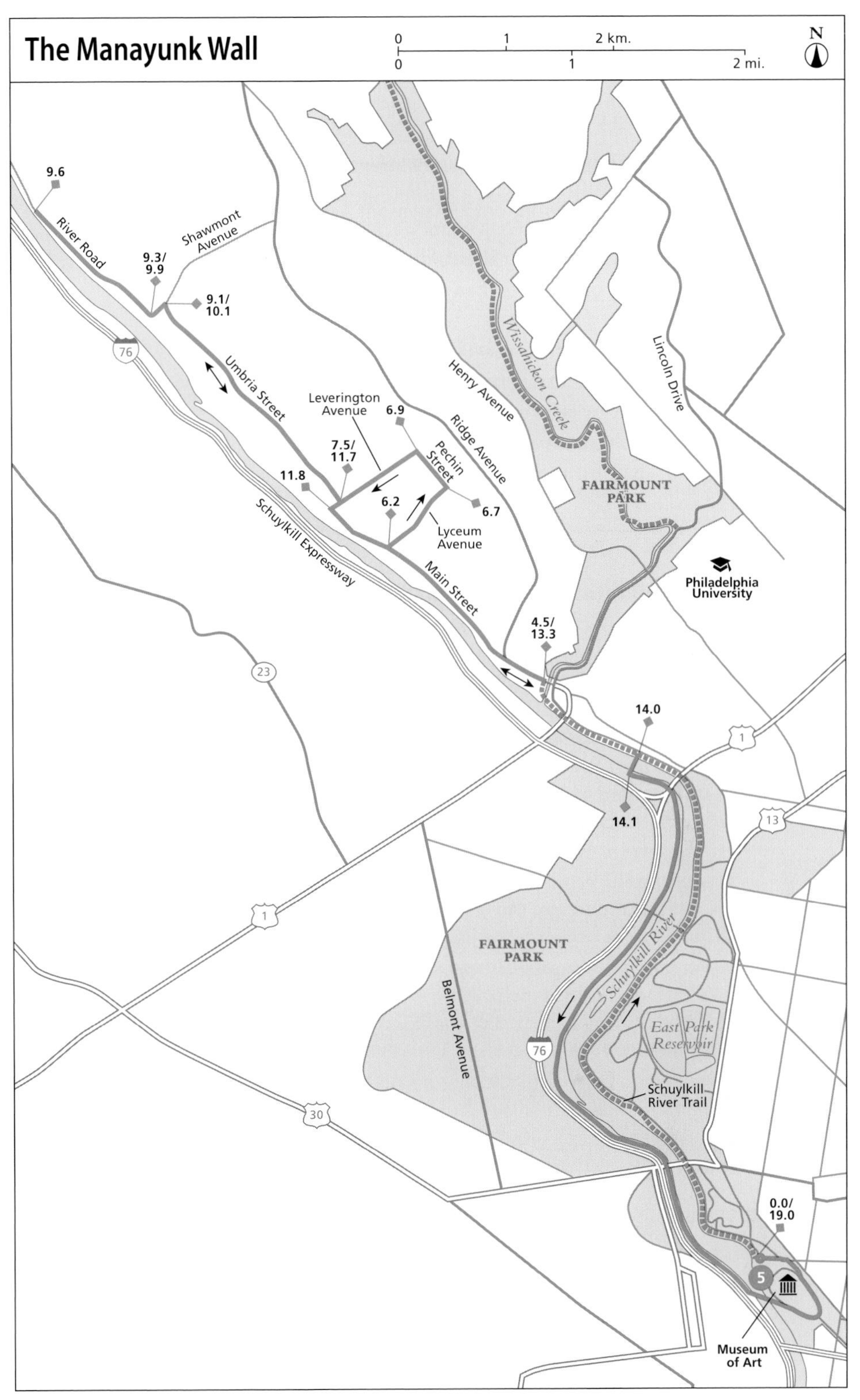
The Manayunk Wall
0 1 2 km.
0 1 2 mi.
N
9.6
River Road
Shawmont Avenue
9.3/
9.9
9.1/
10.1
76
Umbria Street
Leverington Avenue
6.9
7.5/
11.7
11.8
Pechin Street
6.2
6.7
Lyceum Avenue
Schuylkill Expressway
Main Street
Henry Avenue
Ridge Avenue
Wissahickon Creek
Lincoln Drive
FAIRMOUNT PARK
Philadelphia University
4.5/
13.3
23
14.0
1
14.1
13
1
FAIRMOUNT PARK
Schuylkill River
East Park Reservoir
Belmont Avenue
76
Schuylkill River Trail
30
0.0/
19.0
5
Museum of Art

6.9 Turn left onto Leverington Avenue.

7.5 Turn right onto Umbria Street.

9.0 Road changes name to Minerva Street.

9.1 Make a hard left turn onto Shawmont Avenue at bottom of the hill.

9.3 Turn right onto Nixon Street, which will become River Road.

9.6 Turnaround point. This is where the trail splits off to the right from River Road.

9.9 Turn left onto Shawmont Avenue. If you continue straight, you will be on the Schuylkill River Trail, which will require wide tires to negotiate the cobblestones and gravel path.

10.1 Turn right onto Minerva Street, which becomes Umbria Street.

The Philadelphia International Championship

The Philadelphia International Championship has been described as "America's top international cycling classic," and "one of the richest and most prestigious one-day races outside of Europe." At 156 miles it is one of the longest single-day races in the United States.

The race has existed since 1985, but was almost in danger of being canceled when Wachovia withdrew their sponsorship in 2005. With assistance from former Philadelphia mayor and current Pennsylvania governor Ed Rendell, a new corporate sponsor (Commerce Bank now part of TD Bank) was found, allowing the race to continue.

This race starts on the Benjamin Franklin Parkway, outside the Art Museum. After three parade laps around Logan Circle, the riders head off on a 14-mile circuit north on Kelly Drive toward the Manayunk district for the famous climb up "The Wall."

After the Manayunk Wall, the riders make their way back to Kelly Drive then two diversions to tackle additional climbs up Strawberry Mansion and Lemon Hill before making it back to the Art Museum on Benjamin Franklin Parkway.

The men's race completes ten circuits of the 14-mile course and ends the race with three shorter finishing circuits that include Lemon Hill, for a grand total of 156 miles.

You may not be able to qualify for the race, but for a small registration fee you can ride the course in the early morning before the race and get a feel of what the pros face.

11.7 Turn right onto Leverington Avenue.

11.8 Turn left onto Main Street. Watch the traffic here.

13.3 Turn right onto Lincoln Drive and start riding on the Schuylkill River Trail.

14.0 Turn right and ride across the Falls River Bridge.

14.1 Make a left after crossing the bridge back onto the Schuylkill River Trail and follow it along Martin Luther King Jr. Drive

18.8 Cross back over the Schuylkill River and continue to follow the trail around the Art Museum.

19.0 Arrive back at the Italian Fountain.

RIDE INFORMATION

Events/Attractions

The Pro Cycling Tour visits Philadelphia once a year for one of the premier races of the tour. This can be a fun race to watch, and if you get there before the race, you can even ride the course. Check out procyclingtour.com for dates and information about the event.

Manayunk: With over 30 restaurants and bars and many places to shop, Manayunk is a great place to hang out. For a listing of places to shop, eat, and drink check out the official website at manayunk.com.

The name Manayunk comes from the Lenape Indian word for river, *mëneyung* or *manaiung* ("where we go to drink"). For ease of spelling the "i" was changed to a "y" and the "g" to a "k." Manayunk is still a great place to "go to drink" because of its many bars and taverns.

Restrooms

Portable toilets can be found in some of the parking lots along the Schuylkill River Trail.

Maps

Delorme Pennsylvania Atlas & Gazetteer: Page 86, D3

Schuylkill River Trail Ride

The Schuylkill River Trail is the very popular urban escape route to the country roads in the northwest. The trail parallels the river closely from Center City to Valley Forge and beyond.

Start: Southern end of the Schuylkill River Trail, 0.3 mile south of Market Street on the east bank of the Schuylkill River

Length: 26.5 miles one way (53.0 miles round-trip)

Approximate riding time: 3.0 hours one way (6.0 hours round-trip)

Best bike: Cross bike or road bike

Terrain and trail surface: Flat and mostly paved. There are 2.2 miles of gravel on the Manayunk Canal towpath from mile 6.8 to mile 9.0. There is also a short stretch of cobblestones at the north end of the towpath and a short on-road portion for 0.4 mile north of the cobblestones.

Traffic and hazards: The trail can have heavy pedestrian usage, particularly on the segment in Fairmount Park and Center City. There are also brief on-road sections of the trail. Apart from Main Street in Manayunk, the on-road sections are generally quiet.

Getting there: By car: There are a number of access points along the trail. To start at Center City, take I-676 west to the Benjamin Franklin Parkway exit (22nd Street, Museum area) on the right side. At the end of the exit ramp, turn right onto 22nd Street and get into the far left lane. The Benjamin Franklin Parkway is a boulevard with two outer lanes and two inner lanes. Turn left onto the outer lanes of the parkway. The museum will be in front of you on the hill. Stay in the outer lanes and go past the museum to Kelly Drive, then make a left at the light onto Waterworks Drive. The southern end of the trail is 1.5 miles south of the intersection of Kelly Drive and Waterworks Drive. GPS: N39 58.04 / W75 10.98

To start toward the north end of the trail, the most convenient place to start is at the Betzwood Picnic Area in Valley Forge National Historical Park. To get there, drive north from Center City on I-76, and take the ramp for exits 328B-A /327 to 422 West. Keep left on this ramp for exit 328A to US 422 West toward Pottstown. Drive 3.6 miles, and take the PA

363 exit toward Audubon/Trooper. Turn left at the end of the ramp onto South Trooper Road. Drive 0.3 mile, and turn right when South Trooper Road ends in a T intersection. GPS: N40 06.56 / W75 25.24

By train: Take the train to 30th Street Station. Exit 30th Street Station south to Market Street and cross to the south side of Market Street. Ride east on Market Street toward City Hall. On the east side of the bridge over the Schuylkill River, there is a ramp that descends to the Schuylkill River Trail. Descend the ramp to trail level and ride 0.3 mile south to reach the south end of the trail.

Alternatively, the Norristown Line parallels the trail for much of its distance. The trail goes right by the Spring Mill, Conshohocken, and Norristown Transit Center stations.

THE RIDE

The Schuylkill River Trail is a very popular, well-designed multiuse trail and on a nice weekend day can be crowded with joggers, bikers, and pedestrians. The trail can be broken down roughly into three segments: The southern paved segment goes through Center City and Fairmount Park. The middle segment goes through Manayunk and features a variety of road surfaces and conditions: on-road, crushed rock towpath, and cobblestones. The northern paved segment goes through a mix of suburban downtowns and residential neighborhoods, well used but not as busy as Center City.

The southernmost part of the trail proceeds with the Schuylkill River on one side and a set of train tracks on the other, and the cross streets go on bridges over the trail, so you don't get a lot of cross traffic. This changes a little when the trail gets past the Art Museum and starts running along Kelly Drive. This area is known as Boathouse Row for the boathouses that are maintained by area rowing clubs. There are typically a lot of walkers around this area, so you need to be on your guard. When you get past Boathouse Row, you still have a lot of pedestrian traffic, and sometimes you will have cars crossing the trail to get into or out of parking lots, but the traffic becomes somewhat more predictable. The trail continues with the Schuylkill on the west and the sights of Fairmount Park on the east. You will also eventually pass Laurel Hill Cemetery, which is the final resting place of forty-two Civil War generals, including one Confederate general.

Eventually, you will reach the end of the trail, when Kelly Drive meets Ridge Avenue. This turn is known as Hoagie Corner, because the trail becomes thin enough for a large hoagie to bridge across it. There's enough room for two bicycles to pass—just. There are plans to reroute the trail so that the trail can be wider, but for right now, when I return to Center City on the trail, I pull onto

Kelly Drive and ride with traffic so that bicyclists who are heading northbound can have the full path.

The middle segment of the trail starts at Hoagie Corner. The trail turns left to cross the Wissahickon. At that point, the trail intersects with the Wissahickon Bike Trail, which continues to the right. The Schuylkill River Trail continues straight with Ridge Avenue, and then with Main Street in Manayunk. You can choose to continue to follow the trail (more like a wide sidewalk at this point), or you can choose to ride on Main Street as many cyclists do. Be watchful, though, because it's easy to miss the turn to the Manayunk Canal towpath at 6.8 miles. Turn left onto Lock Street at that point, and then turn right onto the towpath. Opinions differ about whether the towpath is suitable for road bicycles. It's a dirt path, and there are rocks and tree roots on it. Personally, I think that it's short enough that it's not a big deal. If you don't want to ride the rough towpath, you can follow the directions from miles 5.0 to 9.3 of Ride 5, which will take you through the streets of Manayunk and get you to Nixon Street at mile 9.0 of this ride.

The towpath ends with a short, steep climb up a cobblestone street. There's a brief on-road section, and then it's off the road onto the northern segment of the trail, which is 100 percent paved. There are some climbs (mostly to get to bridge crossings), but most of the northern segment of the trail is flat. There are also some at-grade crossings of streets, but the trail typically goes over or under the major highways in the area. The main things to watch for are train tracks and the occasional sharp curve. Before you know it, you will have passed through Conshohocken and Norristown and arrived at Betzwood in Valley Forge National Historic Park. This is the traditional turnaround point, so you can choose to get a drink of water here and turn around. Alternatively, you can keep going toward the Perkiomen Trail at Oaks and the current end of the

Bike Shops

Human Zoom Bikes and Boards, 4159 Main St., Philadelphia (in Manayunk); (215) 487-7433; humanzoom.com Human Zoom features a variety of road, mountain, cross, and folding bicycles, and sponsors bike maintenance clinics and group rides. At Mile 6.8 on the route, this shop is opposite Lock Street, which is where you turn to get on the Manayunk Canal towpath, so it would be a good landmark to watch for.

Cadence Cycling, 4323 Main St., Philadelphia (in Manayunk); cadencecycling.com In addition to being a full-service bike shop, Cadence Cycling provides coaching and performance services (such as pedaling analysis and bike and triathlon camps). Cadence is not quite on the route, but you get there from the route by biking 1 block north on Cotton Street in Manayunk and then turning left onto Main Street. Cadence Cycling is the second store on the right.

trail at Port Providence, or you can cross the walkway on the US 422 bridge and take a look around Valley Forge.

MILES AND DIRECTIONS

0.0 Start at the south end of the Schuylkill River Trail and head north.

1.5 Lloyd Hall. Bear left onto the trail that runs alongside Kelly Drive.

5.8 Bear left onto the trail that runs alongside Ridge Avenue.

The Betzwood Story

From 1912 to 1922, the 350-acre Betzwood complex was one of the largest and most advanced motion picture studios of its time.

The Betzwood story started in 1897, when Siegmund Lubin, a Jewish immigrant from Poland, started his film business in Philadelphia. Like most involved in motion pictures at the time, Lubin's company made the equipment, produced the motion pictures, and distributed the finished product. He was very successful, and soon owned a theater chain and exported his films to Europe. He also soon attracted the attention of Thomas Edison, who owned many of the patents related to motion picture cameras. This led to years of lawsuits and other trouble. Finally, Edison, Lubin, and the other major American film companies formed the Motion Picture Patents Company (MPPC), whereby the companies cross-licensed their patents to each other but shut out all other companies.

This effectively created a monopoly on motion picture production in the United States.

With this agreement, Lubin's business empire continued to grow. Lubin opened studios elsewhere in the United States, expanded his studio in Philadelphia, and at the height of his career, purchased the estate in Betzwood and made it into a studio and film lot.

Unfortunately for Lubin, a fire in June 1914 destroyed the negatives for a number of unreleased films, and the start of World War I later that year shut down the market for films in Europe. Changing tastes also eroded the market for Lubin's films. The final blow was the expiration of the patents on which the MPPC was founded. Lubin's company went out of business in 1916, and Siegmund Lubin returned to his previous career as an ophthalmologist. The production of movies resumed at Betzwood in 1918, but by 1922 the successor company also called it quits.

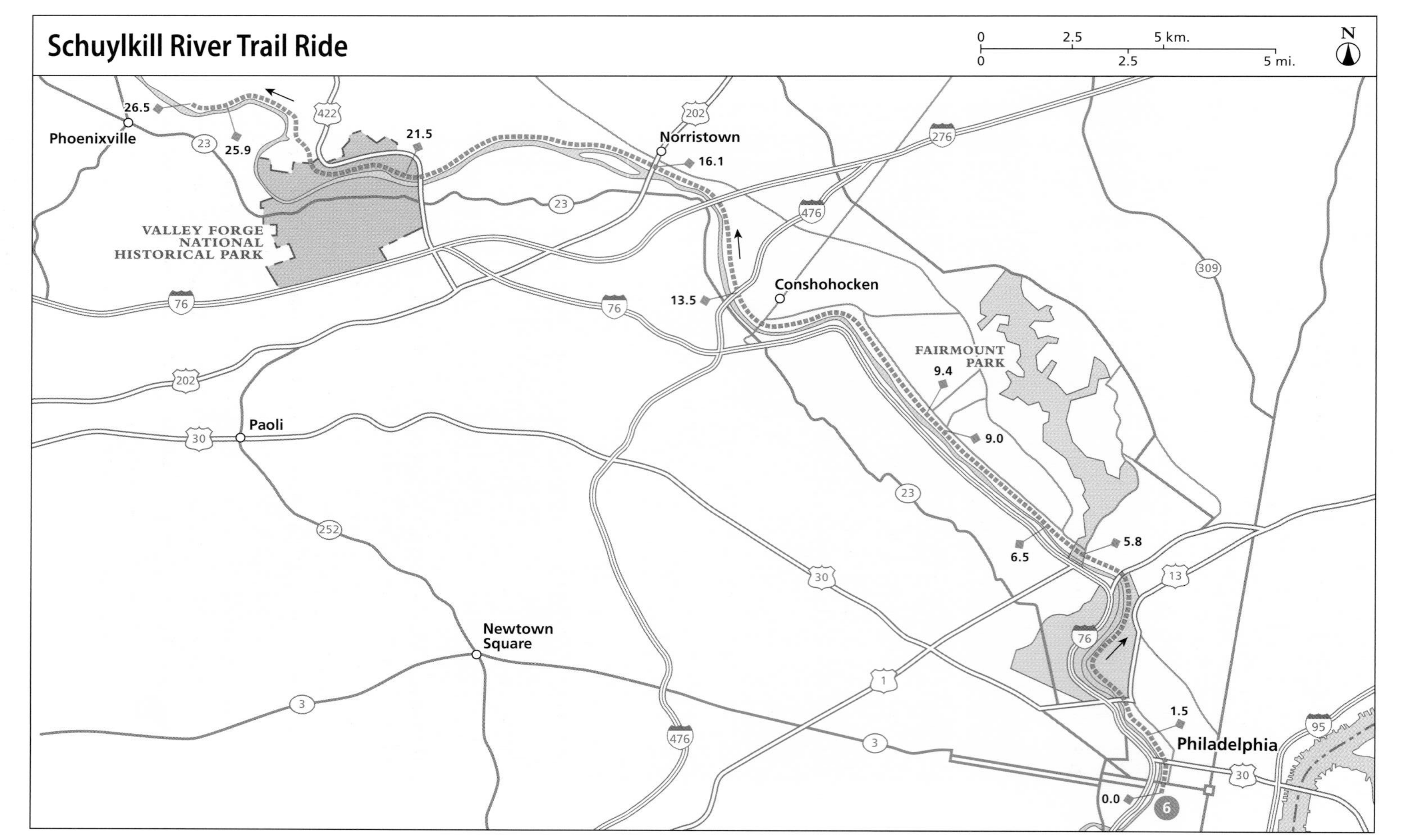

Schuylkill River Trail Ride
0 2.5 5 km.
0 2.5 5 mi.
N
26.5
Phoenixville
23
25.9
422
21.5
VALLEY FORGE NATIONAL HISTORICAL PARK
202
Norristown
16.1
23
276
476
13.5
Conshohocken
76
76
202
Paoli
30
252
309
FAIRMOUNT PARK
9.4
9.0
23
6.5
5.8
30
13
76
1
Newtown Square
3
3
476
1.5
95
Philadelphia
30
0.0
6

5.9 Wissahickon Bike Trail turns right at this point.

6.8 Turn left onto Lock Street and then right onto the Manayunk Canal towpath.

9.0 Ride uphill on a brief section of cobblestones, cross the train tracks, and turn left onto Nixon Street.

9.3 Turn right at the fork (follow the bike route sign).

9.4 Turn left onto the trail.

13.5 Cross County Trail branches off at this point.

16.0 The trail makes a 360-degree turn in descending to Ross Street.

16.1 Turn left onto the trail.

21.5 Betzwood Picnic Area at Valley Forge National Historic Park.

23.9 Perkiomen Trail branches off at this point.

25.9 Longford Park/Port Providence Trailhead. Turn left onto Port Providence Road.

26.5 Arrive at Fitzwater Station on left.

RIDE INFORMATION

Events/Attractions

Valley Forge National Historic Park: At mile 21.5, you can turn off the trail to cross the walkway on the US 422 bridge to the main unit of Valley Forge National Historic Park. Valley Forge features more bike trails, a good on-road biking route, and historical exhibits.

The Schuylkill Navigation System was a series of canals and pools that allowed barges to bypass rapids and shallows in the Schuylkill River and navigate the river successfully. Completed in 1827, the Schuylkill Navigation System opened commerce between Philadelphia and the coal-mining area around Pottsville, and enabled the industrial development of east-central Pennsylvania. Eventually, the system succumbed to competition with the railroads, and most of the canals were eventually filled in. The Manayunk Canal and the section of canal by Fitzwater Station are the only two segments of the system that are still in existence.

Fitzwater Station, 264 Canal St., Phoenixville; (610) 933-9958; fitzwaterstation.com: Fitzwater Station is a tavern that is located in a restored 19th-century canal house. They serve lunch and dinner daily, and they feature a summer concert series on Sunday afternoons. The only knock on this place is that they sometimes take awhile to serve you, but on a nice summer day with the music playing, you might not care so much.

Restrooms

Mile 1.5: Lloyd Hall has restrooms and drinking water.
Mile 3.2: There is a water fountain right next to the Kelly Statue (statue of a rower) by the regatta stands on the river.
Mile 21.5: Betzwood Picnic Area at Valley Forge National Historic Park has restrooms and drinking water.
Mile 25.9: Port Providence Trailhead has restrooms and drinking water.

Maps

Delorme Pennsylvania Atlas & Gazetteer: Page 86, D3

7

Bryn Athyn Cathedral

Historic churches are scattered all in and around Philadelphia. One of the most magnificent ones is Bryn Athyn Cathedral. The cathedral, located just outside the north limits of the city, was built between 1913 and 1919 in the Gothic and Norman styles. This ride will take you through the Pennypack valley for a view of the cathedral and the surrounding area.

Start: The parking area on Pine Road, Philadelphia

Length: 16.1-mile loop

Approximate riding time: 2 hours

Best bike: Road or hybrid bike

Terrain and trail surface: Paved roads; rolling with no real long or steep hills

Traffic and hazards: You will be riding on regular roads with mostly low to moderate traffic. Valley Road can have heavy traffic at times but has a small shoulder to ride on. The roads in and around Jenkintown can be congested during rush hours.

Things to see: Bryn Athyn Cathedral, Pennypack Park, Jenkintown

Getting there: From Philadelphia take I-76 west to the Roosevelt Boulevard exit (US 1). Take US 1 north to State Highway 232 (Oxford Avenue). Go north on 232 for 3.1 miles then make a right onto Pine Road. After 1 mile you will see the Pennypack parking area on your right. GPS: N40 05.39 / W75 04.16

THE RIDE

The northeast suburbs of Philadelphia are one of the most popular areas around the city to live in. This area is a mix of small towns, residential neighborhoods, and a few nice rural parks. The diversity and less crowded nature of this area make it a good area for a bike ride.

To start the ride, head out the entrance of the parking lot and make a right onto Pine Road. This will take you through a few residential neighborhoods as you make your way toward Bryn Athyn. Be careful when you make the left turn onto Tomlison Road because it is a busy intersection where five roads meet, so you have to watch out for cars coming from a couple of different directions.

The Bryn Athyn Cathedral

Once on Tomlison Road, you will pass a country club on your right then enter the area of Bryn Athyn College, which is a small, private Christian liberal arts college. When you make a right onto Ashley Road, you will work your way through part of the college campus and end up on College Road and State Route 232 (Huntington Pike). Straight ahead of you here is the Bryn Athyn Cathedral. Although the route directions say turn left here, feel free to cross the street onto Cathedral Road to get a closer look at the cathedral. The cathedral is open to the public and they do offer tours. You can check the website for details.

Also on the grounds of the cathedral is the Glencairn Museum. This castle-like building was the former house of billionaire businessman Raymond Pitcairn and now houses a collection of over 8,000 pieces of religious art.

Once you're done checking out the cathedral and grounds, you can head back out to the route. As you head away from the cathedral, you will go through a residential neighborhood and pass over the upper part of the Pennypack Creek before coming to Valley Road. This road can be busy at times so stay to the right. Eventually you will veer off Valley Road onto Fairway. There is a shopping mall here so it is a good place to stop if you need a break. Be careful of the cars coming in and out of the driveways of the mall.

From here you will ride through the residential area and town center of Jenkintown. This is one of the oldest towns in Montgomery County. The residential roads will be pretty low traffic, but you will have moderate to heavy traffic in town depending on the time of day. As you leave Jenkintown on Washington Lane, be careful not to miss the turn onto Fairacres Road since the entrance to the road is surrounded by a stone wall that makes it look like a large driveway.

You will then travel through the Fox Chase area, which will lead you back to your starting point on Pine Road. If you still want some more miles and good scenery, you can take a ride down the Pennypack Trail.

Bike Shops

Abington Wheel Wright Bikeshop, 1120 Old York Rd., Abington 19001; (215) 884-6331 Abington Wheel Wright Bikeshop is a full-service bike shop that can help you repair your current bike or help you find a new one that fits your riding style.

MILES AND DIRECTIONS

0.0 Make a right out of the parking lot onto Pine Road.

1.8 Turn left onto Welsh Road.

2.0 Turn right onto Pine Road.

3.1 Turn left onto Tomlinson Road.

4.0 Turn right onto Ashley Road.

4.1 Bear left onto Waverly Road.

4.2 Cross Buck Road. Waverly Road becomes College Drive.

4.6 Turn right onto Cathedral Drive.

4.6 Turn left onto State Route 232 (Huntington Pike).

4.7 Turn right onto Alnwick Road.

4.9 Bear right to stay on Alnwick Road.

5.3 Merge onto Fetters Mill Road.

5.5 Turn left onto Terwood Drive.

5.7 Bear right onto Valley Road.

8.1 Bear right onto The Fairway.

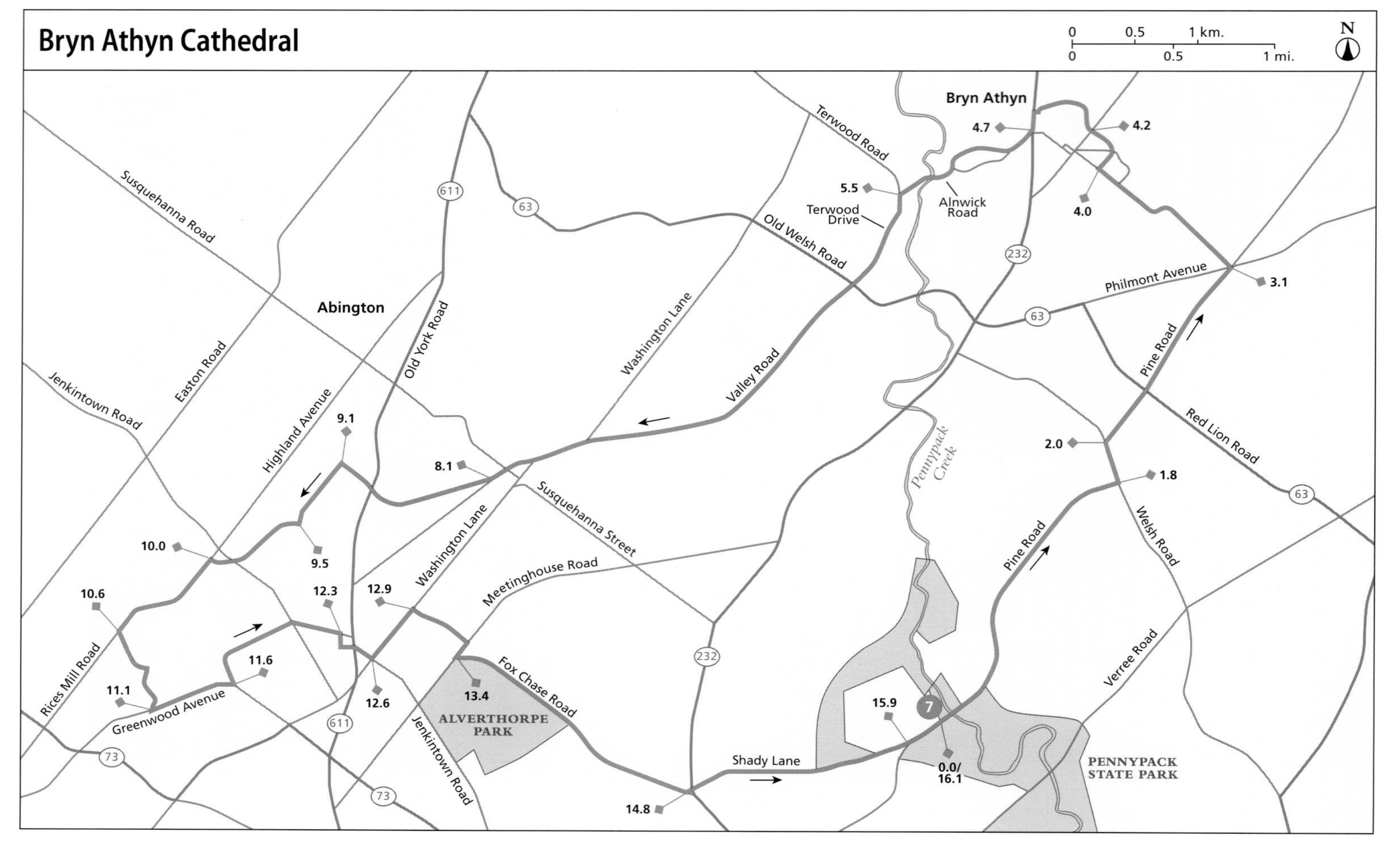
Bryn Athyn Cathedral
0 0.5 1 km.
0 0.5 1 mi.
N
Bryn Athyn
Abington
Susquehanna Road
Easton Road
Jenkintown Road
Highland Avenue
Old York Road
Washington Lane
Valley Road
Old Welsh Road
Terwood Road
Terwood Drive
Alnwick Road
Philmont Avenue
Pine Road
Red Lion Road
Welsh Road
Verree Road
Susquehanna Street
Meetinghouse Road
Fox Chase Road
Shady Lane
Greenwood Avenue
Rices Mill Road
Pennypack Creek
ALVERTHORPE PARK
PENNYPACK STATE PARK
611
63
232
73
7
0.0/16.1
1.8
2.0
3.1
4.0
4.2
4.7
5.5
8.1
9.1
9.5
10.0
10.6
11.1
11.6
12.3
12.6
12.9
13.4
14.8
15.9

8.9 Cross State Route 611. The Fairway becomes Harte Road.

9.1 Turn left onto Glen Road.

9.4 Turn left onto Winding Road.

9.5 Turn right onto Baeder Road.

9.8 Cross Jenkintown Road.

9.9 Turn right onto Wharton Road.

10.0 Turn left onto Highland Avenue.

10.2 Highland Avenue becomes Rices Mill Road.

10.6 Turn left onto Hewett Road.

10.9 Turn right onto Bent Road.

11.1 Turn left onto Greenwood Avenue.

11.6 Turn left onto West Avenue.

12.3 Turn right onto Leedon Street.

12.4 Turn left onto Greenwood Avenue.

12.5 Cross State Route 611.

12.6 Turn left onto Washington Lane.

12.9 Turn right onto Fairacres Road.

13.3 Turn right onto Meetinghouse Road.

13.4 Turn left onto Fox Chase Road.

An Early Innovator

John Pitcairn Jr. (January 10, 1841—July 22, 1916) was a Scottish-born American and one of the main benefactors of the Bryn Athyn Cathedral. Pitcairn made his money by working through the ranks of the Pennsylvania railroad and oil industry. He went on to found the Pittsburgh Plate Glass Company (now PPG Industries), an early industry innovator that quickly grew into the largest manufacturer of plate glass in the United States. The result is that he amassed one of the largest fortunes in the United States at the time.

14.8 Bear left right before crossing State Route 232 (Huntington Pike) onto Shady Lane.

15.9 Turn left onto Pine Road.

16.1 Turn right into Pennypack Park parking area.

RIDE INFORMATION

Events/Attractions

Bryn Athyn Cathedral is a wonderful historic cathedral with a lot of interesting history and architecture. If you're interested in visiting the cathedral or learning more about its history, visit brynathyncathedral.org for more details.

Pennypack Park is a beautiful park that surrounds Pennypack Creek and provides a good place for biking, hiking, and horseback riding. An environmental center provides some educational programs. For more information check out the website fairmountpark.org/pennypackpark.asp.

Bryn Athyn's original college campus and surrounding community of Bryn Athyn were designed in 1893 by Charles Eliot of the firm Olmstead, Olmstead, and Eliot—the firm responsible for the design of Central Park in New York City.

Restrooms

Start/end: There is a portable toilet in the Pennypack parking lot.

Mile 8.2: You should be able to use one of the bathrooms in one of the delis in the shopping mall.

Maps

Delorme Pennsylvania Atlas & Gazetteer: Page 86, B4

8

Fairmount Park

In Philadelphia, Fairmount Park is where people go to escape the urban jungle and enjoy some recreational time in grassy fields or nice walks through wooded areas. The park has everything a big-city park needs, including plenty of open space, lots of different athletic fields for both kids and adults, and many interesting sites and attractions. This ride will take you through some different areas of Fairmount Park to show you the beauty and variety it offers.

Start: Italian Fountain behind the Art Museum

Length: 10-mile loop

Approximate riding time: 1.5 hours

Best bike: Road or hybrid bike

Terrain and trail surface: Flat to rolling as you ride on the pavement of city streets and park roads.

Traffic and hazards: This ride will be on the streets of Philadelphia so you will be doing some urban riding. Most of the streets you will be riding on will have dedicated bike lanes, but you will still have to be cautious of the traffic and pedestrians along the route.

Things to see: Art Museum, Strawberry Mansion, Belmont Plateau, Japanese Tea House, Lemon Tree Hill

Getting there: By car: From I-95 take I-676 west to the Benjamin Franklin Parkway exit (22nd Street, Museum area) on the right side. At the end of the exit ramp, turn right onto 22nd Street and get into the far left lane. The Benjamin Franklin Parkway is a boulevard with two outer lanes and two inner lanes. Turn left onto the outer lanes of the parkway. The Museum will be in front of you on the hill. Stay in the outer lanes and go past the Museum to Kelly Drive then make a left at the light onto Waterworks Drive. The Italian Fountain is at the far end of the parking lot close to the Museum. GPS: N39 58.04 / W75 10.98
By train: Take the train to the 30th Street Station then cross the Schuylkill River on Market Street and take Schuylkill River Trail north to the Art Museum.

THE RIDE

Although Fairmount may sound like one large park, it is really a series of different park areas separated by highways, roads, and other neighborhoods. Each area has its own personality, history, and interesting attractions that can take years to fully explore. To start your tour of the park, head back out of the parking lot and cross Kelly Drive onto Sedgely Road. There is a bike lane here to ride on as you slowly go up a shallow hill. You will stay to the right where Sedgely Road goes left to get onto Poplar Drive. This will take you across Girard Avenue and across a bridge over railroad tracks that will take you through one of the residential neighborhoods near the park. There is still a bike lane here, but there will be a little more traffic so be careful when you make the left onto Reservoir Road to get back into the park.

Once on Reservoir Road, you will be back in Fairmount Park; ride around a reservoir and past some athletic fields before entering the Strawberry Mansion

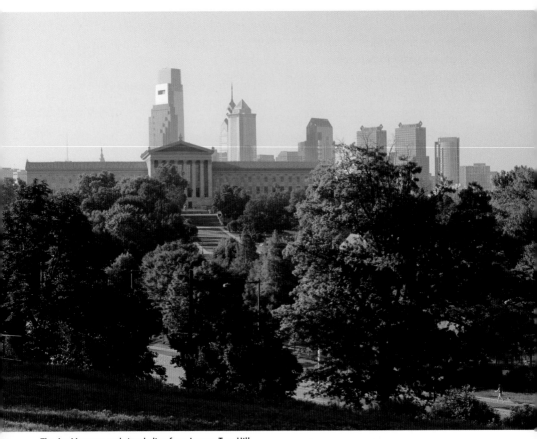

The Art Museum and city skyline from Lemon Tree Hill

part of the park. Strawberry Mansion is a large summer home that was built for Judge William Lewis in 1789. Lewis was a well-known lawyer during Revolutionary times; he was eventually appointed to federal judicial positions by George Washington and also advised Alexander Hamilton on the first national bank. If you want to take a look at the actual mansion, you can take a quick detour to the house by making the next left off Greenland Drive after passing Woodford Road.

Once you are on Strawberry Mansion Bridge Drive, you will pass an open-air theater as you go downhill. At the bottom of the hill you will make a right and cross Strawberry Mansion Bridge. Although the road has a bike lane, you can also use the wooden walkway to ride over the bridge especially if you want to stop and enjoy the view of the Schuylkill River. After crossing the bridge, you will head up hill. Since you crossed the river you are now in West Fairmount Park. At the top of the hill, you will ride along the ridge past a number of athletic fields and parking areas before making your way to the Belmont Plateau.

Halfway down Belmont Mansion Drive you will see Belmont Mansion on your right. It was built in the mid-18th-century by William Peters, an English lawyer and land management agent for the Penn family. The mansion is a beautiful example of Palladian architecture and has been well preserved. It is now an Underground Railroad museum open to the public for tours.

To your left across from the mansion is one of the best views of the Philadelphia skyline. As you continue on you will make a loop out to the Mann Center for the Performing Arts that hosts a number of musical, theatrical, and other entertainment in a beautiful outdoor theater.

After you loop around the Mann, you will head through a gate onto Horticulture Drive, which will take you past the Japanese House and Garden and the Please Touch Museum before you make your way to Lansdowne Drive. Lansdowne Drive will take you to the Girard Avenue Bridge, which will take you back across the Schuylkill River. This is a busy road so it is recommended that you ride on the sidewalk here instead of the road. Right after you cross the bridge, you will make a right onto Sedgely Road. The next turn will take you up Lemon Tree Drive, which is one of the hills the bike racers ride during the International Bicycling championship. Although the hill is steep in spots, it is very short and will give you a nice glimpse of the skyline on your way down.

Bike Shops

Cadence Cycling, 4323 Main St., Philadelphia 19127; (215) 508-4300
Cadence Cycling is a great bike shop for beginning cyclists, enthusiasts, and triathletes of all abilities. They provide all types of service including retail product, coaching, physiological testing, and regular bike repair.

At the end of Lemon Tree Drive you will make a right back to Sedgely Road, which will take you back to your starting point. As you can see by this short ride, Fairmount Park has a lot to offer, which is why people in Philadelphia love it.

MILES AND DIRECTIONS

0.0 Start at the corner of Kelly Drive and Waterworks Drive; cross Kelly Drive onto Sedgely Road.

0.1 Stay to the right where Sedgely Road forks to the left; you will now be on Poplar Drive.

0.6 Cross Girard Avenue, Sedgely Road becomes 33rd Street (US 13).

1.0 Turn left onto Reservoir Drive.

2.2 Turn right onto Dauphin Drive.

2.4 Turn left before leaving the park onto Greenland Drive.

2.5 Greenland Drive becomes Strawberry Mansion Bridge Drive.

2.9 Turn right onto Strawberry Mansion Drive and ride across bridge. (It's OK to ride on the wooden walkway.)

3.1 Road changes name to Greenland Drive on other side of the bridge.

3.7 Bear left at Y then make left onto Chamounix Drive.

4.7 Turn left onto Belmont Mansion Drive.

5.2 Bear right onto Montgomery Drive.

5.3 Cross Belmont Avenue; Montgomery Drive becomes South Georges Hill Drive.

5.4 Bear left onto States Drive.

5.7 Go around circle to the right onto Avenue of the Republic.

6.0 Cross 52nd Street; Avenue of the Republic becomes Georges Hill Drive.

6.3 Turn right onto South Georges Hill Drive.

6.9 Cross Belmont Avenue. South Georges Hill Drive becomes Montgomery Drive then bear right to stay on Montgomery Drive.

6.9 Turn right onto Belmont Mansion Drive.

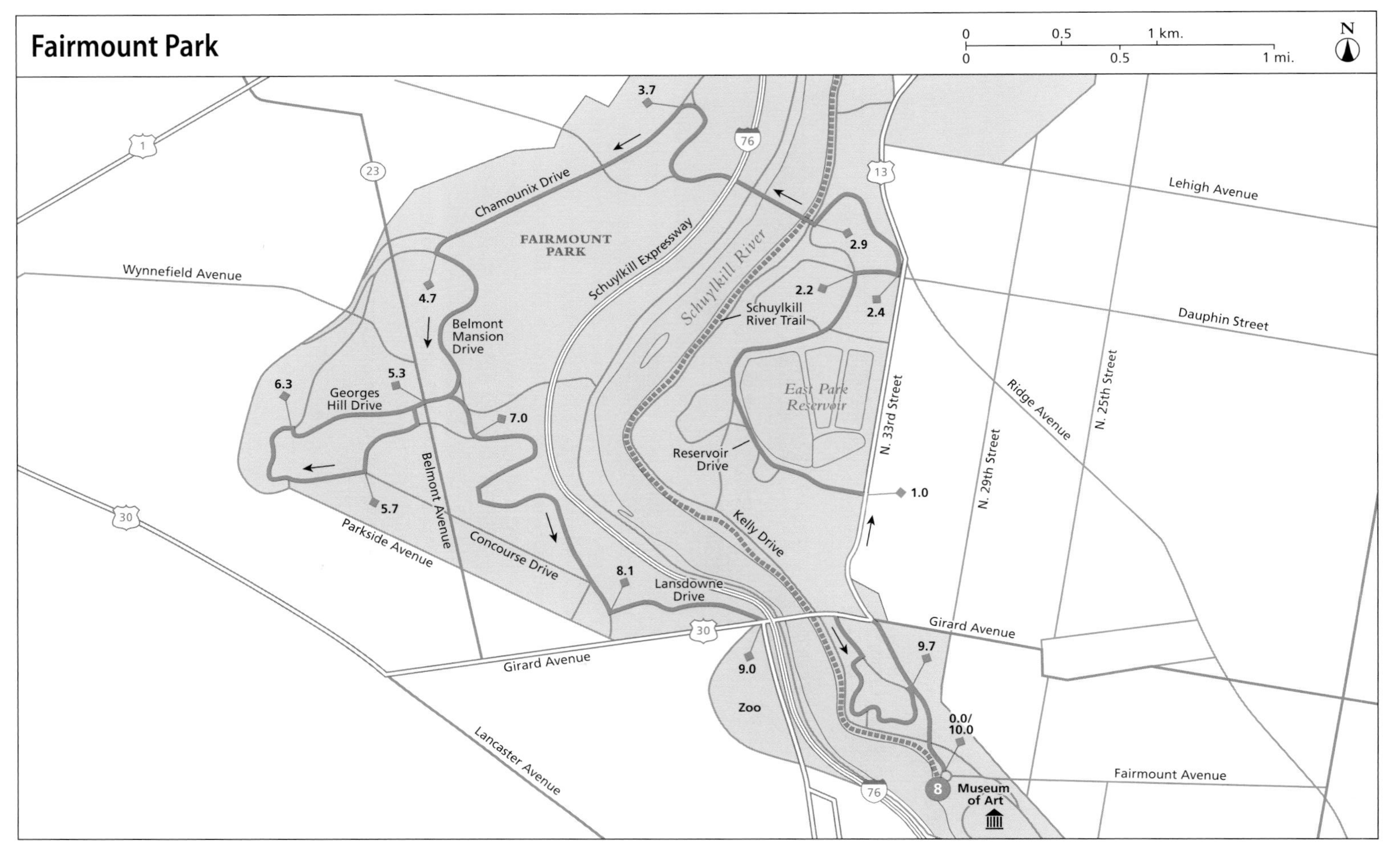

Fairmount Park
0
0.5
1 km.
0
0.5
1 mi.
N
FAIRMOUNT PARK
Chamounix Drive
Schuylkill Expressway
Schuylkill River
Schuylkill River Trail
East Park Reservoir
Reservoir Drive
Kelly Drive
Belmont Mansion Drive
Georges Hill Drive
Belmont Avenue
Concourse Drive
Parkside Avenue
Lansdowne Drive
Girard Avenue
Girard Avenue
Lancaster Avenue
Wynnefield Avenue
Lehigh Avenue
Dauphin Street
Ridge Avenue
N. 33rd Street
N. 29th Street
N. 25th Street
Fairmount Avenue
Zoo
Museum of Art
8
1
23
30
30
76
76
13
0.0/10.0
1.0
2.2
2.4
2.9
3.7
4.7
5.3
5.7
6.3
7.0
8.1
9.0
9.7

7.0 Bear left and go through gates onto Horticultural Drive.

7.5 Turn left onto Belmont Mansion Drive.

7.5 Turn left onto Lansdowne Drive.

8.1 Go a little over halfway around the circle onto Lansdowne Drive.

8.1 Turn left at a T onto Lansdowne Drive.

8.8 Turn left at light and cross Girard Avenue Bridge (stay on sidewalk here).

9.0 Turn right onto West Sedgely Drive.

9.2 Turn right onto Lemon Hill Drive.

9.7 Turn right onto Poplar Drive.

10.0 Cross Kelly Drive to arrive back at starting point.

America's First World's Fair

The area of Fairmount Park by the Avenue of the Republic was the site for the Centennial International Exhibition of 1876. This was a world's fair to celebrate the centennial and showcase America's culture and industry. This was the first world's fair held in the United States and was comprised of over 200 buildings built to house the displays of industrial machines, art, music, tools, furniture, flowers, exotic plants, clothing, and a lot of new technologies of the time. The exhibition was the first time the public saw Alexander Graham Bell's telephone, the typewriter, Heinz Ketchup, and Hires Root Beer to name a few. The main exhibition building covered over 21 acres and was the largest building, in terms of area, at the time. Some states also had their own building for exhibits as did eleven foreign countries. The Centennial International Exhibition of 1876 was open from May 10th until November 10th of 1876 and was a big success with over ten million visitors. This exhibition showed that America was a major industrial power that could compete on the world stage. More details and pictures of the exhibition can be found at liblibrary.phila.gov/CenCol.

RIDE INFORMATION

Events/Attractions

Fairmount Park is a collection of sixty-three parks within Philadelphia that comprise over 9,200 acres. The park contains many historic sites as well as athletic fields, picnic areas, hiking trails, open spaces, and many other opportunities for outdoor activities. For more information about the parks, check out the website at fairmountpark.org.

The Please Touch Museum is housed in Memorial Hall, which was built for the Centennial Exhibition to house the art exhibits.

Restrooms

Mile 0.1: Corner of Kelly Drive and Waterworks Drive

Maps

Delorme Pennsylvania Atlas & Gazetteer: Page 86, D3

9

Airport Loop

It might not seem at first that an airport would be a good place for a ride. When you consider that airports are generally flat and have limited access points (and therefore limited places where traffic can cross), you can see that the idea has potential. And when you further consider that Philadelphia International Airport was built on the banks of the Delaware River and might harbor some numbers of wild creatures, then you can see that it might not be a bad idea at all to ride around the airport.

Start: Parking lot of John Heinz National Wildlife Refuge at Tinicum

Length: 12.6-mile loop

Approximate riding time: 1 hour

Best bike: Road bike

Terrain and trail surface: Flat, with two climbs over an overpass. The route runs entirely on paved streets and roads.

Traffic and hazards: This ride uses mostly streets with paved shoulders. The portions of the route that are north of I-95 are moderately busy. The portions of the route that are south of I-95 are used mainly by delivery trucks and are somewhat less busy. Because the route circles Philadelphia International Airport, you will see and hear frequent low-flying aircraft.

Things to see: Fort Mifflin

Getting there: By car: Drive south on I-95, and take exit 12B to Cargo City. At the stoplight, turn right onto Bartram Street. Drive on Bartram Street for 0.8 mile, then turn left onto South 84th Street. Drive on S 84th Street for 0.7 mile, then turn left onto Lindbergh Boulevard. Drive 0.2 mile to the entrance to John Heinz National Wildlife Refuge at Tinicum. GPS: N39 53.35 / W75 15.25
By train: Take the train to 30th Street Station, and then transfer to the Airport Line. Take the Airport Line train to Eastwick Station. The route runs right by the station.

THE RIDE

Philadelphia International Airport serves over 30,000 people a year, which makes it the twelfth busiest airport in the United States. Although this area is busy with people getting to and from the airport, the road you will be riding on will not be too congested and most of the roads have wide shoulders to ride on. You will start the ride from John Heinz National Wildlife Refuge. Ride out of the refuge the same way that you drove in, biking north on Lindbergh Boulevard, and turn right at the light onto 84th Street. You will then go over an overpass and turn right at the T intersection onto Bartram Avenue. Continue south on the shoulder on Bartram Avenue, under I-95 and through the next light, and turn right at the stop sign at Tinicum Island Road. Continue on the shoulder of Tinicum Island Road until you see a concrete barrier in the middle of the road. When you see the barrier, pick a spot to move into the left-turn lane, and turn left onto Fort Mifflin Road. This will take you around

Airplane above Fort Mifflin

the south and east side of the airport, where you will get good views of the airport runways and the Delaware River.

After you pass the northern end of the airport, you will see Fort Mifflin on your right. If you have the time, you can stop and explore the fort. There is also a bathroom here if you need it. When Fort Mifflin Road ends in a T intersection, you will turn left onto Enterprise Avenue. In turn, Enterprise Avenue ends, and you will turn right onto Island Avenue. Take extra care on Island Avenue because of the extra traffic. When you go under I-95 again, pick a spot to move into the left lane so that you can turn left onto Bartram Avenue. Continue on Bartram Avenue to 84th Street and turn right. At this point, all you need to do is retrace your steps back to John Heinz.

MILES AND DIRECTIONS

0.0 Start in the parking lot of John Heinz National Wildlife Refuge at Tinicum and head northeast toward Lindbergh Boulevard.

0.2 Turn left onto Lindbergh Boulevard.

0.4 Turn right onto South 84th Street.

1.1 Turn right onto Bartram Avenue.

1.2 Eastwick Station is on the right.

2.8 Turn right onto Tinicum Island Road.

4.3 Turn left onto Fort Mifflin Road (at the barriers in the middle of the road).

8.6 Fort Mifflin is on the right.

9.8 Turn left onto Enterprise Avenue.

10.4 Turn right onto Island Avenue.

11.2 Turn left onto Bartram Avenue.

11.5 Turn right onto South 84th Street, or continue another 0.1 mile to Eastwick Station on the right.

12.2 Turn left onto Lindbergh Boulevard.

12.4 Turn right into John Heinz National Wildlife Refuge.

12.6 Arrive back at John Heinz National Wildlife Refuge at Tinicum.

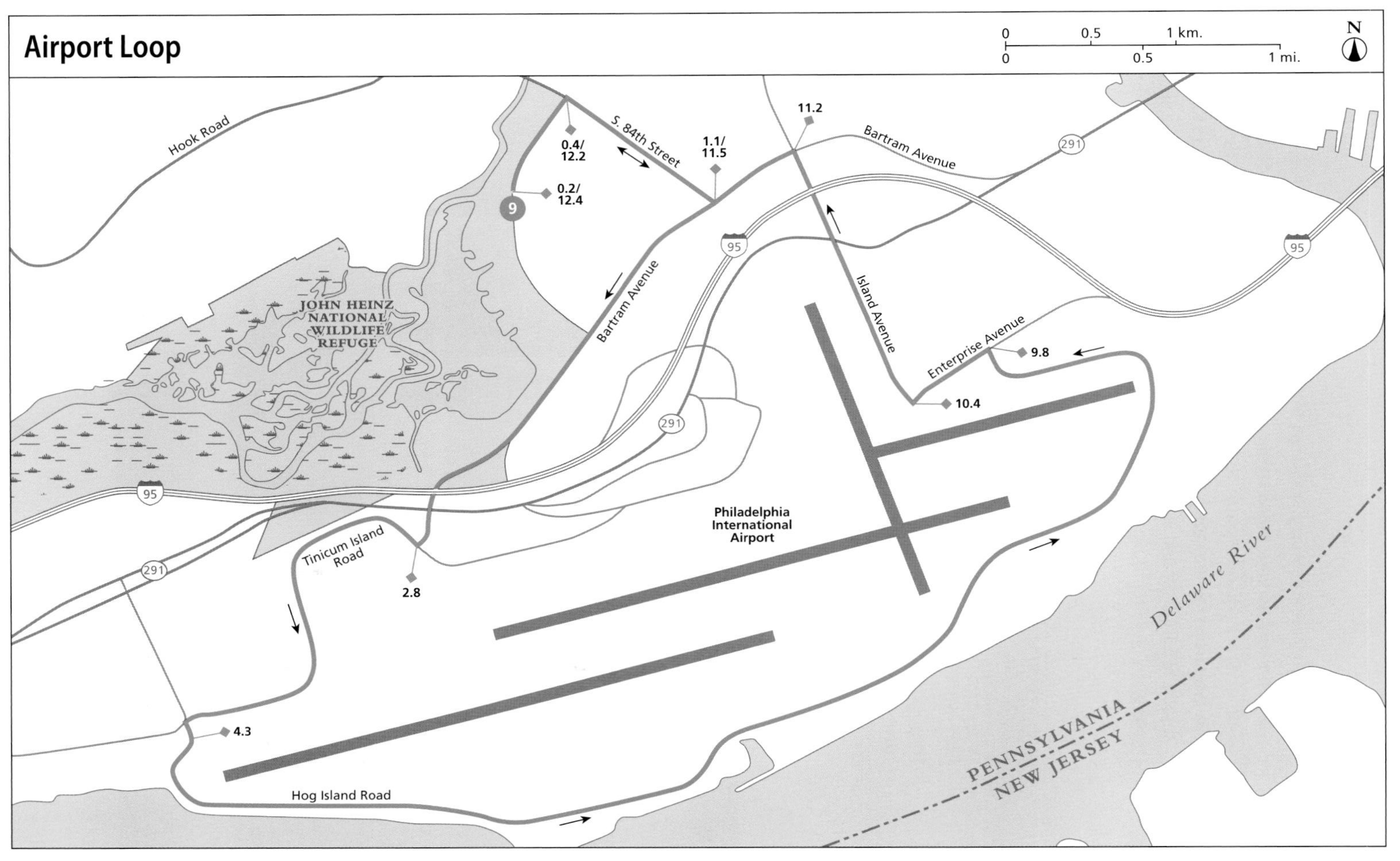
Airport Loop
0 0.5 1 km.
0 0.5 1 mi.
N
Hook Road
S. 84th Street
0.4/ 12.2
0.2/ 12.4
9
1.1/ 11.5
11.2
Bartram Avenue
291
95
JOHN HEINZ NATIONAL WILDLIFE REFUGE
Island Avenue
Enterprise Avenue
9.8
10.4
Philadelphia International Airport
Tinicum Island Road
2.8
4.3
Hog Island Road
Delaware River
PENNSYLVANIA
NEW JERSEY

9

After the Revolutionary War, Fort Mifflin was rebuilt but never again saw enemy fire. Like many other forts, Fort Mifflin was used to house Confederate prisoners during the Civil War. The land on which the fort sits was used for various defense-related purposes over the years but finally fell into disuse and was deeded to the City of Philadelphia in 1962.

RIDE INFORMATION

Events/Attractions

Fort Mifflin is open to the public March 1 to December 15, Wednesday through Sunday 10 a.m. to 4 p.m. There is an admission charge.

John Heinz Wildlife Refuge is a 1,000-acre wildlife refuge spanning Philadelphia and Delaware Counties. The refuge is a great place for hiking, fishing,

The Hospital at Fort Mifflin

Fort Mifflin under Siege

After the British defeated the Continental Army at Brandywine in 1777, the British advanced and took Philadelphia. However, the Royal Navy could not follow the army to Philadelphia, because the citizens of Philadelphia had prepared a line of defense against naval attack downstream from the city. They finished the construction of Fort Mifflin (which had been started by the British in 1771) and constructed Fort Mercer on the New Jersey side of the river. The citizens of Philadelphia also constructed a line of underwater obstacles in the river so that ships could proceed only through narrow channels in the river, which of course were closely guarded by the forts. Because ships could not land supplies at Philadelphia itself, the British were forced to haul their supplies overland from Chester and dedicate a substantial escort to protect their supply line. The British therefore placed Fort Mifflin under siege. The garrison held out for five weeks under the heaviest bombardment of the Revolutionary War. Over half the garrison were killed or wounded, but their stand prevented the British from resuming the offensive in 1777 and ultimately allowed the Continental Army to retire safely to winter quarters at Valley Forge.

canoeing, and wildlife observation. It has 10 miles of trails, a good portion of which are open to biking. The refuge also contains an environmental center that hosts a number of educational programs.

Restrooms

Mile 0.0: The Cusano Environmental Education Center at John Heinz National Wildlife Refuge has toilets and water. There is also a portable toilet outside if the Cusano Center is closed.

Mile 8.6: Fort Mifflin has toilets for visitors.

Maps

Delorme Pennsylvania Atlas & Gazetteer: Page 86, B2

10

Pennypack Park

In the northeast part of Philadelphia is one of the jewels of the Fairmount Park system, Pennnypack Park. This 1,600-acre park is a beautiful mix of woodlands, meadows, and wetlands. The park has hiking, biking, and bridle trails that make it easy to explore all the different natural and historic features. The main feature of this park is Pennypack Creek, which runs the length of the park and eventually drains into the Delaware River. This ride will take you along the main paved trail of the park and show you the main sights.

Start: The parking area on Pine Road, Philadelphia

Length: 19.2 miles out and back

Approximate riding time: 2.5 hours

Best bike: Road, mountain, or hybrid bike

Terrain and trail surface: Paved park trail. It's well-maintained and even plowed when it snows so this is a place that can be ridden year-round. The park terrain is flat to rolling with a couple of very short steep hills.

Traffic and hazards: There will be no car traffic on the paved trail, but this trail is shared by hikers, joggers, inline skaters, etc., so on a nice sunny weekend day the trail may be a little crowded.

Things to see: Fox Chase Farm, Pennypack Environmental Center, King's Highway Bridge, Pennypack Bandshell, Delaware River

Getting there: From Philadelphia take I-76 west to the Roosevelt Boulevard exit (US 1). Take US 1 north to State Highway 232 (Oxford Avenue). Go north on 232 for 3.1 miles then make a right onto Pine Road. After 1 mile you will see the Pennypack parking area on your right. GPS: N40 05.39 / W75 04.16

THE RIDE

Pennypack Park was officially established in 1905 by an ordinance from the city, but this area has a rich history that started back with the Lenni-Lenape Indians, who hunted and fished along the creek. This land which is now the park was acquired in 1683 by William Penn and was the center of industry

The Pennypack Trail

A Park Teeming with Nature

Pennypack Park is home to more than 150 species of nesting and migrating birds, including the tiny ruby-throated hummingbird, the great blue heron, warblers, the pileated woodpecker, several kinds of seabirds, ducks, geese, hawks, great horned owls, and the little screech owl to name only a few. This makes the park a nice place to hang out and do some bird watching. The park is also famous for its large, scattered deer herd, as well as other mammals, including several kinds of bats, the red and gray fox, rabbits, chipmunks, mice, muskrats, woodchucks, raccoons, skunks, opossum, and weasels. Those interested in reptiles will find snakes, turtles, frogs, the common toad, and several kinds of salamanders in the park. This makes this park a great place to come to commune with nature. For more information on the flora and fauna, check out the Pennypack Environmental Center located on Verree Road.

throughout the 19th and early 20th centuries with many mills and factories dotting its banks. The remains of some of these factories can still be located throughout the park if you look carefully.

To start the ride, go down the paved road and head away from the parking area. You will soon be riding along Pennypack Creek. The area along the creek is heavily forested, so there is a lot of shade to keep you cool on a hot day or block the wind on a cold, windy day. This is a popular park so you will be sharing the path with other walkers, runners, and bicyclists. On occasion the path will branch off and you may not be sure which way to go. Most of these branches lead to the roads near or crossing over the park. To stay on the path, always choose the way that keeps you close to the creek.

To your left just before you pass under Verree Road is the Pennypack Environmental Center. This was started in 1958 as a bird sanctuary and today hosts exhibits, a reference library, and a number of programs to teach adults and children about the local environment.

As you continue to ride along the creek, you will cross under a number of bridges of the main roads that cross the park. At 3.5 miles you will briefly emerge from the park where the path meets Winchester Avenue and parallels it for about 50 feet. The next bridge that you go under will be for Roosevelt Boulevard (US 1), one of the main north-south roads in the area.

At 5.4 miles the path will split. If you go right and stay along the creek, you will cross under Rhawn Street and take the loop along the creek that will get you back to the main trail in just under a mile. After this you will ride through a meadow where you will see the Concert Stage where almost weekly concerts are held throughout the summer months.

Your next main stop on the trail is at Frankford Avenue. This is where most people choose to turn around. Although it is hard to see, the bridge that Frankford Avenue goes over to your right is the oldest stone bridge still used in this country and was built in 1697. If you want to continue down the trail toward the Delaware River, you will have to cross the street here and go to your right and get back on the path just before the bridge.

From here you will have a 0.4-mile ride past a couple of ball fields before you reach another break in the trail where it runs into Torresdale Avenue. Here you will see a large stone wall that is part of Holmesburg Prison, built in 1896 and part of the Philadelphia prison system. To continue your trek toward the Delaware River, make a right and ride the bike lane over the bridge. A few hun-

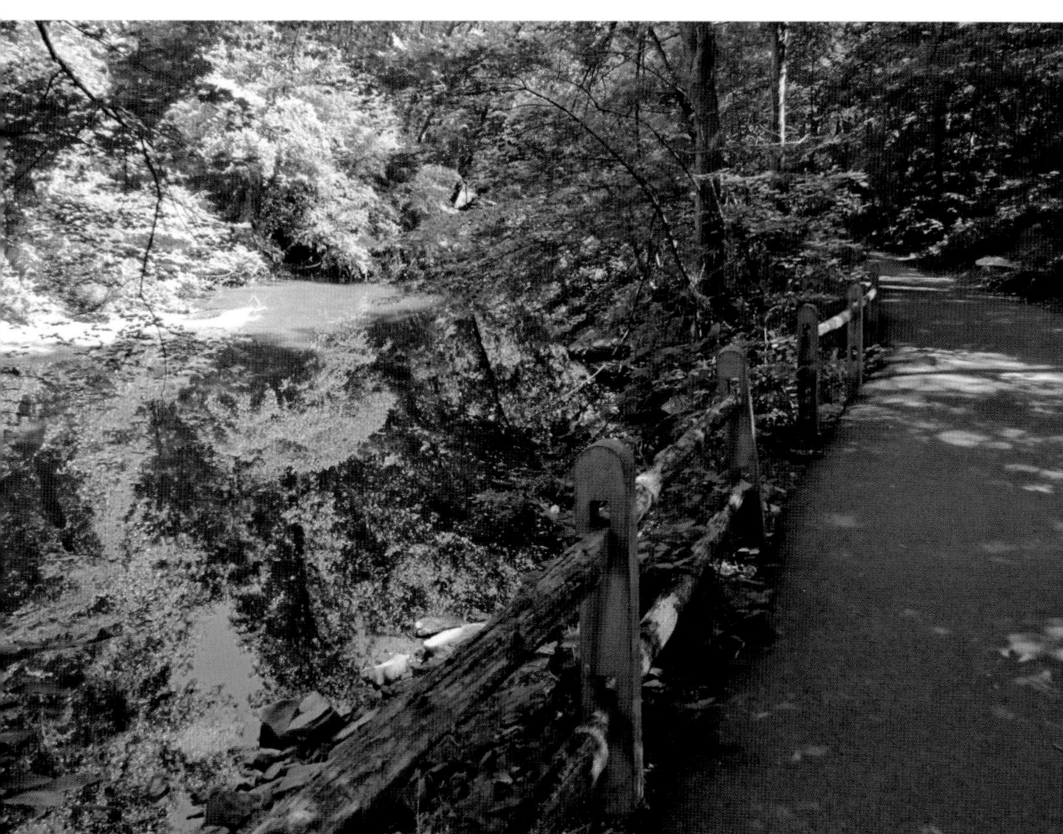

The Pennypack Creek

dred feet after crossing the bridge you will see the entrance to the trail on the other side of the road. This road can have heavy traffic at times, so be careful as you cross the road and continue down the trail. As you ride down this next 0.5 mile of the trail, you will go under I-95 and end up at State Street. From here ride down the wide sidewalk and cross over to the other side at the light at Rhawn Street. Then continue down to the sidewalk and make a left down the next road, which after passing another "Correctional Facility" will get you to Pennypack on the Delaware.

This park on the Delaware is a beautiful contrast to the surrounding highways and urban area and provides a good place to enjoy a view of the river. There are picnic tables here as well as a gazebo on a little peninsula where people fish from. If you follow the bike path here to the end, you will see where Pennypack Creek empties into the river.

Once you are done exploring, you can reverse your path back to where you started from. Even through you will be retracing your steps, Pennypack is one of those trails that is fun to explore over and over again throughout the seasons.

Bike Shops

Abington Wheel Wright Bikeshop, 1120 Old York Rd., Abington 19001; (215) 884-6331 Abington Wheel Wright Bikeshop is a full-service bike shop that can help you repair your current bike or help you find a new one that fits your riding style.

MILES AND DIRECTIONS

0.0 Start down the paved trail away from the parking lot .

0.8 Cross under Verree Road. (If you want to go to the Pennypack Environmental Center, stay to the right where the trail branches then make a left onto Verree Road.)

3.6 Trail meets Winchester Avenue.

4.2 Cross under US 1 (Roosevelt Boulevard).

5.3 Bear right where trail splits.

6.3 Bear right to continue on trail.

6.5 Pass Concert Stage.

7.7 Cross Frankford Avenue then make right and walk down sidewalk.

7.7 Get back on the trail right before the bridge.

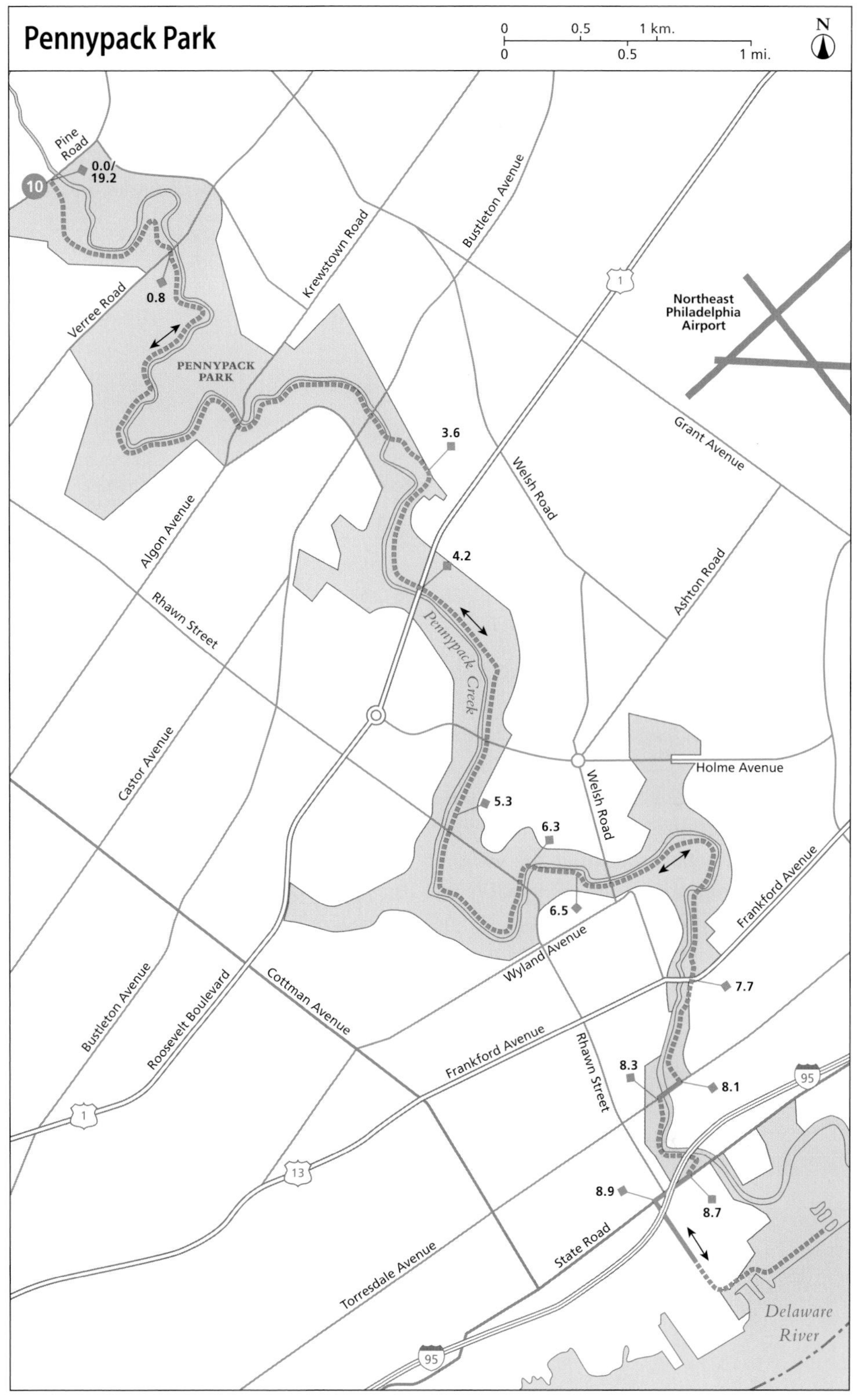
Pennypack Park
0
0.5
1 km.
0
0.5
1 mi.
N
Pine Road
0.0/
19.2
10
0.8
Verree Road
PENNYPACK PARK
Krewstown Road
Bustleton Avenue
1
Northeast Philadelphia Airport
Grant Avenue
3.6
Welsh Road
Algon Avenue
4.2
Rhawn Street
Pennypack Creek
Ashton Road
Castor Avenue
Holme Avenue
Welsh Road
5.3
6.3
6.5
Frankford Avenue
Wyland Avenue
7.7
Cottman Avenue
Bustleton Avenue
Roosevelt Boulevard
Frankford Avenue
Rhawn Street
8.3
8.1
95
1
13
8.9
8.7
State Road
Torresdale Avenue
Delaware River
95

8.1 Make right and ride down the bike lane on Torresdale Avenue over the bridge.

8.3 Cross Torresdale Avenue and get back on trail.

8.7 Trail ends at State Road. Bear right and ride down sidewalk under the bridge.

8.8 Cross State Road at light by Rhawn Street.

8.8 Make right and ride down sidewalk to the entrance to Pennypack Park on the Delaware.

8.9 Make left into park entrance.

9.6 Arrive at the Delaware River.

9.6 When done enjoying the river retrace your steps back to the start.

19.2 Arrive back at the starting point.

RIDE INFORMATION

Events/Attractions

Pennypack Park is a beautiful park that surrounds Pennypack Creek and provides a good place for biking, hiking, and horseback riding. An environmental center provides some educational programs. For more information check out the website fairmountpark.org/pennypackpark.asp.

Frankford Avenue Bridge, built in 1697, is the oldest stone arch bridge in continuous use in America. The bridge is on what was once called the King's Highway, the main route from Philadelphia to Trenton and New York.

Restrooms

Start/end: A portable toilet is located in the parking lot on Pine Road.
Mile 6.3: There is a portable toilet at the parking lot at the trail intersection.

Maps

Delorme Pennsylvania Atlas & Gazetteer: Page 86, B4

John Heinz Ride

The John Heinz National Wildlife Refuge at Tinicum is a small but significant remnant of the freshwater tidal marsh that used to stretch for miles around the mouth of Darby Creek. The refuge is a good place to do some canoeing, hiking, bird watching and of course biking. This ride will take you around and through the refuge and show you the main sites.

Start: Parking lot of John Heinz National Wildlife Refuge at Tinicum

Length: 9.5-mile loop (or 8.2 miles out and back on the trail)

Approximate riding time: 1 hour

Best bike: Mountain bike

Terrain and trail surface: The terrain is mostly flat. The route outside of the refuge runs on paved streets and roads, and contains three climbs over overpasses. The route inside the refuge is dirt and gravel, which can be rutted.

Traffic and hazards: The ride outside of the refuge uses four-lane streets with moderate traffic. Most of these streets have paved shoulders. The trail inside of the refuge is shared with hikers, birders, and photographers.

Getting there: **By car:** Drive south on I-95 and take exit 12B to Cargo City. At the stoplight, turn right onto Bartram Street. Drive on Bartram Street for 0.8 mile, then turn left onto South 84th Street. Drive on South 84th Street for 0.7 mile, then turn left onto Lindbergh Boulevard. Drive 0.2 mile to the entrance to John Heinz National Wildlife Refuge at Tinicum. GPS: N39 53.35 / W75 15.25
By train: Take the train to 30th Street Station, and then transfer to the Airport Line. Take the Airport Line train to Eastwick Station. The route runs right by the station.

THE RIDE

Despite its urban location the John Heinz National Wildlife Refuge supports a large variety of wildlife. Hundreds of species of birds either nest here or stop in on their migration. This area is also home to a lot of small mammals and reptiles. There is a lot of wildlife to see if you take the time to look around. This ride will start with a loop around the roads outside the park to its east trailhead then take you back to the starting point through the refuge itself. If you don't want to do the road part of the ride, you can just do an out-and-back on the John Heinz bike trail.

To start the ride, head out of the refuge the same way that you drove in, bike north on Lindbergh Boulevard, and turn right at the light onto 84th Street. You will then go over an overpass and turn right at the T intersection onto Bartram Avenue. Continue south on the shoulder on Bartram Avenue and under I-95. Immediately after passing under I-95, turn right at the light onto PA 291. Apart from a short hop over an overpass, the street has a paved shoulder that you can use. Ride for 2.3 miles until you reach Wanamaker Avenue (State Highway 420).

After you turn right onto Wanamaker Avenue, you will have to cross the I-95 interchange. Be careful as you cross the ramps on the interchange to ensure that traffic is clear or that it is yielding to you. The parking lot and east trailhead are just on the other side of the interchange.

The main trail in the John Heinz National Wildlife Refuge

Tidal Marsh Wins Its Day

Back when the first Europeans reached what was to become Pennsylvania, tidal marsh covered over 5,700 acres of land at the mouth of Darby Creek (almost 9 square miles). As it does now, the tidal marsh supported many species of plants and animals, and it also provided an important stopping point for birds that migrated in the Atlantic Flyway. For the European settlers, the marsh was conveniently located astride key transportation routes through the area. Additionally, the marsh could be easily drained, cleared, and used for grazing land, unlike the hillier country farther inland. The marsh could not always be contained by dikes that used 18th- and 19th-century technology, but the farms were profitable enough that the settlers continued to repair the dikes and use the land for agriculture until the early 20th century.

It was only after the population of Philadelphia started to explode in the early 20th century that the marsh as a whole was threatened. Dry land was needed for rail lines, houses, warehouses, the Philadelphia International Airport, and other uses. Soil that was dredged from the bottom of the Delaware River was dumped into the marsh. Ditches were dug in the marsh to control mosquitoes. Even in cases where the land use did not drain the marsh, the land use would often disrupt the tidal flow between the Delaware Estuary and the marsh, or wastewater would run off and poison the marsh.

Gradually, those who enjoyed visiting the marsh realized that they would need to fight to save any portion of the marsh at all for future generations. The main catalysts for action were the proposed construction of the Delaware Expressway (I-95) through the marsh and the improper management of the Folcroft Landfill on the edge of the marsh. After many public hearings, injunctions, and grassroots action by local groups, the Delaware Expressway was rerouted, the Folcroft Landfill was closed, and funds were authorized for the acquisition of 1,200 acres for a wildlife refuge.

From here you will take the trail back to the visitor center. Bicycles are allowed only on the main trail that goes around the perimeter of the refuge. The trails that head into the interior of the refuge are for foot traffic only. The trail is not always of the best quality. Refuge employees use the trail as an access road, so you will find occasional tire ruts in the trail. The trail also gets washed out occasionally, so there might be areas with a thick coat of loose gravel.

A variety of different landscapes are encompassed by the refuge. The interior is a mixture of marsh, impounded water, and meadow, and the western and eastern ends are fringed with woods. You can see anglers out most any time that the refuge is open, and you can see canoeists paddling through the water at high tide. As the seasons change, so do the landscape and birds you will see, so this is a place worth visiting a number of times during the year.

MILES AND DIRECTIONS

0.0 Start in the parking lot of John Heinz National Wildlife Refuge at Tinicum and head northeast toward Lindbergh Boulevard.

0.2 Turn left onto Lindbergh Boulevard.

0.4 Turn right onto South 84th Street.

1.1 Turn right onto Bartram Avenue.

1.2 Eastwick Station is on the right.

2.6 Turn right onto PA 291 going west.

2.7 Merge carefully into the right lane before you cross the overpass. The shoulder will reappear when you reach the other side of the overpass.

4.9 Turn right onto Wanamaker Avenue.

5.4 Turn right into the John Heinz parking lot and continue biking on the John Heinz trail.

9.5 Arrive at the parking lot of John Heinz National Wildlife Refuge at Tinicum.

RIDE INFORMATION

Events/Attractions

John Heinz Wildlife Refuge is a 1,000-acre wildlife refuge spanning Philadelphia and Delaware Counties. The refuge is a great place for hiking, fishing, canoeing, and wildlife observation. It has 10 miles of trails, a good portion of which are open to biking. The refuge also contains an environmental center that hosts a number of educational programs.

The town of Essington that is southwest of the refuge is the site of Fort New Gothenburg, which was the capital of the Swedish colony of New Sweden in the mid 17th century.

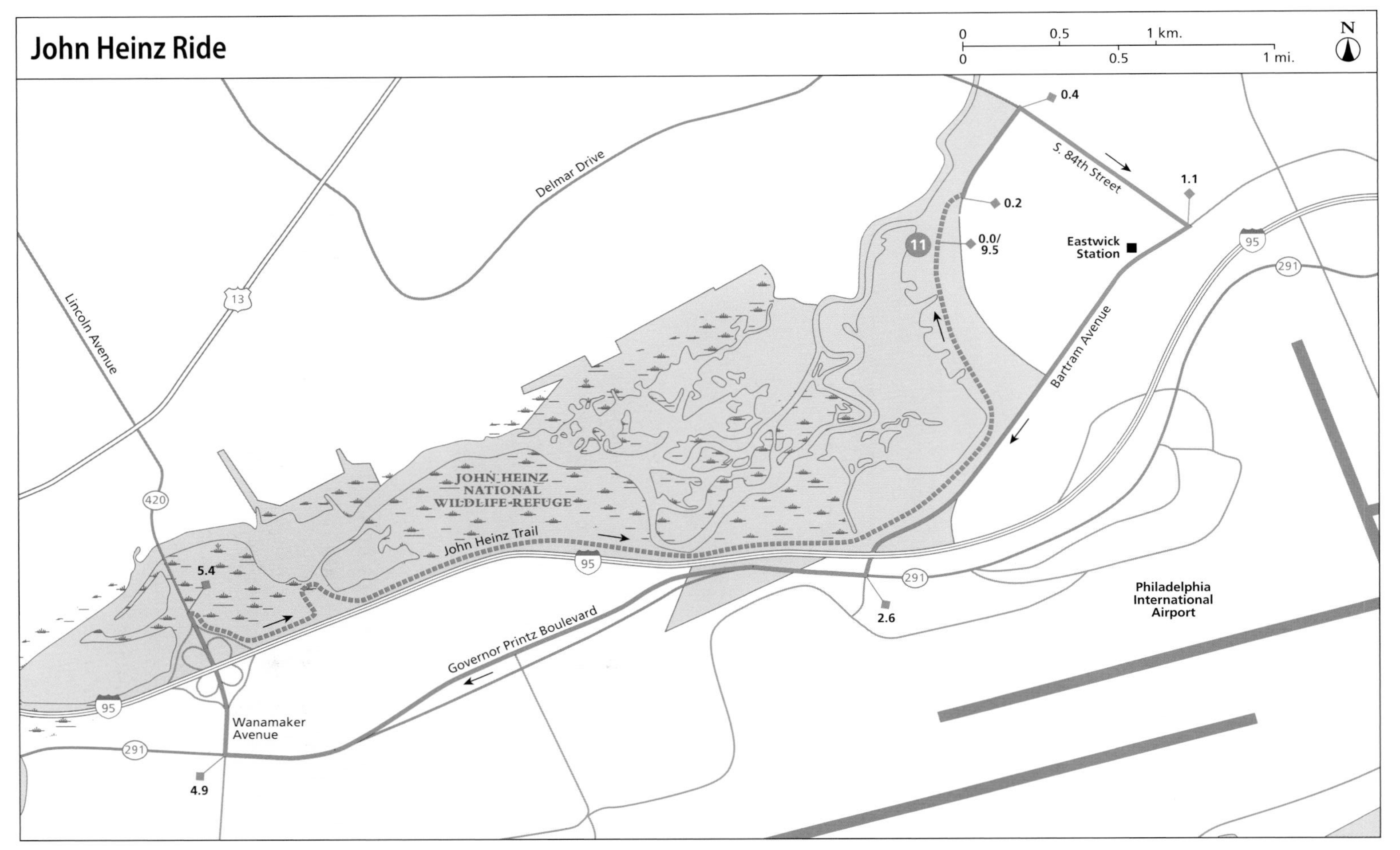
John Heinz Ride
0
0.5
1 km.
0
0.5
1 mi.
N
Delmar Drive
Lincoln Avenue
13
420
S. 84th Street
0.4
1.1
0.2
0.0/
9.5
11
Eastwick
Station
95
291
Bartram Avenue
JOHN HEINZ
NATIONAL
WILDLIFE REFUGE
John Heinz Trail
5.4
2.6
Philadelphia
International
Airport
Governor Printz Boulevard
Wanamaker
Avenue
4.9

The refuge serves to protect the largest remaining freshwater tidal marsh in Pennsylvania.

Restrooms

Start/end: The Cusano Environmental Education Center at John Heinz National Wildlife Refuge has toilets and water. There is also a portable toilet outside if the Cusano Center is closed.

Maps

Delorme Pennsylvania Atlas & Gazetteer: Page 86, E2

View of the trail along the marshlands

Center City Connector

Philadelphia is a great city to bike in partly because of the many bike lanes and trails that make it easy to get to the different parts of the city. This ride will take you from Pennypack Park in the north through Center City and all the way to the airport by John Heinz Park. This will help you understand the best way to get around the city and connect to the other rides in the book.

Start: The parking area on Pine Road, Philadelphia

Length: 26.5 miles one way

Approximate riding time: 2 hours

Best bike: Road, mountain, or hybrid bike

Terrain and trail surface: The ride will be on paved roads and trails. The terrain will be flat to rolling.

Traffic and hazards: You will be spending most of the ride on bike lanes along main roads so you will have moderate to heavy traffic most of the way, but the dedicated bike lanes make riding with traffic not too bad as long as you are comfortable riding in an urban environment. Just be careful at busy intersections where cars and pedestrians will be crossing the bike lane.

Things to see: Pennypack Park, Holmesburg prison, Art Museum, University City, John Heinz Wildlife Refuge

Getting there: From Philadelphia take I-76 west to the Roosevelt Boulevard exit (US 1). Take US 1 north to State Highway 232 (Oxford Avenue). Go north on 232 for 3.1 miles then make a right onto Pine Road. After 1 mile you will see the Pennypack parking area on your right. GPS: N40 05.39 / W75 04.16

THE RIDE

Philadelphia is the top city for bicycle commuters per capita. One of the reasons for this is the many bike lanes and bike paths that have been added in and around the city. This makes it relatively easy to get around. Some of the roads you will be riding on will be high traffic, but as long as you are careful and don't mind a little urban riding, it is no problem coexisting with the traffic.

In fact during rush hour or major events in the city, getting around by bike is a much quicker and enjoyable option.

This ride starts at the top of Pennypack Park on Pine Road, which is also where Ride 7 Bryn Athyn Cathedral starts. Since this route is meant as a way to connect, help you get around town, or get to the starting point of a lot of rides in the book, you can start the ride anywhere along the route.

From Pine Road, head away from the parking area of Pennypack Park along Pennypack Creek. The trail along the creek is heavily forested which provides a lot of shade to keep you cool on a hot day or block the wind on a cold, windy day. On occasion the path will branch off and you may not be sure which way to go. Most of these branches lead to the roads near or crossing over the park. To stay on the path always choose the way that keeps you close to the creek.

At 3.5 miles you will briefly emerge from the park where the path meets Winchester Avenue and parallels it for about 50 feet. At 5.4 miles the path will split. Go right and stay along the creek as you cross under Rhawn Street. After this you will ride through a meadow where you will see the Concert Stage.

The Bicycle Mural at Spring Garden and 2nd

At 7.7 miles the trail will come to a T at Frankford Avenue. To continue down the trail you will have to cross the street here and go to your right and get back on the path just before the bridge. From here you will have 0.4 mile before you reach another break in the trail where it runs into Torresdale Avenue. Here you will make a right onto the bike lane on Torresdale Avenue.

The rest of your ride to Center City will be on bike lanes on roads with moderate to heavy traffic. You'll be riding through urban neighborhoods in northern Philadelphia, which consist of mostly tightly spaced houses, apartments, small shops, and restaurants. It's not the most scenic ride, but the occasional mural here and there brightens the neighborhood.

Once on Spring Garden it's an easy ride to the Art Museum, where a number of rides in the book start. You can also connect to the Schuylkill Trail here, which can get you out to Forbidden Drive or all the way out to Valley Forge.

Bike Shops

Liberty Bell Bicycle, 7741 Frankford Ave., Philadelphia 19136; (215) 624-7343 A friendly neighborhood bike shop that is happy to spend the time to help you find a bike that fits your needs or help you maintain your current bike.

You will pass in front of the Art Museum and continue up a ramp to continue on Spring Garden into University City. Located here are the University of Pennsylvania, Drexel University, and 30th Street Station, the main rail terminal in Philadelphia.

University City can have heavy traffic at times, especially later in the day. Just be careful on the turn onto Woodland Avenue. Also watch out for the train tracks here. From here you will make a few turns and eventually end up on Lindbergh Boulevard, which will take you through some industrial sections of town before ending at John Heinz National Wildlife Refuge.

Like most large cities Philadelphia is an urban jungle, but bicycle commuters have a lot to like about the riding here, and through the efforts of the Bicycle Coalition of Greater Philadelphia and other bike advocates, things should only get better.

MILES AND DIRECTIONS

0.0 Start down the paved trail away from the parking lot.

0.8 Cross under Verree Road. (If you want to go to the Pennypack Environmental Center, stay to the right where the trail branches then make a left onto Verree Road.)

3.6 Trail meets Winchester Avenue.

4.2 Cross under US 1 (Roosevelt Boulevard).

5.3 Bear right where trail splits.

6.3 Bear right to continue on trail.

6.5 Pass Concert Stage.

7.7 Cross Frankford Avenue then turn right and walk down sidewalk.

7.7 Get back on the trail right before the bridge.

8.1 Make right and ride down the bike lane on Torresdale Avenue.

9.9 If you want to go over the Tacony Palmyra Bridge, you can make a left at Magee.

12.0 Turn left onto Church Street.

12.5 Turn right onto Aramingo Avenue.

14.9 Turn left onto Lehigh Avenue.

15.3 Go under I-95 and turn right onto Richmond Street.

15.9 Bear left where road splits onto Delaware Avenue. Watch the intersections here.

17.1 Turn right onto Spring Garden Street.

19.1 Cross 23rd Street. Stay left where Spring Garden Street goes down into a tunnel. Cross Kelly Drive and ride past the front of the Art Museum. You can ride on the sidewalk here to avoid traffic.

19.5 Follow the right-most ramp at the end of the Art Museum to continue on Spring Garden and over the Schuylkill River.

19.8 Turn left onto 32nd Street.

20.0 Turn right onto Powelton Avenue.

20.5 Turn left onto 38th Street (US 13).

21.3 Turn right onto Baltimore Avenue then quickly bear left onto Woodland Avenue.

22.2 Turn left onto 49th Street.

22.4 49th Street becomes Grays Avenue.

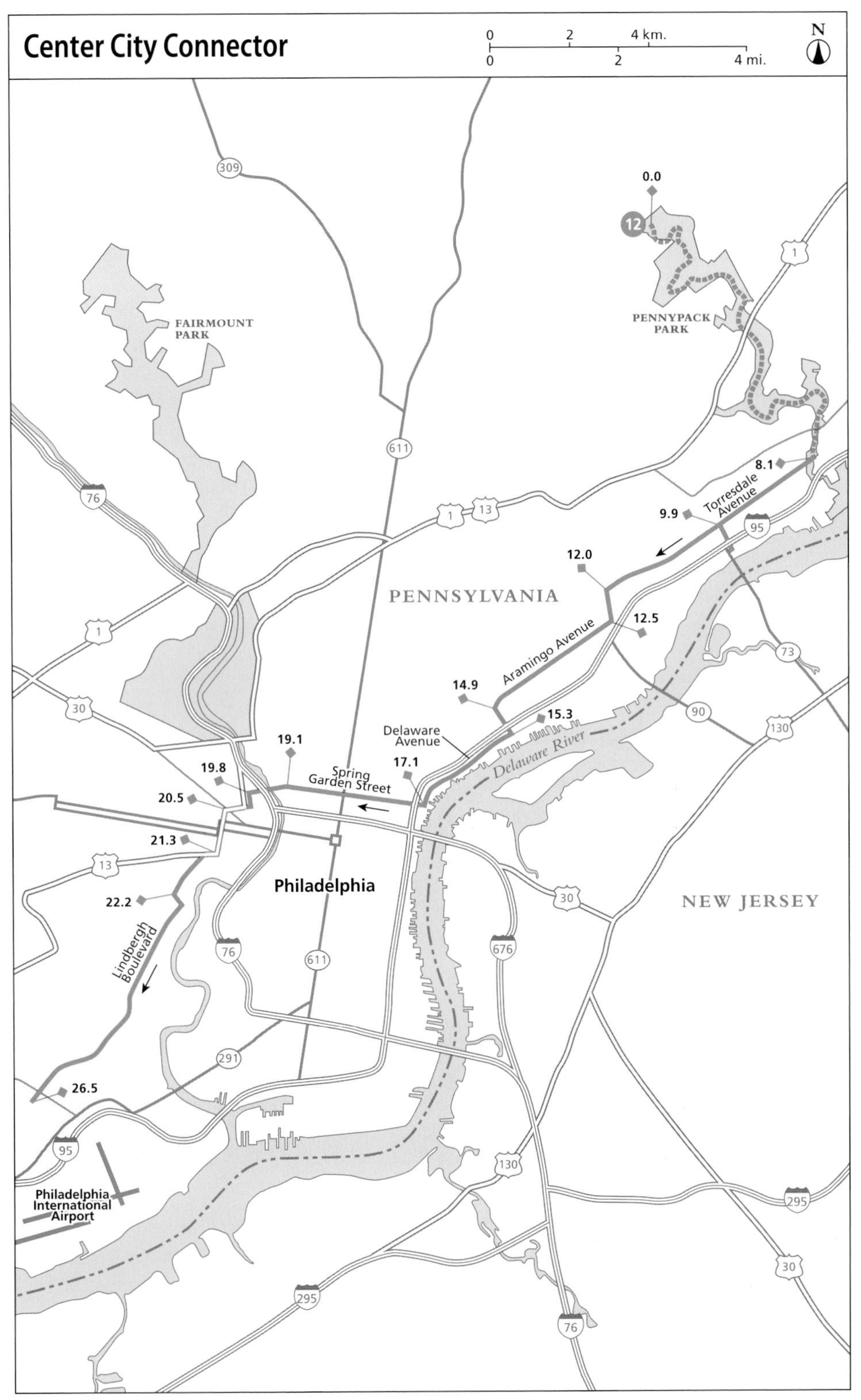

Center City Connector
0
2
4 km.
0
2
4 mi.
N
0.0
12
PENNYPACK PARK
FAIRMOUNT PARK
8.1
9.9
Torresdale Avenue
12.0
PENNSYLVANIA
12.5
Aramingo Avenue
14.9
15.3
Delaware Avenue
Delaware River
19.1
17.1
Spring Garden Street
19.8
20.5
21.3
Philadelphia
22.2
Lindbergh Boulevard
NEW JERSEY
26.5
Philadelphia International Airport

Mural Arts Program

Although there are a lot of scenic attractions that can be found riding around Philadelphia, a lot of the city's residential and industrial areas are, shall we say, less scenic. However, if you look carefully around as you ride, you will notice a number of extraordinary murals on many buildings around the city. These murals were created by the Mural Arts Program (muralarts.org), which was started in 1984 to help eradicate the graffiti that was plaguing the city. This program redirects destructive graffiti writing to constructive mural painting and provides a structure to help young men and women use their artistic talents in a way that helps beautify the community. This program has been very successful and has produced over 3,000 murals. So keep your eyes open as you ride around the urban landscape, and you will discover a lot of amazing works of art.

22.7 Stay left. Grays Avenue becomes Lindbergh Boulevard.

26.5 Turn right into the John Heinz Wildlife Refuge.

RIDE INFORMATION

Events/Attractions

Pennypack Park is a beautiful park that surrounds Pennypack Creek and provides a good place for biking, hiking, and horseback riding. An environmental center provides some educational programs. For more information check out the website fairmountpark.org/pennypackpark.asp.

For more information on commuter routes for bikes, check out the Bicycle Coalition of Greater Philadelphia Bike Maps page (bicyclecoalition.org/resources/maps), which has a complete Philadelphia Bike Map as well as recommended routes and other useful information.

John Heinz Wildlife Refuge is a 1,000-acre wildlife refuge spanning Philadelphia and Delaware Counties. The refuge is a great place for hiking, fishing, canoeing, and wildlife observation. It has 10 miles of trails, a good portion of which are open to biking. The refuge also contains an environmental center that hosts a number of educational programs.

Restrooms

Mile 0.0: A portable toilet is located in the parking lot on Pine Road.
Mile 6.3: There is a portable toilet at the parking lot at the trail intersection.
Mile 19.1: There is a restroom behind the Art Museum at the back end of the parking lot where Waterworks and Kelly Drives meet.
Mile 26.5: There is a bathroom at the John Heinz Wildlife Refuge visitor center.

Maps

Delorme Pennsylvania Atlas & Gazetteer: Page 86, B4

Ambler Ramble

If you're looking for a good long training ride from Center City, then the Ambler Ramble is what you want. This favorite route of the Philadelphia Bike Club will take you past the city limits to some of the outlying suburbs for a nice long ride with enough variety of terrain and scenery to make this a ride you will want to do again and again.

Start: Italian Fountain behind the Art Museum

Length: 45.1-mile loop

Approximate riding time: 3.5 hours

Best bike: Road bike

Terrain and trail surface: Rolling terrain through paved city streets, park and suburban roads

Traffic and hazards: This ride will be on the streets of Philadelphia and the outlying suburbs, so you will be doing some urban riding. Some of the streets you will be riding on will have dedicated bike lanes or shoulders, but you will still have to be cautious of the traffic.

Things to see: Art Museum, Ambler, Carson Valley School

Getting there: By car: From I-95 take I-676 west to the Benjamin Franklin Parkway exit (22nd Street, Museum area) on the right side. At the end of the exit ramp, turn right onto 22nd Street and get into the far left lane. The Benjamin Franklin Parkway is a boulevard with two outer lanes and two inner lanes. Turn left onto the outer lanes of the parkway. The Museum will be in front of you on the hill. Stay in the outer lanes and go past the Museum to Kelly Drive then make a left at the light onto Waterworks Drive. The Italian Fountain is at the far end of the parking lot close to the Museum. GPS: N39 58.04 / W75 10.98
By train: Take the train to the 30th Street Station then cross the Schuylkill River on Market Street and take Schuylkill River Trail north to the Art Museum.

THE RIDE

Since the mid-1800s Philadelphians have been taking day trips to Ambler to escape the city for a few hours and see the local countryside. Today Ambler and the surrounding area are much more developed, but it is still a good destination for a bike ride. To start the ride, head back out of the parking lot and cross Kelly Drive onto Sedgely Road. There is a bike lane here to ride on as you slowly go up a shallow hill. You will stay to the right where Sedgely Road goes left to get onto Poplar Drive. This will take you across Girard Avenue and across a bridge over railroad tracks that will take you through one of the residential neighborhoods near the park. There is still a bike lane here, but there will be a little more traffic here so be careful when you make the left onto Reservoir Road to get back into the park.

Once on Reservoir Road, you will be back in Fairmount Park; ride around a reservoir and past some athletic fields before passing the Strawberry Mansion part of the park. Eventually you will leave the park and head out to Hunting Park Avenue and Henry Drive. These streets will be busy, so just use caution as you ride through the traffic. The traffic will be lighter on the second stretch of Henry Drive as you ride on the outskirts of Wissahickon Valley Park.

The ride from here on will be a mix of neighborhood streets and small parks. There are a lot of turns here, but this is necessary to keep off the busier streets. Keep an eye on the cue sheet and look ahead for the next few turns so you don't lose your way.

At mile 17.1 you will enter Carson Valley School. This nonprofit child welfare agency provides special education and a number of other programs to help the local community. You will wind your way through its parklike campus.

As you continue you will see some more open farm fields. These roads will eventually lead you into the town of Ambler as you head up Butler Avenue into town. There will be a little more traffic here until you turn off Butler. Right after the turn onto Main Street, you will see Toto's Gelateria and Caffe, which is a great place for a break. They have pastries, sandwiches, hot soup, coffee, and anything else you need to fuel up. One thing to note: Do not lean your bike against the fence or wall on either side of the driveway next to the Caffe as the driveway is narrow and parking your bike here will prevent cars from getting to the parking lot in back.

Bike Shops

Keswick Bicycle Shop, 4040 Locust St., Philadelphia; (215) 397-4191 Keswick Bicycle Shop is a friendly neighborhood bike shop that can help you with all your biking needs.

After your break you will start to work your way back to Philadelphia. The way back will be a little more direct. At mile 33 you will be on River Road and will be riding along the Schuylkill River for the rest of the ride. This will take you through the town of Manayunk. There is no bike lane here and usually heavy traffic, but traffic moves slow here and drivers are used to bike riders, so as long as you keep your eyes open and stay to the right as much as you can, it's not too bad.

After you pass through Manayunk, you will approach Lincoln Drive, where you will pick up the Schuylkill River Trail that will take you the last 5 miles back to the starting point. If you ride this route on a Saturday or Sunday between April and October, then MLK Drive will be closed to traffic and you will be able to ride along the road instead of having to stick to the bike path.

MILES AND DIRECTIONS

0.0 Start at the corner of Kelly and Waterworks Drives. Cross Kelly Drive onto Sedgely Road.

0.1 Stay to the right where Sedgely Road forks to the left; you will now be on Poplar Drive.

0.6 Cross Girard Avenue; Sedgely Road becomes 33rd Street (US 13)

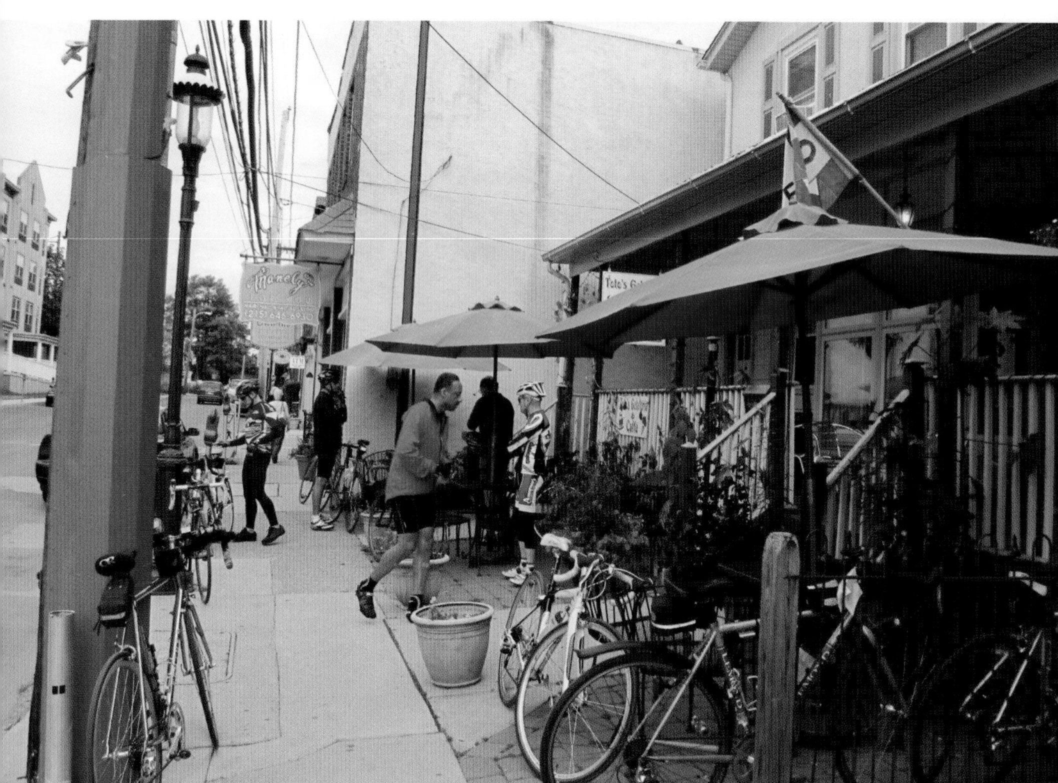

Toto's Caffe in Ambler

1.0 Turn left onto Reservoir Drive.

2.2 Turn right onto Dauphin Drive.

2.4 Turn left before leaving the park onto Greenland Drive.

2.5 Merge onto Strawberry Mansion Bridge Drive then make an immediate right onto Cumberland Drive.

2.6 Turn left onto US 13 (Ridge Avenue). You may encounter some heavy traffic here so stay to the right.

3.5 Turn left onto Henry Avenue. This is a busy 5-way intersection.

3.8 Turn right onto Roberts Avenue.

4.1 Turn left onto Fox Street.

4.9 Turn left onto Coulter Street.

5.1 Turn right onto Netherfield Road.

5.4 Turn left onto School House Lane.

5.5 Turn right onto Henry Avenue.

6.5 Turn right onto Walnut Lane.

7.1 Go three quarters around the circle onto Park Line Drive.

7.2 Turn right onto Upsal Street.

7.4 Turn left onto Wissahickon Avenue.

7.8 Turn right onto Westview Street.

8.1 Turn left onto Sherman Street.

8.3 Sherman Street becomes Mount Pleasant Road.

8.6 Turn left onto McCallum Street.

9.3 Turn right onto Mermaid Lane.

9.4 Turn left onto Cherokee Street.

9.8 Cherokee Street becomes Hartwell Lane.

10.1 Turn left onto Saint Andrews Road.

10.7 Road bends right and becomes Glengary Road.

11.0 Turn left onto Cherokee Street.

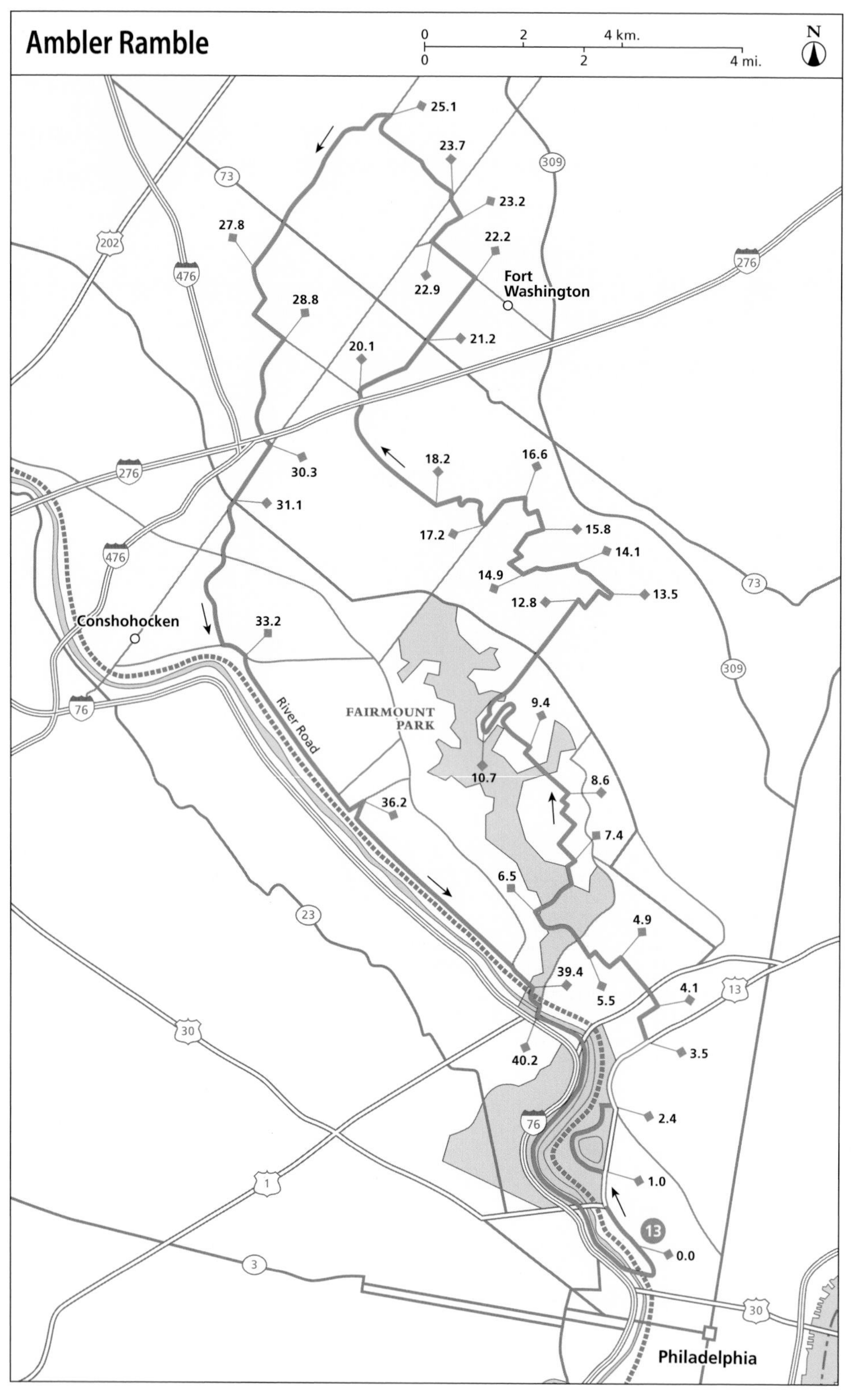

Ambler Ramble
0
2
4 km.
0
2
4 mi.
N
25.1
23.7
23.2
22.2
22.9
27.8
28.8
Fort Washington
21.2
20.1
18.2
16.6
30.3
31.1
17.2
15.8
14.1
14.9
12.8
13.5
Conshohocken
33.2
River Road
FAIRMOUNT PARK
9.4
10.7
8.6
36.2
7.4
6.5
4.9
39.4
5.5
4.1
40.2
3.5
2.4
1.0
13
0.0
Philadelphia

11.1 Cherokee Street becomes Gravers Lane.

12.8 Turn right onto Flourtown Avenue.

13.0 Turn left onto Southampton Avenue.

13.2 Turn right onto Southampton Avenue.

13.4 Turn left onto Churchill Road.

13.5 Turn left onto Hull Drive (nice downhill).

14.1 Turn left onto Patton Road.

14.7 Turn right onto Carlisle Road.

14.8 Turn left onto Paper Mill Road (busy road; stay right).

14.9 Quick right onto Montgomery Avenue.

15.2 Turn left onto Terminal Avenue.

15.6 Turn right onto Longfield Road.

15.8 Turn left onto Preston Road.

16.1 Turn right onto Haws Lane.

16.3 Turn right onto Chestnut Lane.

16.4 Turn left onto McCloskey Road.

16.5 Quick right onto Kopley Road.

16.6 Quick left onto Wissahickon Avenue.

16.8 Cross Bethlehem Pike.

17.2 Turn right into Carson Valley School.

17.4 Bear left around circle.

17.9 Turn left onto Mill Road.

18.2 Turn right onto Stenton Avenue.

20.1 Turn right onto Sheaff Lane right after going under I-276.

21.2 Turn right onto SR 73 (Skippack Pike) followed by a quick left to stay on Sheaff Lane.

22.2 Turn left onto Morris Road.

22.9 Turn right onto Butler Avenue.

23.3 Turn left onto Short Race Street right after crossing railroad tracks.

23.4 Turn left onto Main Street (Toto's Caffe is on the right).

23.6 Turn right onto Reiffs Mill Road.

23.7 Turn left onto Spring Garden Street.

24.3 Bear left onto Pen Ambler Road.

25.1 Turn hard left onto Penllyn Pike.

27.8 Road bends left and becomes Stenton Avenue.

28.2 Merge with Walton Road.

28.3 Bear left to stay on Stenton Avenue.

28.8 Turn right onto Narcissa Road.

30.3 Turn right onto Butler Pike.

31.1 Turn left onto Germantown Pike.

31.1 Quick right onto Butler Pike.

31.2 Turn left onto Spring Mill Road.

32.3 Turn left onto Cedar Grove Road.

33.0 Turn left onto Barren Hill Road.

33.2 Turn right onto River Road.

34.3 Turn right onto Harts Lane, which quickly becomes River Road again.

35.6 River Road becomes Nixon Street.

35.9 Turn left onto Shawmont Avenue.

36.2 Turn right onto Minerva Street. Becomes Umbria Street.

37.8 Turn right onto Leverington Avenue.

37.9 Turn left onto Main Street. Watch the traffic here.

39.4 Turn right onto Lincoln Drive and start riding on the Schuylkill River Trail.

40.1 Turn right and ride across the Falls River Bridge.

40.2 Make a left after crossing the bridge back onto the Schuylkill River Trail and follow it along Martin Luther King Jr. Drive.

Mary Johnson Ambler

The town of Ambler is named for Mary Johnson Ambler for her generosity and community leadership.

On July 17, 1856, a northbound train collided head-on with a southbound train between Fort Washington station and Camp Hill station, resulting in the death of 59 people. Mary Ambler, who was already known for helping ill people in the town, walked 2 miles to the site of the accident and directed the relief efforts. In July 1869, because of her efforts the town officials renamed the local railroad station Ambler in her honor. Later, the village and post office adopted the name.

As you ride along Main Street on this ride near Reiff's Mill Road, you will come to one of the oldest houses in Ambler Borough, the home of Mary Ambler.

44.9 Cross back over the Schuylkill River and continue to follow the trail around the Art Museum.

45.1 Arrive back at the Italian Fountain.

RIDE INFORMATION

Events/Attractions

Toto's Gelateria & Caffe, 35 N. Main St., Ambler; (215) 628-3980: Toto's Caffe is a good place to get a cup of coffee or a sandwich to help you fuel up before, during, or after a ride.

Restrooms

Mile 23.7: Toto's Caffe has a bathroom they let patrons use.

Maps

Delorme Pennsylvania Atlas & Gazetteer: Page 86, B4

On July 2, 1855, the Wissahickon railroad station, in what is now Ambler, was opened. Besides allowing farmers to ship their produce to market at a much lower cost, it also allowed people from Philadelphia an easy way to spend a day in the country, which is why the northbound train from Philadelphia was known as the "picnic special."

Cobbs Creek Ride

For those who live in West Philadelphia, Cobbs Creek is one of the few places to go to hike, swim, rest in the shade of trees, and otherwise enjoy nature. This ride will take you from the John Heinz National Wildlife Refuge up the Cobbs Creek Trail to 63rd Street and back.

Start: Parking lot of John Heinz National Wildlife Refuge at Tinicum

Length: 13.6 miles out and back

Approximate riding time: 1.5 hours

Best bike: Cross bike or road bike

Terrain and trail surface: The terrain is paved and mostly flat, though there's a 50-foot dip down to creek level and back up between 59th and 61st Streets.

Traffic and hazards: The on-road portion of the route has moderate traffic and can contain trolley tracks. The on-trail portion of the route can have heavy pedestrian usage, particularly from users of the adjoining park facilities.

Getting there: By car: Drive south on I-95, and take exit 12B to Cargo City. At the stoplight, turn right onto Bartram Street. Drive on Bartram Street for 0.8 mile, then turn left onto South 84th Street. Drive on South 84th Street for 0.7 mile, then turn left onto Lindbergh Boulevard. Drive 0.2 mile to the entrance to John Heinz National Wildlife Refuge at Tinicum. GPS: N39 53.35 / W75 15.25
By train: Take the train to 30th Street Station, and then transfer to the Market-Frankford Line. Take the Market-Frankford Line train to 63rd Street Station. The northern end of the route ends at 63rd Street Station.

THE RIDE

The ride starts at John Heinz National Wildlife Refuge (or at 63rd Street Station, if you take the train). If you start at John Heinz, you ride out the same way that you drove in and bike north on Lindbergh Boulevard. This part of the route uses the Cobbs Creek Bikeway, so you can follow the bikeway signs to guide you to the bike trail. The bikeway meanders generally north and west to the bike path. You must be attentive when you reach Elmwood Avenue

Riding along the Cobbs Creek Trail

because 1) you will start to see trolley tracks in the road, and 2) the sign for the turn onto 70th Street is hard to see. Always cross trolley tracks at a right angle so that your front tire doesn't get caught. When you reach Cobbs Creek Parkway, the trail is on the far (west) side of the parkway. Cross the parkway carefully and ride onto the trail.

The southern part of the trail is the quietest part, mainly because there aren't so many playgrounds, basketball courts, and other facilities in this area. The main features of this area are the trees and Mount Moriah Cemetery. The trail runs along Cobbs Creek Parkway at this point, and there are very few traffic crossings on the trail.

The usage of the trail picks up when you get north of Whitby Avenue, since there are a number of basketball and tennis courts available. There is also a parking lot at the intersection of South 59th Street and Thomas Avenue. It is around this area that the trail splits from Cobbs Creek Parkway and descends to the level of Cobbs Creek. The trail runs underneath the SEPTA Media/Elwyn Line bridge over Cobbs Creek, and then crosses Baltimore Avenue (US 13) at grade. The trail runs along 61st Street and then along Cobbs Creek Parkway again. Once you reach the 63rd Street Station, you just retrace your steps to get back to the start.

MILES AND DIRECTIONS

0.0 Start in the parking lot of John Heinz National Wildlife Refuge at Tinicum. Head northeast toward Lindbergh Boulevard.

0.2 Turn left onto Lindbergh Boulevard.

0.9 Turn left onto South 80th Street.

Bike Shops

Firehouse Bicycles, 701 S. 50th St.; (215) 727-9692, firehousebicycles.com Firehouse Bicycles carries quality used bicycles and new and used parts and accessories. Firehouse Bicycles also offers repair and wheel-building services for all makes. The shop is visible from Baltimore Avenue (US 13) and located just across from Cedar Park (1.3 miles east of the bike trail).

Swaray's Bike Shop, 612 S. 52nd St.; (215) 476-0903, swaraysbikeshop.com Swaray's Bike Shop specializes in used bicycles, bicycle repair, and bicycle accessories. The shop is on the west side of the street, about 0.5 block south of Cedar Avenue.

1.1 Turn right onto Buist Avenue.

1.4 Turn left onto South 77th Street.

1.6 Turn right onto Elmwood Avenue.

2.5 Turn left onto South 70th Street.

3.1 Cross Cobbs Creek Parkway and turn right onto Cobbs Creek Trail.

6.8 Arrive at 63rd Street Station. Retrace route to return to beginning.

13.6 Arrive back at John Heinz National Wildlife Refuge.

RIDE INFORMATION

Events/Attractions

John Heinz Wildlife Refuge is a 1,000-acre wildlife refuge spanning Philadelphia and Delaware Counties. The refuge is a great place for hiking, fishing, canoeing, and wildlife observation. It has 10 miles of trails, a good portion of which are open to biking. The refuge also contains an environmental center that hosts a number of educational programs.

The first European water-powered mill in Pennsylvania was built on Cobbs Creek by Johan Printz, governor of New Sweden, in 1645. The mill provided flour and cornmeal to the residents of New Gothenburg (present-day Essington). The mill was located near the Blue Bell Inn, at the intersection of Island and Woodland Avenues, 2 blocks south of the bike route.

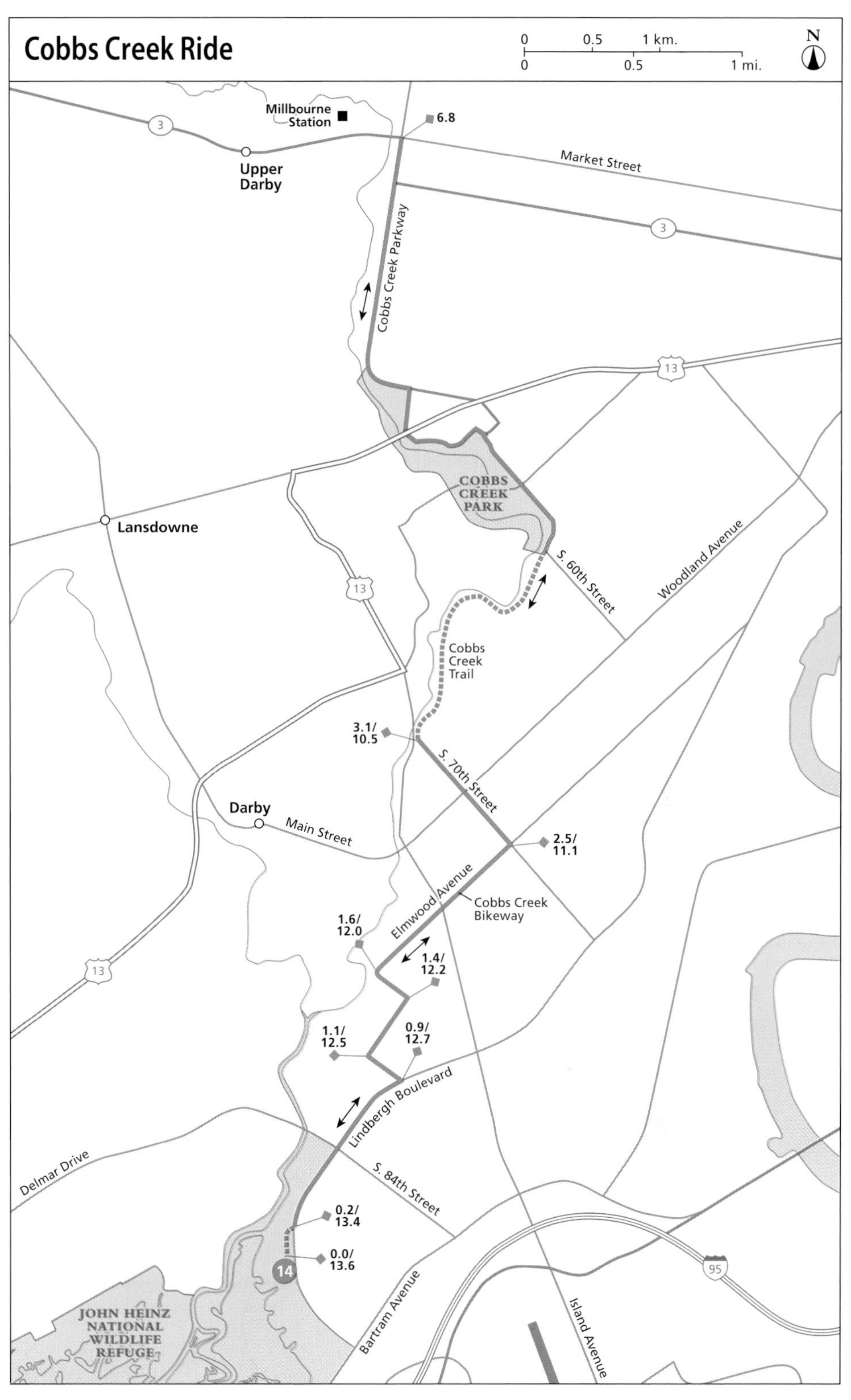
Cobbs Creek Ride
0
0.5
1 km.
0
0.5
1 mi.
N
Millbourne Station
6.8
3
Upper Darby
Market Street
Cobbs Creek Parkway
13
COBBS CREEK PARK
Lansdowne
S. 60th Street
Woodland Avenue
Cobbs Creek Trail
3.1/ 10.5
S. 70th Street
Darby
Main Street
2.5/ 11.1
Elmwood Avenue
Cobbs Creek Bikeway
1.6/ 12.0
1.4/ 12.2
1.1/ 12.5
0.9/ 12.7
Lindbergh Boulevard
Delmar Drive
S. 84th Street
0.2/ 13.4
0.0/ 13.6
14
95
Bartram Avenue
Island Avenue
JOHN HEINZ NATIONAL WILDLIFE REFUGE

Cobbs Creek Keeps Its Open Spaces

Cobbs Creek's open spaces and proximity to Center City make it a popular destination for urban dwellers today. It's interesting to note, though, that these same characteristics made Cobbs Creek a popular location for proposed superhighways in the mid-20th century. Even as far back as 1932, plans were drawn up to build a limited access parkway similar to the parkways built in New York City. The plans floundered, however, because of a lack of funding.

Enter the National Interstate and Defense Highways Act of 1956. With a source of funding secured, new plans were drawn to build a network of limited access highways throughout the region and a loop highway around the Center City business district. The first highways to be built were the Delaware Expressway (now I-95), the Schuylkill Expressway (now I-76), and the Vine Street Expressway (now I-676). With the construction of these highways complete or well under way in 1960, attention turned to the southern part of the loop. The proposed Cobbs Creek Expressway would start at Philadelphia International Airport and travel north along Cobbs Creek to Baltimore Avenue (US 1). The Cobbs Creek Expressway would then turn west to meet the proposed Crosstown Expressway, which would cross the Schuylkill River south of University City and follow South Street to the Delaware Expressway.

Fortunately for those who enjoy Cobbs Creek Park today, opposition to the plan was vocal, and funding was diverted to projects elsewhere in Pennsylvania. The plans were resurrected a number of times through the late 1960s and early 1970s, but in 1977 the Pennsylvania Department of Transportation halted funding of all proposed highway projects, and the Cobbs Creek Expressway was shelved for good.

Restrooms

Mile 0.0: The Cusano Environmental Education Center at John Heinz National Wildlife Refuge has toilets and water. There is also a portable toilet outside if the Cusano Center is closed.

Mile 6.0: A water fountain and portable toilet are available at the jungle gym across from Webster Street.

Mile 6.8: Restrooms are available at 63rd Street Station.

Maps

Delorme Pennsylvania Atlas & Gazetteer: Page 86, B2

Montgomery and Bucks Counties

If you head out of the city proper to the northern and western suburbs of Montgomery and Bucks County, you leave some of the hustle and bustle of the city behind you and find some less-traveled roads. This area is rich with history. Here there are many parks that capture everything from famous battles of the Revolutionary War to the industrial evolution of our country.

This area includes parks—like Valley Forge, Washington Crossing, and Tyler—that were created to preserve the history of the Revolutionary War and the Colonial era. As you ride around the rural roads in the area, you can occasionally get a glimpse of what it was like in those early days.

The other main attraction of this area is the many covered bridges that are still left along the roads. This is especially true in Bucks, where they have their own covered bridge society as well as a popular bike ride that celebrates the preservation of these bridges.

Dotted around the parks and covered bridges are some nice scenic vistas and beautiful historic towns. As long as you don't mind some hillier terrain and a little bit of travel, this area makes a perfect day trip for a bike ride.

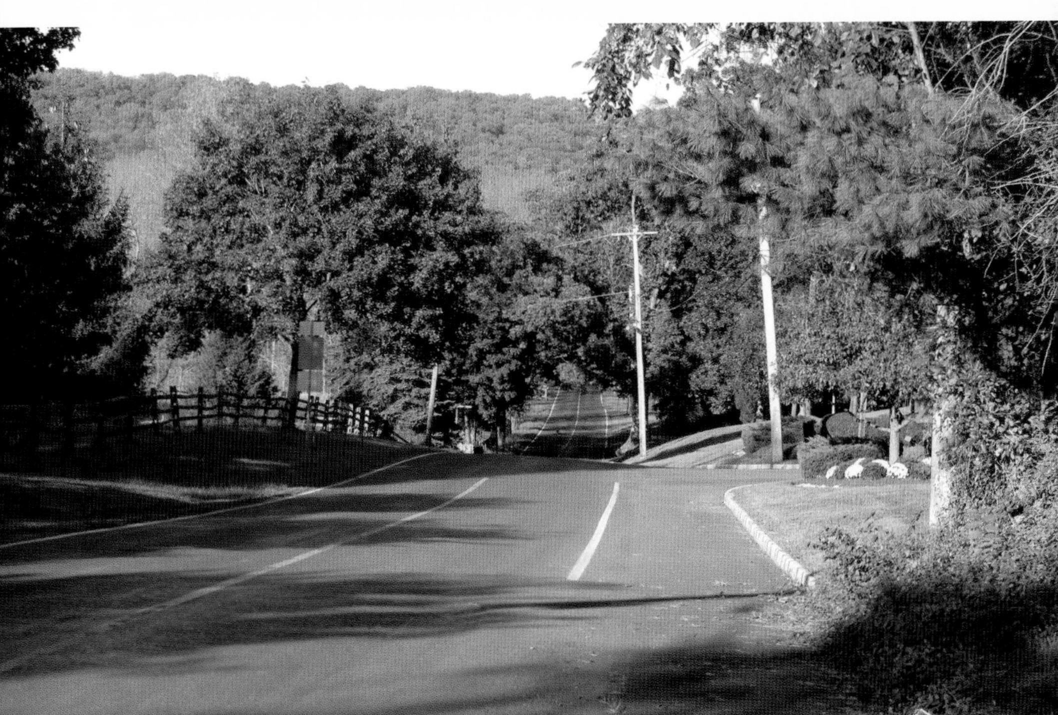

Heading down Wrightstown Road. See Ride 17.

Valley Forge Ride

The words "Valley Forge" conjure up images of hardship and cold. Nowadays, however, Valley Forge is just as well-known as an oasis of countryside in the middle of an ocean of suburbs and office parks. If you live or work close by and are in the mood for a few hills, Valley Forge is the place to go.

Start: Parking lot of Valley Forge National Historical Park

Length: 9.4-mile loop (road) or 5.1-mile loop (trail)

Approximate riding time: 1 hour

Best bike: Road bike or cross bike

Terrain and trail surface: The terrain is paved, with a few cobblestones around the memorial arch. The bicycle path is less hilly than the road route, but you can expect some amount of climbing either way.

Traffic and hazards: The bicycle path can have heavy pedestrian usage, particularly where there are stops along the Encampment Tour. The roads typically have moderate traffic, but the traffic can be heavy at times (particularly on PA 23). If you are not comfortable biking on PA 23, there is a paved bike path that parallels the road through most of its length in the park.

Getting there: From Center City, drive north on I-76, and take the ramp for exits 328B-A /327 to 422 West. Keep left on the ramp to exit 328A to US 422 West toward Pottstown. In 2.8 miles, take the exit to PA 23 toward Valley Forge. At the light at the end of the ramp, turn left onto PA 23. Continue straight into the park. The parking lot will be on both sides of the road beyond the welcome center. GPS: N40 06.14 / W75 25.37

THE RIDE

Valley Forge National Historical Park was created to commemorate the sacrifices and perseverance of the soldiers who encamped here during the winter of 1777–78. The park features historic and re-created buildings from that era as well as a number of memorials. The park can easily be explored on bike by using the bike trails or riding on the roads in and around the park. Two routes are given in the Miles and Directions sections so you can choose whether to stay on the trail or use the roads.

The ride starts in the parking lot at Valley Forge National Historical Park. You will bike out the way that you came in, east toward the welcome center. When you reach the welcome center, turn right and start climbing to the top of the outer line ridge. Before long, you will pass some replicas of the huts that the soldiers constructed for shelter at the beginning of the winter of 1777–78. Continue biking until you reach the National Memorial Arch. There are cobblestones on the road and path

Bike Shops

Bike Line of Valley Forge/Wayne, 111 E. Swedesford Rd., Wayne; 610-688-5880
Bike Line is the world's largest Trek bicycle retailer, with stores throughout the lower Delaware Valley.

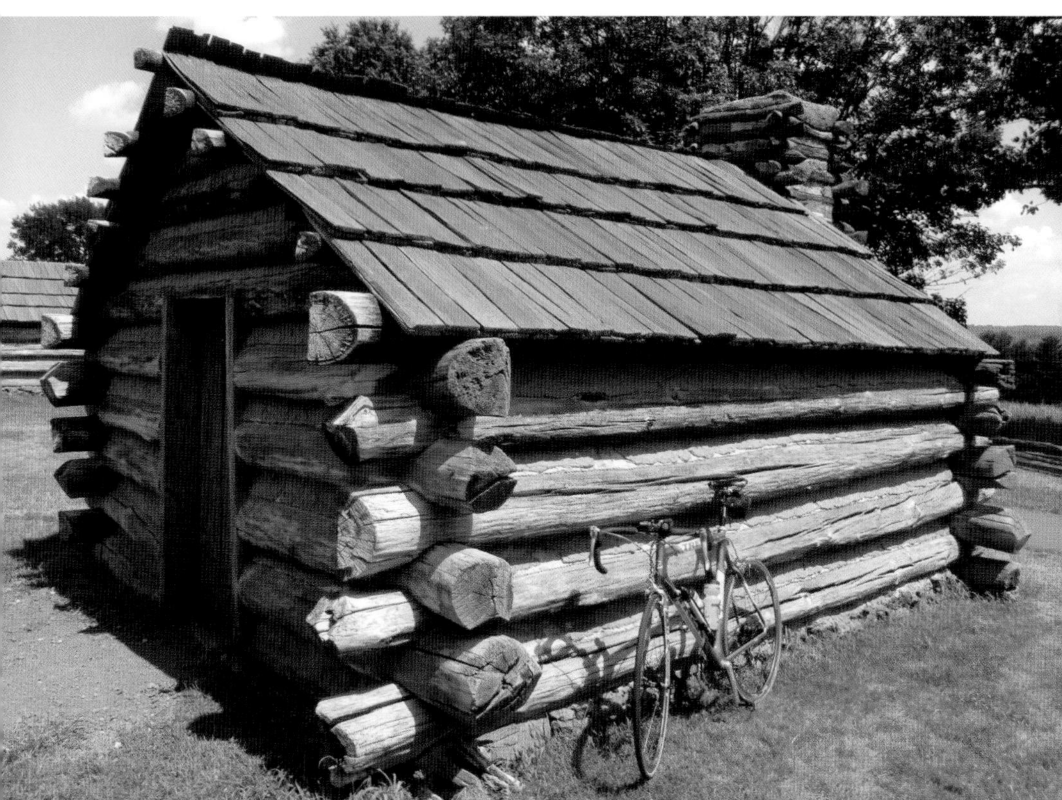

One of the huts used by the soldiers

that go by the arch, so you might find it prudent to circle around the arch or walk your bike through the arch.

After 2.0 miles, you will reach Wayne's Woods, where General Anthony Wayne was stationed with his Pennsylvania troops. At this point, the bike path splits from the road. You can continue along the road to see a statue of Anthony Wayne, or you can continue on the trail, which is more level. The road and bike path come together at 2.3 miles, but then diverge again at 2.5 miles. You can take the bike path to cut across the park back to Valley Forge Road and avoid the traffic and the big hills. Alternatively, you can take the road to enjoy better scenery and get a better workout.

If you continue on the road, it will double back on itself. About 0.2 mile after the road doubles back, turn right onto Valley Creek Road, which will continue west and then north, past a covered bridge and through the valley at the base of Mount Joy. When Valley Creek Road ends in a T intersection, turn right at Valley Forge Road and continue to follow the Encampment Tour route. If you want to climb some hills, turn right on Inner Line Road to double back and climb Mount Joy. Mount Joy will give you a 100-foot climb and a 150-foot climb after that. Otherwise, you can continue on Valley Forge Road and rejoin the route later.

After all the routes have rejoined each other, you will continue on (or along) Valley Forge Road, past the Washington Memorial Chapel and the parade ground, and down the hill to the welcome center area. At the bottom of the hill, turn right onto County Line Road to take the back way in to the parking lot.

MILES AND DIRECTIONS

Road ride:

0.0 Start in the parking lot of Valley Forge National Historical Park; head east toward the welcome center.

0.1 Turn right onto Outer Line Drive (follow the Encampment Tour).

3.0 Turn right onto Valley Creek Road.

3.4 Continue right on Valley Creek Road.

4.5 Turn right onto Valley Forge Road (PA 23).

4.9 Turn right onto Inner Line Drive. Inner Line Drive doubles back, climbs Mount Joy, and then descends back to Valley Forge Road. If you prefer, you can continue on Valley Forge Road.

7.8 Turn right onto Valley Forge Road.

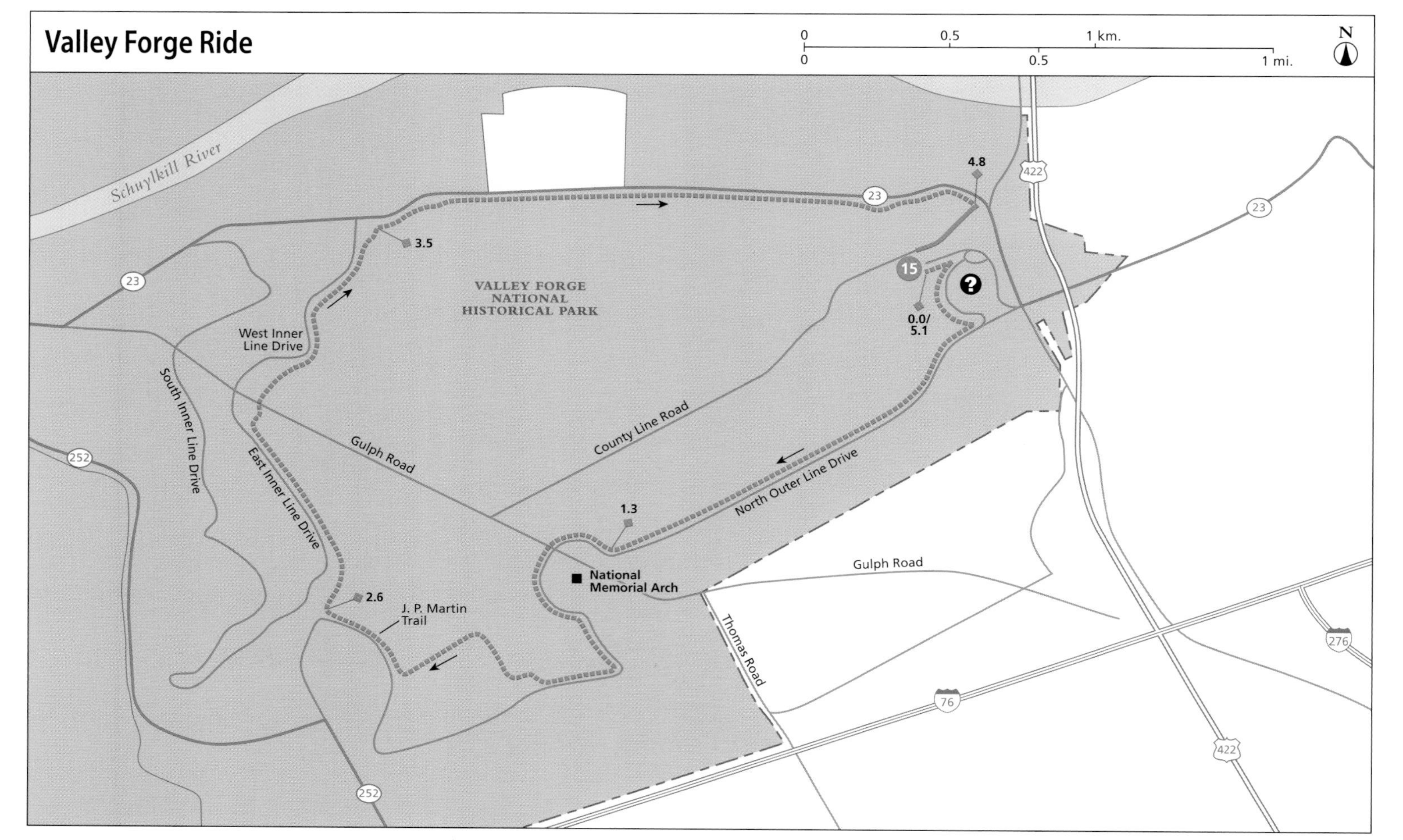
Valley Forge Ride
0
0.5
1 km.
0
0.5
1 mi.
N
Schuylkill River
VALLEY FORGE
NATIONAL
HISTORICAL PARK
23
422
276
76
252
4.8
3.5
15
0.0/
5.1
1.3
2.6
West Inner
Line Drive
South Inner Line Drive
East Inner Line Drive
Gulph Road
County Line Road
North Outer Line Drive
National
Memorial Arch
J. P. Martin
Trail
Thomas Road

9.1 Turn right onto County Line Road.

9.4 Arrive at parking lot of Valley Forge National Historical Park (on left).

Trail ride:

0.0 Start in the parking lot of Valley Forge National Historical Park; head east on the bike path toward the welcome center.

1.3 Turn right to take the path that goes around the memorial arch.

2.6 Turn right at the branch in the trail.

3.5 Turn right at the bike path that follows Valley Forge Road.

4.8 Turn right onto County Line Road.

5.1 Arrive at parking lot of Valley Forge National Historical Park (on left).

Location, Location, Location

Washington picked Valley Forge because 1) it was close enough to Philadelphia to pose a threat to the occupying British, 2) it was far enough from Philadelphia that a surprise attack would be unlikely, and 3) the ridges and bluffs that surround the area form a strong natural defense against attack. When the British saw the strength of the Continental Army's position, they returned to Philadelphia and set up camp for the winter.

Although life was harsh and supplies were short at Valley Forge, it was not uniquely so. There were worse winters than the winter of 1777–78, and it was a constant challenge throughout the war to acquire adequate clothing and supplies from the Continental Congress and the states. Morale was also good. Some of those encamped at Valley Forge had helped to force a British army to surrender at Saratoga earlier in the year. Even those who had been defeated at Brandywine and Germantown had shown their ability to fight and willingness to return to the fight once the weather took a turn for the better. All that was needed to defeat the British was the training.

It was therefore fortunate that Friedrich Wilhelm August Heinrich Ferdinand von Steuben arrived in America to volunteer his services to the Continental Congress because he gave them the needed training to become professional soldiers, which helped win the war.

The park includes the former site of an asbestos insulation plant, where imported asbestos fibers were mixed with magnesium carbonate from the native dolostone to make the insulation. The waste was then dumped into the dolostone quarries. The park acquired this land and discovered the asbestos contamination only in 1997. The contaminated areas of the park are currently closed, and there are plans under way to remediate the area and reopen the area for public use.

RIDE INFORMATION

Events/Attractions

Valley Forge National Historic Park was created to preserve the history of the sacrifices and perseverance of the soldiers who encamped here during the winter of 1777–78. The park features historic and re-created buildings from that era as well as a number of memorials.

Restrooms

Start/end: Water and toilets are available in the parking lot.
Mile 2.0: Toilets are available at Wayne's Woods.

Maps

Delorme Pennsylvania Atlas & Gazetteer: Page 85, B8

16

Fort Washington

Fort Washington was an encampment made by George Washington and the Continental Army in the late autumn of 1777, prior to their movement to winter quarters at Valley Forge. The area of Fort Washington is now a state park with a variety of recreational options.

Start: Mill Road parking lot of Flourtown Day Use Area, Fort Washington State Park

Length: 25.4 miles out and back

Approximate riding time: 3.0 hours

Best bike: Road bike

Terrain and trail surface: Paved roads over rolling hills

Traffic and hazards: The traffic on this route is mainly light, with some brief segments on busy roads. The busiest section of the route is the 0.4 mile the route travels on Welsh Road.

Getting there: By car: From City Hall, drive north 7.7 miles on Broad Street (PA 611) and turn left onto the ramp to Cheltenham Avenue (PA 309). Drive 1.4 miles, then turn right on Ogontz Avenue to continue on PA 309. Drive 3.9 miles, then take the PA 73 exit, and turn left onto PA 73. Drive 0.2 mile, turn left onto Mill Road, and drive 1.0 mile farther. The parking lots for Fort Washington State Park will be on the right side of Mill Road. GPS: N 40 06.38 / W75 13.08
By train: Take the train to 30th Street Station, and then transfer to the Lansdale/Doylestown Line. Take the Lansdale/Doylestown Line train to Ambler Station. The route passes by Ambler Station and Gwynedd Valley Station on the Lansdale/Doylestown Line.

THE RIDE

Fort Washington State Park is a cozy, well-kept neighborhood park that is a popular place for picnicking, hiking, bird watching, and fishing. It's also a popular place to watch the raptor migration in September and October. To start the ride, make a right out of the parking lot onto Mill Road and follow the road for 0.8 mile until it ends at Stenton Avenue. Turn right at the T intersection and continue on Stenton Avenue for 1.9 miles. On the way, you will pass by the Flourtown grounds of the Philadelphia Cricket Club, which is the oldest country club in the United States (founded in 1854).

After you pass under the Pennsylvania Turnpike, turn right onto Sheaff Lane and continue for 2.1 miles. (About halfway through, you will need to jog to the right on Skippack Pike to stay on Sheaff Lane.) When Sheaff Lane ends at Morris Road, turn left and continue 0.7 mile to West Butler Pike. Turn right at the light, cross Wissahickon Creek, and continue past the train station to downtown Ambler. Turn left onto Main Street in Ambler and continue 0.2 mile. When you get to the Do Not Enter signs on Main Street, turn right onto Reiff's Mill Road., and then turn right onto Tennis Avenue at the next intersection. Tennis Avenue will take you northeast out of town.

After about 2 miles on Tennis Avenue, turn left onto Norristown Road. Bike 1 mile on Norristown Road and turn right onto McKean Road. This area has a number of office parks and country clubs, so the traffic shouldn't be too bad on the weekend. After about 1.5 miles, McKean Road will descend a small hill. At the bottom of this hill, turn left onto Stongs Lane, which will feature a short

Historic farmhouse

climb. At the top of that climb, turn right onto Cedar Hill Road and continue biking until the road ends at Horsham Road. Turn left onto Horsham Road, bike 0.7 mile, and then turn left again onto Lower State Road. This marks the approximate halfway point of the ride. From this point, you will ride generally south back to the park.

Bike 1.6 miles on Lower State Road until you reach Welsh Road (PA 63) at the stoplight. Turn right onto Welsh and bike 0.4 mile until you reach Evans Road, where you will turn left. In this stretch of road, you will cross an interchange on PA 309 and pass by a major shopping area, so be careful. The intersection with Evans Road is at a stoplight at the bottom of a slight downhill.

After you turn left onto Evans Road, continue biking for 2.3 miles. Evans Road will jog a little to the west and then continue in a southwesterly direction until it ends in a T intersection at Plymouth Road. Turn left onto Plymouth Road and continue southeast. After 0.2 mile, you will cross Wissahickon Creek again and pass by the Gwynedd Valley SEPTA station. Continue biking on Plymouth Road for 1.3 more miles until you reach the stoplight at Morris Road. There will be a country club ahead of you and to your left. Turn left onto Morris Road to go along the north side of the country club, then turn right on Plymouth Road to go along the east side. Plymouth Road will end at an angle with Penllyn Blue Bell Pike. Stop and look carefully to the left before turning right onto the pike.

Continue southwest on Penllyn Blue Bell Pike for 1 mile. At this point, the road curves to the left. When you take the curve, you will be on Stenton Avenue. After about 0.4 mile, Stenton Avenue will meet Walton Road, run with Walton Road for 0.1 mile, and then turn to the left. Continue to follow Stenton Avenue across Norristown Road and Butler Pike and past Sheaff Lane and the Pennsylvania Turnpike. Beyond this point, retrace your steps back to Mill Road, turn left, and continue on to the parking lot at the park.

Bike Shops

Erdenheim Cycle & Fitness Center, 821 Bethlehem Pike, Erdenheim; (215) 233-3883; erdenheimbicycle.com
Erdenheim Cycle & Fitness Center is a full service bike shop with a helpful staff that will give you honest advice on all your biking needs.

Performance Bicycle, 1210 Bethlehem Pike, Gwynedd Crossing Shopping Center, North Wales; (215) 654-9088; performancebike.com This shop is one of the retail stores of the popular online site.

Land for Recreation and More

The railroads brought many things with them when they expanded into the countryside around Philadelphia. To the areas along the Main Line to the west of the city, the railroads brought wealthy citizens who wanted to purchase country estates. To the areas along the North Pennsylvania Railroad, on which Fort Washington and Ambler are located, the railroad brought daytrippers and industry. During the summer, daytrippers would ride up to picnic along the relatively cool, shady Wissahickon and to swim and play. The small communities in this area would also send products such as lime to Philadelphia for use in mortar.

Daytrippers were welcomed by people such as Elmer Dungan, who bought a field in Fort Washington in 1904 and allowed anybody who followed the rules to use the field free of charge. Dungan's Field eventually included a baseball diamond, a bowling green, and tennis courts. Dungan even installed a large clock on the side of his house so that his guests knew how long they had before it was time to go home.

At around the same time, Ambler was becoming a center for the production of asbestos products. The Keasbey and Mattison Company moved to the town in 1881 to produce asbestos building materials, including asbestos insulation for pipes. Company literature proclaimed that they were "the BEST in asBESTos." Dr. Richard Mattison, a founder of the company, was responsible for initiating or at least partially financing many improvements to Ambler, including a library, an opera house, electric lighting, and a water system.

Eventually, the people of Philadelphia realized that the area around Fort Washington was developing and that they could not indefinitely rely on the generosity of people such as Elmer Dungan for access to recreational facilities. The Fairmount Park Commission therefore started to purchase land in Fort Washington in the early 1920s, even though these lands were outside the municipal boundaries of Philadelphia. The commission administered these lands with the assistance of the Pennsylvania State Department of Forests and Waters until 1953. At that time, the Department of Forests and Waters assumed full responsibility for the land and turned the land into a state park.

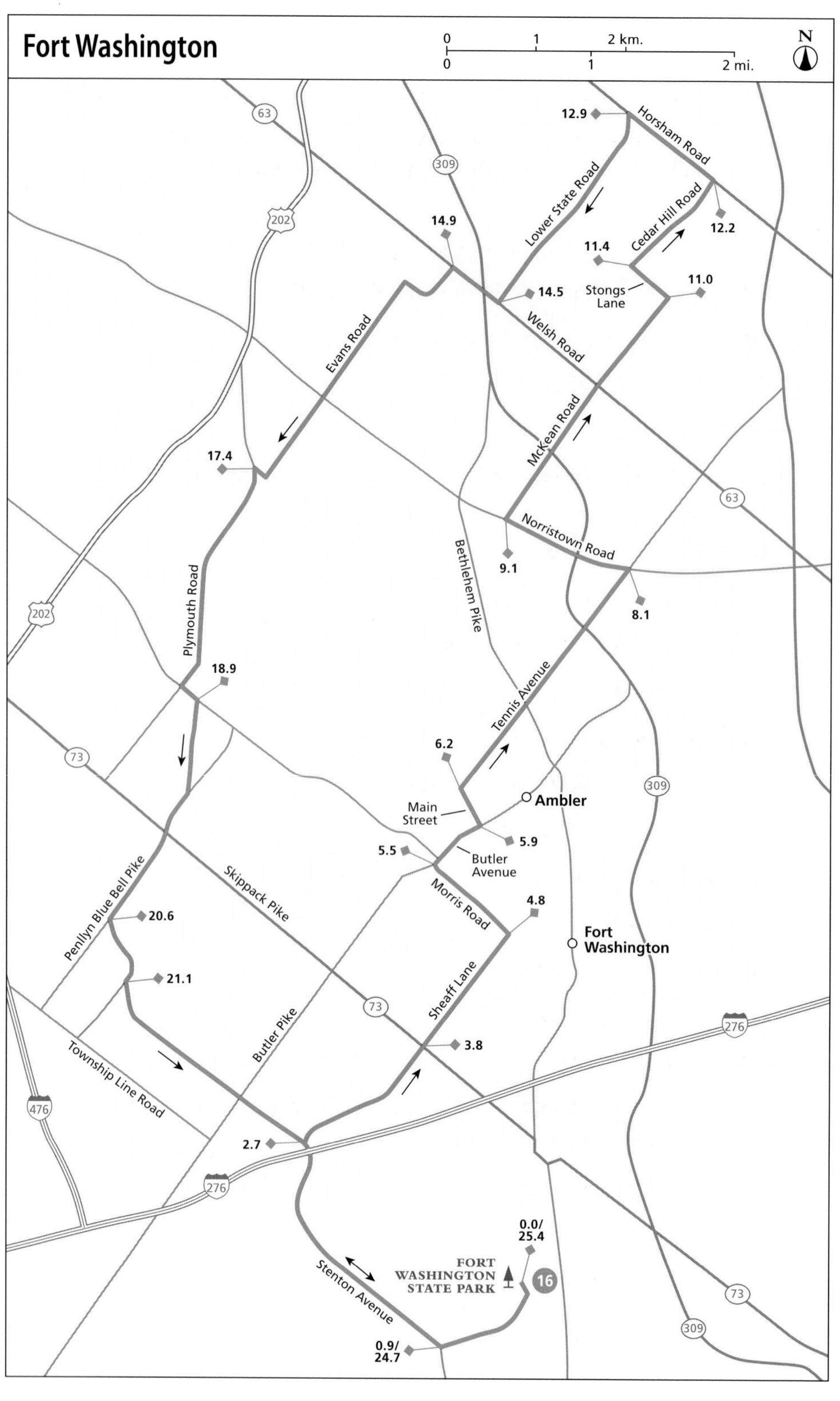
Fort Washington
0
1
2 km.
0
1
2 mi.
N
Horsham Road
12.9
Lower State Road
Cedar Hill Road
12.2
14.9
11.4
11.0
14.5
Stongs Lane
Welsh Road
Evans Road
McKean Road
17.4
Norristown Road
9.1
Bethlehem Pike
8.1
Plymouth Road
18.9
Tennis Avenue
6.2
Main Street
Ambler
5.9
5.5
Butler Avenue
Morris Road
Skippack Pike
Penllyn Blue Bell Pike
20.6
4.8
Fort Washington
21.1
Sheaff Lane
Butler Pike
3.8
Township Line Road
2.7
0.0/
25.4
FORT WASHINGTON STATE PARK
16
Stenton Avenue
0.9/
24.7
63
309
202
73
276
476

MILES AND DIRECTIONS

0.0 Start in the Mill Road parking lot of Flourtown Day Use Area, Fort Washington State Park; turn right and head southwest on West Mill Road.

0.8 Turn right onto Stenton Avenue.

2.7 Turn right onto Sheaff Lane (just past the turnpike).

3.8 Turn right onto East Skippack Pike, then left onto Sheaff Lane.

4.8 Turn left onto Morris Road.

5.5 Turn right onto West Butler Pike.

5.8 The route passes the Ambler station on the SEPTA Lansdale/Doylestown Line.

5.9 Turn left onto North Main Street.

6.1 Turn right onto Reiffs Mill Road.

6.2 Slight right onto Tennis Avenue.

8.1 Turn left onto Norristown Road.

9.1 Turn right onto McKean Road.

11.0 Turn left onto Stongs Lane (at the bottom of the hill).

11.4 Turn right onto Cedar Hill Road.

12.2 Turn left onto Horsham Road.

12.9 Turn left onto Lower State Road.

14.5 Turn right onto West Welsh Road.

14.9 Turn left onto Evans Road.

17.2 Left onto Plymouth Road.

17.4 The route passes the Gwynedd Valley station on the SEPTA Lansdale/Doylestown Line.

18.7 Turn left onto Morris Road.

18.9 Turn right onto Plymouth Road.

19.6 Right onto Penllyn Blue Bell Pike.

20.6 Curve left onto Stenton Avenue.

21.1 Turn left to stay on Stenton Avenue.

24.7 Turn left onto West Mill Road.

25.4 Finish at Mill Road parking lot of Flourtown Day Use Area, Fort Washington State Park.

RIDE INFORMATION

Events/Attractions

Fort Washington State Park (500 South Bethlehem Pike, Fort Washington; 215-591-5250; dcnr.state.pa.us/stateparks/findapark/fortwashington) incorporates Fort Hill (the original location of the encampment and the western end of the Continental Army positions), Militia Hill (the position that was occupied by the Pennsylvania Militia west of Wissahickon Creek), and the Flourtown and Sandy Run areas. The park features hiking and biking trails, a disc golf course, and organized group camping.

In the late 19th century, many roads in this area were made into turnpikes, and tolls were charged to pay for road improvements (such as gravel surfaces). Butler Pike was one of those roads. By 1860, toll gates were set up on both sides of the North Pennsylvania Railroad, so that you could not access the railroad without paying a toll. When Ambler became incorporated as a borough in 1888, 125 citizens petitioned for the toll gates to be removed. The petition was granted in 1890.

Restrooms

Start/end: Water and restrooms are available at Fort Washington State Park.

Mile 5.9: There are a number of businesses in downtown Ambler that have toilets.

Maps

Delorme Pennsylvania Atlas & Gazetteer: Page 86, A2

17

Washington Crossing Ride

Washington Crossing, Pennsylvania, is a beautiful residential community in Upper Makefield Township, Bucks County, named for the famous crossing General George Washington made on Christmas night 1776. This area is a mix of residential community and farmland, and as long as you don't mind a few hills, it is a fun area to explore.

Start: Parking lot of Washington Crossing State Park by the Delaware Canal

Length: 15.1-mile loop

Approximate riding time: 1.5 hours

Best bike: Road bike

Terrain and trail surface: The terrain is paved with some climbing.

Traffic and hazards: The roads in this route have light to medium traffic, with a brief stretch of busy highway in Wrightstown.

Getting there: **By car:** From Center City, drive north on I-95, and take exit 51 to New Hope. Turn left at the stop sign on Taylorville Road, drive 2.9 miles, and turn right onto PA 532. The parking lot is 0.2 mile on the left (just on the other side of the canal). GPS: N40 17.46 / W74 52.57
By train: Take the train to 30th Street Station, and then transfer to the West Trenton Line. Take the West Trenton Line train to Yardley Station. Turn left (northwest) on Main Street by the station, turn right onto Letchworth Avenue (the first right at 0.2 mile), and then turn left onto Delaware Avenue when Letchworth Avenue ends in a T intersection at the Delaware River (in 0.3 mile). Ride northwest on Delaware Avenue 4.4 miles to Washington Crossing.

THE RIDE

The ride starts by Washington Crossing State Park. This is the area where Washington made his crossing of the Delaware River and marched to Trenton to defeat the Hessian troops there. It was one of the major victories in the war. To start the ride you will make a left out of the parking lot onto PA 532 and then make a left onto PA 32 (River Road).

As you ride along River Road, you will pass Washington Crossing State Park on your right. This is the official historic site where Washington made his crossing. This is also the location where the Friends of Washington Crossing Park do the reenactment every year. As you continue on you will get some nice views of the river until the road curves away from it. Be careful where PA 32 and Taylorsville Road meet as this can sometimes be a busy intersection.

After Taylorsville Road you will make the next left onto Stonybrook Road. This will take you past some of the nice rural farms in the area as you slowly head uphill deeper into Bucks County. Eventually Stonybrook will merge with Brownsburg then Eagle Road before you make the right onto Pineville Road. You will continue to ride through some nice spread-out residential areas and will see a few historic barns and old stone houses.

When you make the left onto Brownsburg Road from Pineville, the hill will be a little steeper until you reach Wrightstown Road. You will have a short

The McConkey Ferry Inn in Washington Crossing State Park

stretch on Durham Road (PA 413) that can have moderate to heavy traffic at times, so stay in the large shoulder on the right side of the road until you make the left at a light onto Wrightstown Road.

Once you are on Wrightstown Road, you will have almost 5 miles of riding mostly downhill on a relatively quiet road. On a nice day you will be able to get an occasional glimpse of the valley below. Eventually you will cross Taylorsville Road and be back at the starting point. If you are interested in seeing more of scenic Bucks County, you can try Ride 23, which will take you past some of the wonderful covered bridges in the area.

Bike Shops

Newtown Bicycle Shop, 30 N. State St., Newtown 18940; (215) 968-3200
Whether you need a child's bike, a mountain bike, beach cruiser, or a racing bike, this is a bike shop that can meet all your needs.

MILES AND DIRECTIONS

0.0 Start in the parking lot of Washington Crossing Historic Park by the Delaware Canal; turn left onto PA 532 North/General Washington Memorial Boulevard.

0.4 Turn left onto PA 32 North/River Road.

3.0 Turn left onto Stonybrook Road/Brownsburg Road/Eagle Road.

5.2 Turn right onto Pineville Road.

6.3 Turn left onto Brownsburg Road.

8.6 Slight left onto PA 413 South/Durham Road.

9.0 Turn left onto Wrightstown Road.

14.7 Turn left onto PA 532 North/Washington Crossing Road.

15.1 Finish at Washington Crossing Historic Park.

RIDE INFORMATION

Events/Attractions

Washington Crossing Historic Park, at mile 0.4, was founded in 1917 to preserve the site where Washington crossed the Delaware. Today the park offers tours of a number of historic buildings in the park. They also stage a reenactment of the crossing every year on Christmas Day. Details about the park can be found at ushistory.org/washingtoncrossing.

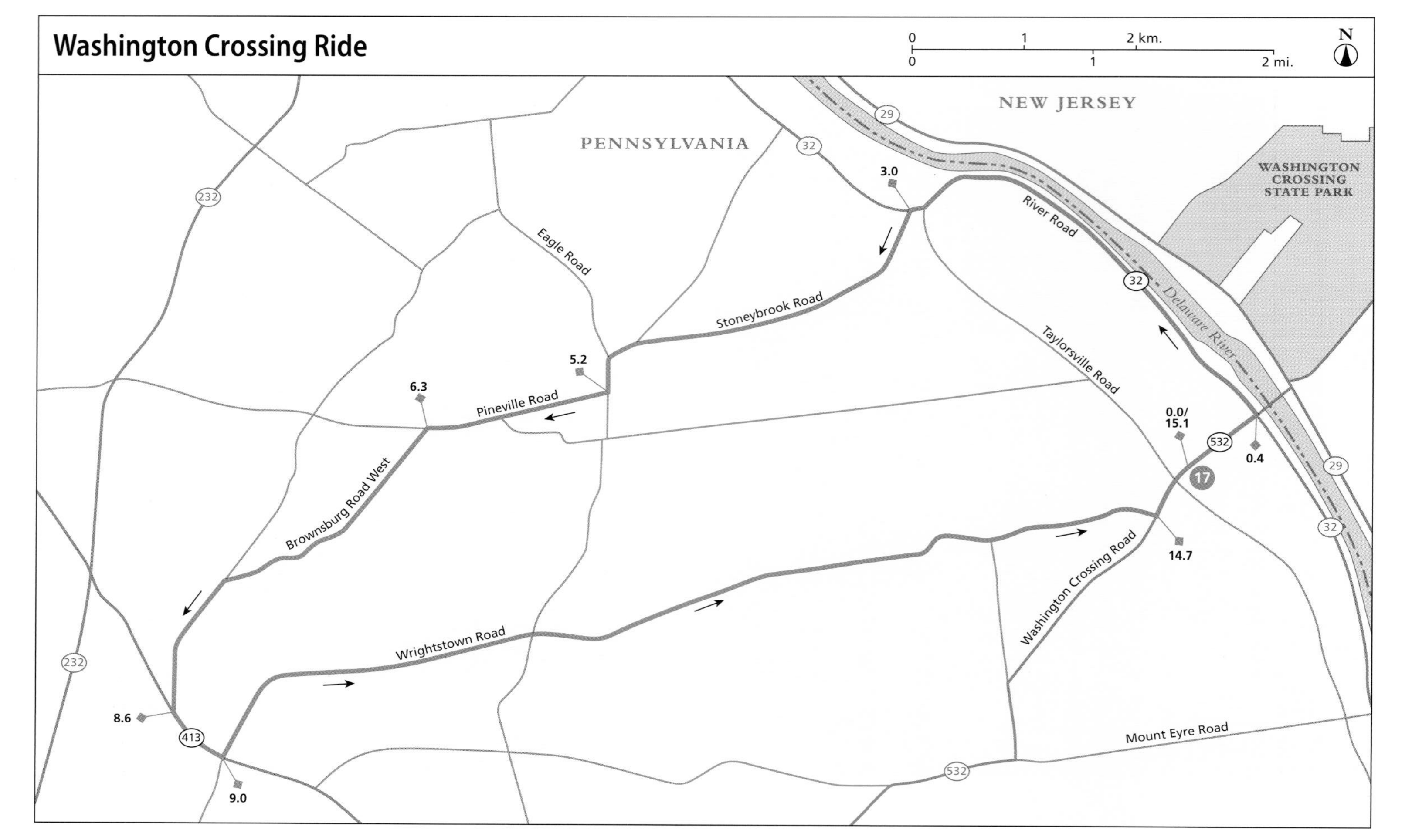
Washington Crossing Ride
0
1
2 km.
0
1
2 mi.
N
NEW JERSEY
PENNSYLVANIA
WASHINGTON
CROSSING
STATE PARK
Delaware River
River Road
Taylorsville Road
Eagle Road
Stoneybrook Road
Pineville Road
Brownsburg Road West
Wrightstown Road
Washington Crossing Road
Mount Eyre Road
29
32
232
413
532
17
0.0/
15.1
0.4
3.0
5.2
6.3
8.6
9.0
14.7

A Daring Move Claims Trenton

In the winter of 1776, General George Washington and his army were at a low point. The war for independence was going badly. A series of defeats had forced Washington to retreat across New Jersey to Pennsylvania. A harsh winter had set in and the soldiers were forced to deal with a lack of both food and warm clothing. Now, more than ever, the war for independence needed a victory.

Washington decided on a surprise attack against the Hessians at the Trenton garrison. So on the night of December 25 under the cover of darkness, Washington and his men crossed the river and headed for Trenton. The crossing was not easy because of worsening weather during the night. In fact the supporting divisions, led by Generals Cadwalader and Ewing, were unable to cross at southern points along the Delaware and help support Washington's attack.

Despite the bad weather and lack of support, Washington and his men successfully completed the crossing and marched into Trenton on the morning of December 26, achieving a resounding victory over the Hessians. This daring plan reignited the cause of freedom and gave new life to the American Revolution.

Restaurants

OWowCow Creamery, 591 Durham Rd. (Rte. 413), Wrightstown, PA, on the right side of the road: A great little shop that serves coffee, cookies, pastries, and some great homemade premium ice cream.

Washington Crossing Inn, 1295 General Washington Memorial Blvd., Washington Crossing 18977; (877) 882-1776 or (215) 493-3634, washingtoncrossinginn.com: This beautifully preserved 1817 home provides a nice backdrop for a restaurant that serves traditional American cuisine. They also have a popular Sunday brunch.

Restrooms

Mile 0.4: Washington Crossing Historic Park has toilets and water at the visitor center (by the Delaware River).

The back of the New Jersey quarter shows a representation of Washington crossing the Delaware.

Maps

Delorme Pennsylvania Atlas & Gazetteer: Page 73, F5

Doylestown

The pastoral settings of the gentle country life are not far away from Philadelphia. Nestled in the hills above the Delaware River lies Doylestown. This town was home to James A. Michener, Oscar Hammerstein, and a number of other notable people. The area around Doylestown is filled with farmland and forests, which makes for some good scenery as long as you don't mind a few hills along the way. This ride will lead you through this area by a few covered bridges and show you some nice countryside.

Start: Hansell Park, Doylestown

Length: 33.9-mile loop

Approximate riding time: 3 hours

Best bike: Road bike

Terrain and trail surface: Paved roads with mostly light traffic. The area you will be riding in is hilly so most of the terrain will be rolling with a few small climbs. Make sure you have done some hill training before you do this ride. There is no one tough climb on this ride, but the constant up-and-downs will have a cumulative effect.

Traffic and hazards: You will encounter light traffic on most roads. The area in and around Doylestown and Perkasie can be busy so there may be some heavy traffic here at times.

Things to see: Moods, South Perkasie, and Pine Valley Covered Bridges, Peace Valley and Doylestown

Getting there: From Center City Philadelphia take I-95 north to exit 49. Take CR 332 (Newtown Bypass) west around Newtown to CR 413. Take CR 413 for just over 11 miles past Newtown then make a left onto Hansell Road. The entrance to the park is on the left in 1/4 mile. GPS: N40 20.99 / W75 5.06

THE RIDE

There are many nice small towns around the Delaware River north of Philadelphia that make great day trips. The most popular is probably New Hope with its many art galleries and good restaurants. A close second is probably

The Moods Covered Bridge

Doylestown. During the spring and summer, there are many arts and crafts and music festivals around here, so it is always easy to find something to do.

To start the ride, make a left out of the parking lot onto Hansell Road and follow it to Burnt House Hill Road. From here you will travel through some woodlands and farmlands. There will be a couple of short climbs here as you make your way along the ridge above the Delaware River. Once you cross Stump Road, you will have some gradual downhills and the riding will get easier.

At 13 miles you will turn right onto Blooming Glen Road and start to enter the town of Perkasie. After making a quick jog on Branch Road to stay on Blooming Glen Road, you will ride through Moods Covered Bridge. This bridge was originally built in 1874 to cross the Perkiomen Creek. This bridge is heavily used and required a lot of upkeep over the years. In 2004 the bridge was destroyed by arson, but luckily the community rallied to have it rebuilt.

After you go through the bridge, you will pass Bucks County Community College on your left before making the left onto 5th Street. There is a shopping center here that is a good place to take a break. To get into the shopping center make the left at Hillendale Road and you will see some stores on your left that include a pizzeria and a place to grab something to eat.

Once you're done with your break, continue on 5th Street. You are now going through the main part of town, which can be a little busy at times. If you watch the names of the cross streets, you will notice that the names and order match the layout of Center City. When you make the left onto Walnut Street, you will pass Lenape Park on your right and see the South Perkasie Covered Bridge just sitting on the ground in the park. This bridge to nowhere used to cross the Pleasant Spring Creek but was condemned in 1959. Instead of destroying it, the local historical society raised enough money to have it moved to the park and restored.

Bike Shops

High Road Cycles, 73 Old Dublin Pike, Suite 4, Doylestown 18901; (215) 348-8015 Good bike shop with a friendly and knowledgeable staff to help you with all your biking needs.

The ride will continue as you make a few more turns and head out of town and end up on Callowhill Road. From here you will have a slow, steady climb as you head back toward Doylestown. About 1.5 miles before the turn onto Creek Road, you will see a stop sign where Callowhill Road meets Myers Road. You will stay to the right here on Callowhill Road and enjoy a nice downhill as you enter Peace Valley.

When you make the left onto Creek Road, you will ride along the edge of Peace Valley Park. The park consists of 1,500 acres of public land surrounding the 365-acre Lake Galena. The lake was created by damming the north branch

The Peace Valley Reservoir

of the Neshaminy Creek. The park has a paved trail you can use to ride around the lake and over the dam. The bike trail can be accessed from any of the parking lots on Creek or New Galena Roads. The park also has a nature center and a place to rent rowboats, sailboats, and kayaks.

After passing Peace Valley you will head down Iron Hill Road and go through the last covered bridge of the ride, Pine Valley Covered Bridge. This bridge was built in 1842 and is painted in the traditional red and white style. This is a heavily used bridge so watch out for oncoming cars as you go through it.

From the bridge you will cross over US 202 and head through the backside of Doylestown. The town can be a little busy, so use caution as you cross through the lights and intersections. If you need some food or water, there are plenty of places in town to stop. Once you get back to the starting point, if you are looking for a post-ride meal, you can head back into Doylestown or down to New Hope. Both are quaint little towns with plenty of food and interesting places to shop.

MILES AND DIRECTIONS

0.0 Turn left out of the parking lot onto Hansell Road.

1.0 Turn right onto Burnt House Hill Road.

3.2 Turn left onto Point Pleasant Pike.

3.4 Turn right onto Old Easton Road.

4.7 Turn left onto Curly Hill Road.

4.9 Bear right onto SR 611 (Easton Road) then quick left onto Haring Road.

6.5 Haring Road becomes Log Cabin Road.

7.5 Log Cabin Road becomes Deep Run Road.

7.9 Turn left onto Derstine Road.

8.3 Turn left onto Irish Meetinghouse Road.

9.5 Turn right onto Elephant Road.

10.0 Turn left onto Blue School Road.

13.1 Turn right onto Blooming Glen Road.

13.8 Turn left onto Branch Road.

14.0 Turn right onto Blooming Glen Road.

14.4 Turn left onto 5th Street.

15.8 Turn left onto Walnut Street.

16.5 Turn left onto Main Street.

17.1 Turn right onto Callowhill Road.

17.6 Steep downhill; watch out for stop at bottom of the hill. Continue on Callowhill Road.

19.8 Turn left onto Rickert Road.

19.8 Quick right onto Callowhill Road.

23.4 Turn left onto Creek Road.

24.1 Turn right onto Old Ironhill Road.

25.0 Old Ironhill Road becomes Keeley Avenue.

25.2 Turn right onto Sioux Road.

25.3 Turn left onto Tamenend Avenue.

25.8 Tamenend Avenue becomes Almshouse Road.

27.0 Almshouse Road becomes Lower State Road.

28.6 Lower State Road becomes Court Street.

29.0 Turn right onto West Street.

29.2 Turn right onto Union Street.

29.8 Cross Main Street, then turn left onto Lacey Avenue.

29.9 Bear left onto North Street.

30.6 North Street becomes Cold Spring Creamery Road.

31.5 Turn right onto Church School Road.

32.0 Turn left onto Fell Road.

32.8 Turn right onto Burnt House Hill Road.

32.9 Quick left onto Hansell Road.

33.9 Turn right into parking lot of park.

Lake Galena was enlarged to its current size when a dam was built by the county in 1972. Before that time, much of the current lakebed had been part of the village of Leven, the economy of which was based largely on lead ore (galena) mining.

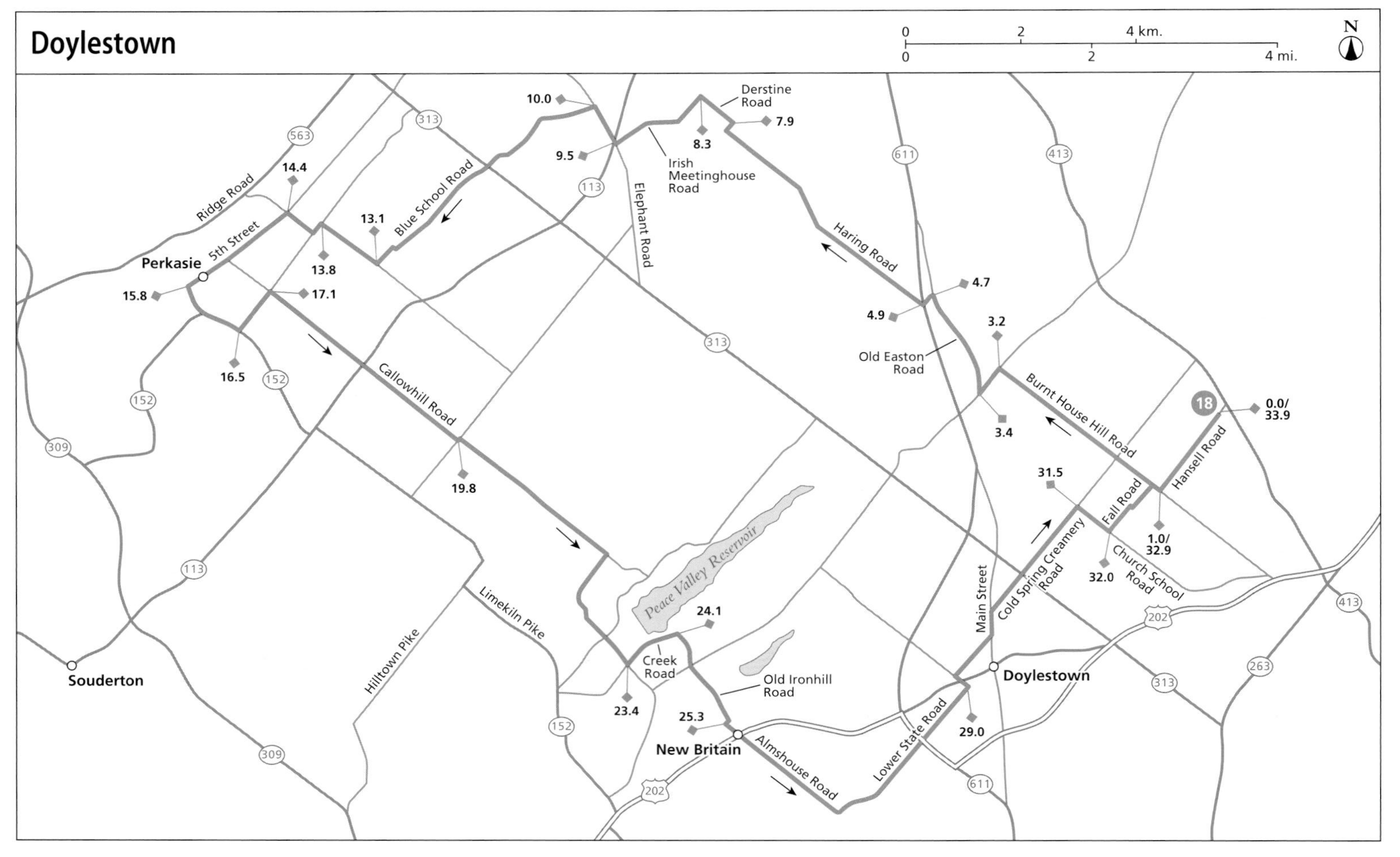

Doylestown
0
2
4 km.
0
2
4 mi.
N
Ridge Road
5th Street
Perkasie
Blue School Road
Callowhill Road
Elephant Road
Irish Meetinghouse Road
Derstine Road
Haring Road
Old Easton Road
Burnt House Hill Road
Hansell Road
Fall Road
Church School Road
Cold Spring Creamery Road
Main Street
Doylestown
Lower State Road
Almshouse Road
New Britain
Old Ironhill Road
Creek Road
Peace Valley Reservoir
Limekiln Pike
Hilltown Pike
Souderton
18
0.0/ 33.9
1.0/ 32.9
3.2
3.4
4.7
4.9
7.9
8.3
9.5
10.0
13.1
13.8
14.4
15.8
16.5
17.1
19.8
23.4
24.1
25.3
29.0
31.5
32.0
563
313
113
611
413
152
309
202
263

Art Museum in Doylestown

Besides being a Pulitzer Prize–winning writer, James Michener was also a very charitable person. He contributed more than $100 million to universities, libraries, museums, and other charitable causes. One of the museums he helped found was the art museum in Doylestown that bears his name. Michener was very involved in all the details needed to establish the art museum. He helped establish the endowment, as well as donating $500,000 and some paintings from his own private collection.

The museum was opened in 1988 and is housed in the old Bucks County Prison. The museum has 3,000 paintings, sculptures, and works on paper from the Bucks County visual arts tradition, dating from Colonial times to the present. The collection includes works by painters of the Pennsylvania Impressionist or New Hope school, American primitive painters, limners, and modernists. In addition to the permanent exhibitions, the museum presents fifteen changing exhibitions each year. These exhibitions feature a broad spectrum of artistic styles and media.

RIDE INFORMATION

Events/Attractions

Peace Valley Park is built around scenic Lake Galena and is a nice place to spend a summer day. This park has a paved bike path, some walking trails, and a boat rental center. For more information about the park check out buckscounty.org/government/departments/parksandrec/Parks/PeaceValley.aspx.

Doylestown is a quaint historic town with some unique shopping and nice restaurants as well as the world-class James A. Michener Art Museum. For more information, including places to shop and eat, check out the town's official website at doylestownborough.net.

Restrooms

Mile 14.5: The pizzeria and deli in the shopping center have bathrooms for patrons.

Maps

Delorme Pennsylvania Atlas & Gazetteer: Page 72, E3

19

Lake Nockamixon

Tohickon Creek's long run through Bucks County feeds and takes it through Lake Nockamixon. This beautiful 7-mile-long man-made lake is a nice place for boating, biking, fishing, and hiking. This ride will take you on a 29.4 loop around the quieter roads in the area and get you a couple views of the lake.

Start: Nockamixon State Park, Quakertown

Length: 29.4-mile loop

Approximate riding time: 2.5 hours

Best bike: Road or hybrid bike

Terrain and trail surface: Rolling, paved roads with mostly light traffic. The area you will be riding in has a lot of rolling hills so this ride will have a lot of small ups and downs with a few little climbs. Make sure you have done some hill training before you do this ride. There are no long or steep hills, but there aren't many flat spots either. The constant ups and downs will have a cumulative effect so just make sure you are ready for this type of ride.

Traffic and hazards: You will encounter light traffic on most roads. The short stretch on PA 412/611 can be busy so there may be some heavy traffic here at times. Be careful crossing PA 313 as this can be a busy road with a lot of fast-moving cars at times.

Things to see: Lake Nockamixon, Sheard's Mills Covered Bridge, and the Nockamixon Dam

Getting there: From Center City Philadelphia take I-476 north to PA 663 east (John Fries Highway). After 3.8 miles the road will change to PA 313. In another 4.7 miles turn left onto PA 563 (Mountainview Drive). The entrance to the park will be ahead 3.3 miles on the right. You can park in the parking lot right behind the park office as you enter the park or in one of the other many parking lots the park has. GPS: N40 27.67 / W75 14.63

THE RIDE

Nockamixon State Park is a hidden gem in Bucks County. Not only does the lake offer great boating and fishing but the park also contains rental cabins, a large marina, and a large swimming pool, as well as numerous hiking, mountain biking, and horse riding trails. And its out-of-the-way location means this park is never very crowded.

Although the park does contain a short 2.8-mile bike path, for this ride we are going to explore some of the roads in the surrounding area. To start the ride, make a left out of the park entrance followed by a right onto Deerwood Lane.

From here you will be riding up and down some rolling hills as you circle around Maycock and Haycock Mountains. These are some nice tree-covered roads with almost no traffic. There are a few slow gentle uphills here but also some downhills. When you make the right onto Haycock Run Road, you will cross over then ride along Haycock Creek, which is one of the other creeks that feed Lake Nockamixon.

Haycock Run Road will turn into Top Rock Road and end at PA 563, which is the road that goes along the north part of the lake. In about 1.25 miles you will make a right onto PA 413 (Durham Road). Across the street from the intersection of PA 563 and PA 413, there is an ice cream shop with good coffee. A half mile down PA 413 on the right is a mini mart and CVS store. This is the only place on the ride where you can get food or water, so make sure you have enough supplies to make the rest of the trip.

The Marina on Lake Nockamixon

You will most likely encounter heavy traffic, so stay to the right. There is a shoulder most of the way, especially after the merge with PA 611, so as long as you are careful you should have no problem with the traffic. To avoid some of the traffic you can make a right onto Tower Road, which will become Fink Road and take you to South Park Road. The only problem here is that there is a 0.75-mile section of road that is packed gravel. If you are riding a hybrid bike, this is not a problem. If you are riding a road bike, you can still ride through the packed gravel; you just will have to take it slow and avoid the looser sections.

Bike Shops

High Road Cycles, 73 Old Dublin Pike, Suite 4, Doylestown 18901; (215) 348-8015 A good bike shop with a friendly and knowledgeable staff to help you with all your biking needs.

Once on South Park Road you get a couple of quick views of the lake through the woods. The most interesting view will be by the dam that formed the lake and the spillway, which looks like a terraced waterfall. This dam was built in 1958 by the US Army Corps of Engineers and turned this part of the fast-moving Tohickon Creek into Lake Nockamixon.

From here you will continue along South Park Road, which will turn into Ridge Road and go past some farmland, rural homes, and churches. When you make the right onto Old Bethlehem Road, you will head down a steep hill then ride along the lake and the Three Mile Run Creek, which also feeds the lake. Be careful when you cross PA 313 as the cars on the road are moving fast.

You will have to cross PA 313 again at the end of West Rock Road. After you cross the road, you will have to ride up the shoulder for a short stretch before making a right onto PA 563 followed by a quick left onto Clymer Road.

Once on Clymer Road you will be heading into some rolling hills and quiet roads. Along the way you will see a small retirement community and a few wellness centers as well as a white building with large columns that looks like a Greek temple. After you make the left onto Richlandtown Road, you will head mostly downhill until you go through the Sheard's Mill Covered Bridge that goes over the Tohickon Creek. As with most covered bridges, the wooden boards of the road part of the bridge are rough and bumpy so use caution as you ride through the bridge. This bridge was built in 1835 and was named after Levi Sheard, the owner of the mill at the time. You will see the old mill on the right just before you cross the bridge.

From here you will slowly make your way back to PA 563 and back to your starting point. If you have not explored much of the park yet, you should head down to the marina and enjoy the view of the sailboats that are usually in the lake. If you want a bite to eat, there is a small snack bar by the pool area.

MILES AND DIRECTIONS

0.0 Turn left out of the entrance to the park onto PA 563.

0.2 Turn right onto Deerwood Lane.

2.4 Turn right onto Saw Mill Road.

2.5 Stay left where Saw Mill turns off to the right. Becomes Stoney Garden Road.

5.2 Turn right onto Haycock Run Road.

7.4 Haycock Run Road becomes Top Rock Road.

8.5 Turn left onto PA 563 (Mountainview Drive).

9.8 Turn right onto PA 412 (Durham Road).

10.3 PA 611 merges in from the left.

11.5 Turn right onto South Park Road.

14.6 South Park Road becomes Ridge Road.

18.3 Turn right onto Old Bethlehem Road.

19.1 Bear left toward bottom of hill onto Sterner Mill Road (unmarked) then turn left onto Three Mile Run Road.

Tohickon Creek

The area around Tohickon Creek was always a good place for hunting, but early settlers to this area realized that this fast-moving creek could be used for water-powered mills. A number of them sprung up on the lower part. The most notable one was the Ralph Stover gristmill in Plumstead Township. By the 1930s most of these mills had been shut down for a long time. The heirs of Ralph Stover donated the mill and land around it to the Commonwealth of Pennsylvania, and in 1935 this area was converted to Ralph Stover State Park.

The creation of the state park started the shift of the area around the Tohickon Creek from industrial to recreational. In 1958 land was acquired and the dam built that created Nockamixon State Park. More land has been added over time, and with the creation of the Tohickon Valley County Park, much of the area along the Tohickon Creek has been preserved for people to enjoy the unique and natural beauty of this area.

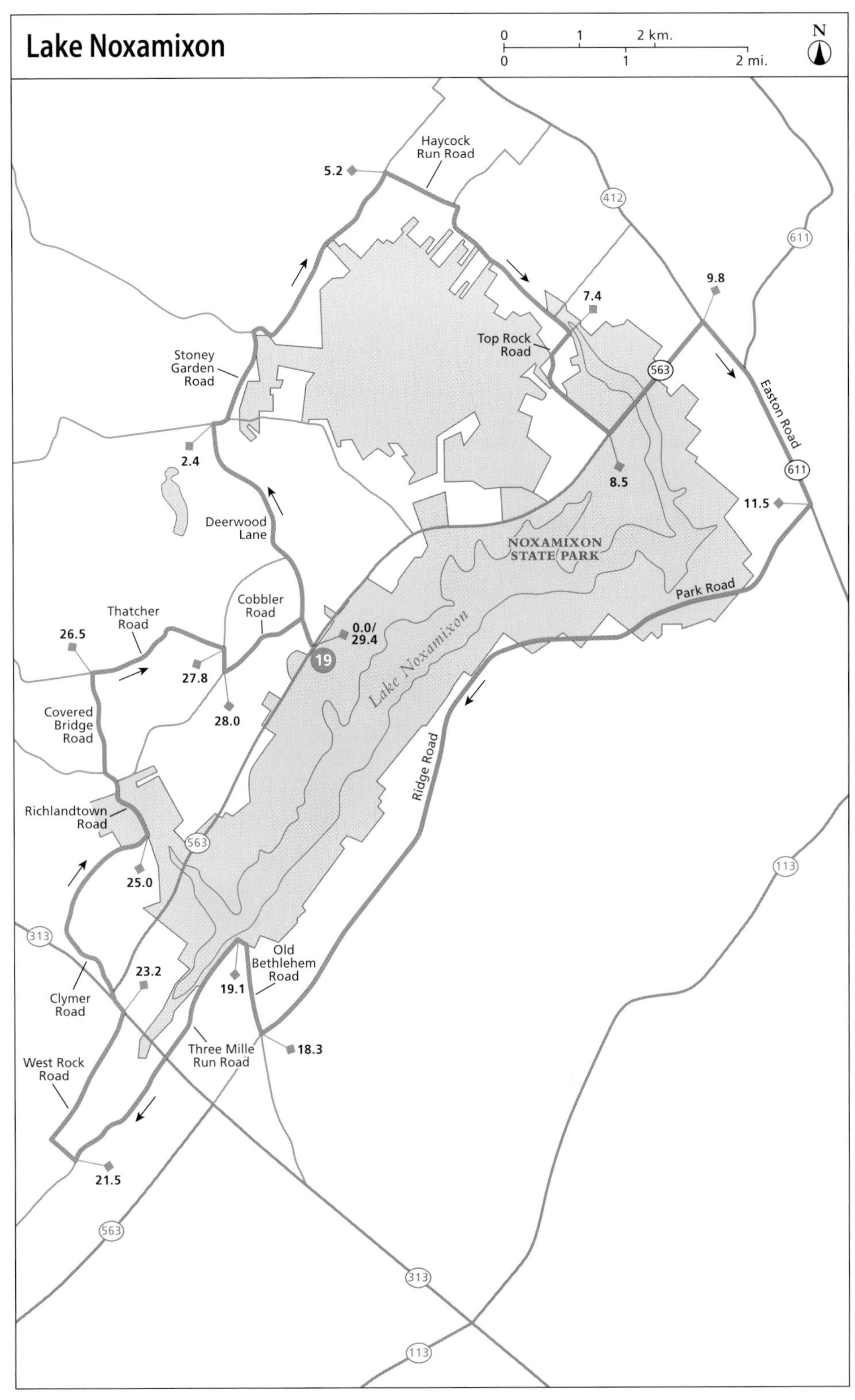
Lake Noxamixon
0
1
2 km.
0
1
2 mi.
N
Haycock Run Road
5.2
412
611
9.8
7.4
Top Rock Road
563
Easton Road
Stoney Garden Road
2.4
8.5
611
11.5
Deerwood Lane
NOXAMIXON STATE PARK
Park Road
Thatcher Road
Cobbler Road
26.5
0.0/ 29.4
19
27.8
Lake Noxamixon
Covered Bridge Road
28.0
Ridge Road
Richlandtown Road
563
25.0
113
313
Old Bethlehem Road
23.2
19.1
Clymer Road
18.3
Three Mille Run Road
West Rock Road
21.5
563
313
113

21.5 Turn right onto West Rock Road.

23.0 Turn left onto PA 313.

23.2 Turn right onto PA 563.

23.2 Quick left onto Clymer Road.

23.9 Cross Sterner Mill Road. Continue on Clymer Road.

25.0 Turn left onto Richlandtown Road.

25.7 Turn right onto Covered Bridge Road. You will cross Sheard's Mill Covered Bridge in 0.6 miles

26.5 Turn right onto Thatcher Road.

You may see some arrows on the road with an N underneath them. This is from the Lake Nockamixon century ride that is run by the Suburban Cyclists Club. If you are interested in doing the ride, check out their website, suburbancyclists.org.

A view of Lake Nockamixon

27.8 Turn right onto Mission Road.

28.0 Turn hard left onto Cobbler Road.

28.9 Turn right onto Deerwood Lane.

29.2 Turn left onto State Route 563 (Mountainview Drive).

29.4 Turn right into entrance to park.

RIDE INFORMATION

Events/Attractions

Nockamixon State Park is a beautiful 5,286-acre park that surrounds Lake Nockamixon. Besides boating and fishing, there are also a swimming pool, picnic areas, and numerous hiking and biking trails. For more information about the park, check out dcnr.state.pa.us/stateparks/findapark/nockamixon/index.htm.

Restaurants

OWowCow Creamery, 4105 Durham Rd., Ottsville: A great little shop that serves coffee, cookies, pastries, and some great homemade premium ice cream.

Restrooms

Mile 10.3: The mini mart has a bathroom that you can use.

Maps

Delorme Pennsylvania Atlas & Gazetteer: Page 72, C2

Tyler State Park

If you're looking for a good place to take the family for a day outdoors, just head to Tyler Park in Newtown. This 1,711-acre park is nestled along the Neshaminy Creek in Bucks County and provides a diverse environment that is a mix of woodlands, farmlands, wetlands, and historic sites. The park has a nice network of paved biking trails that make exploring the park easy. This 9-mile loop will take you around the park and show you the main sights.

Start: Tyler Park, Newtown

Length: 8.9-mile loop

Approximate riding time: 1.5 hours

Best bike: Mountain or hybrid bike, although the paved paths are fine for road bikes, too.

Terrain and trail surface: The ride will be on the paved biking trails. If you decide to visit the Schofield Ford Covered Bridge, you will have to ride a few hundred feet along a packed gravel trail. The terrain is relatively flat by the boathouse on the east side of the Neshaminy Creek, but once you cross over to the west side, you will encounter some rolling hills.

Traffic and hazards: You will be riding on paved bike paths, which are well maintained. The bike path is also a multiuse path so besides other bikers you will encounter pedestrians and joggers along the path. The path is 8 feet wide in most areas, so it is easy to share; just be sure to slow down on some of the curvier sections so you don't run into anybody.

Things to see: Schofield Ford Covered Bridge, Boathouse, Neshaminy Creek

Getting there: From Center City Philadelphia take I-95 north to exit 49. Take CR 332 (Newtown Bypass) west around Newtown and to the park. The main park entrance is on the left at the intersection of Swamp Road and the bypass. Follow the Main Park Road into the park. Continue straight across the first intersection and park in parking lot at the end of the road. GPS: N40 13.55 / W74 57.27

THE RIDE

No matter what time of year it is, if you want to enjoy some outdoor activities, Tyler State Park is a nice place to go. The park is large with a good trail system so it is easy to explore, but you never feel isolated because there are usually other people around walking the trails. This makes it a safe place for a family.

To start the ride, leave the parking lot and head out the way you came in. At the first intersection, make a right and follow the park road. In just under 0.5 mile you will pass another parking lot on your right. Right after the parking lot you will see a path. Make a right here and you will now be riding the Tyler Drive Trail.

This trail is wide and flat and will take you to the boathouse area. Here you will find a picnic area by the Neshaminy Creek. There are also a couple of pavilions and a canoe rental (during the summer). This is the most popular area of the park, so you will see a lot of people milling around the trail and creek. By the boathouse area you will cross the pedestrian causeway to get to the other side of the river. At the end of the bridge you will make a right onto the Mill Dairy

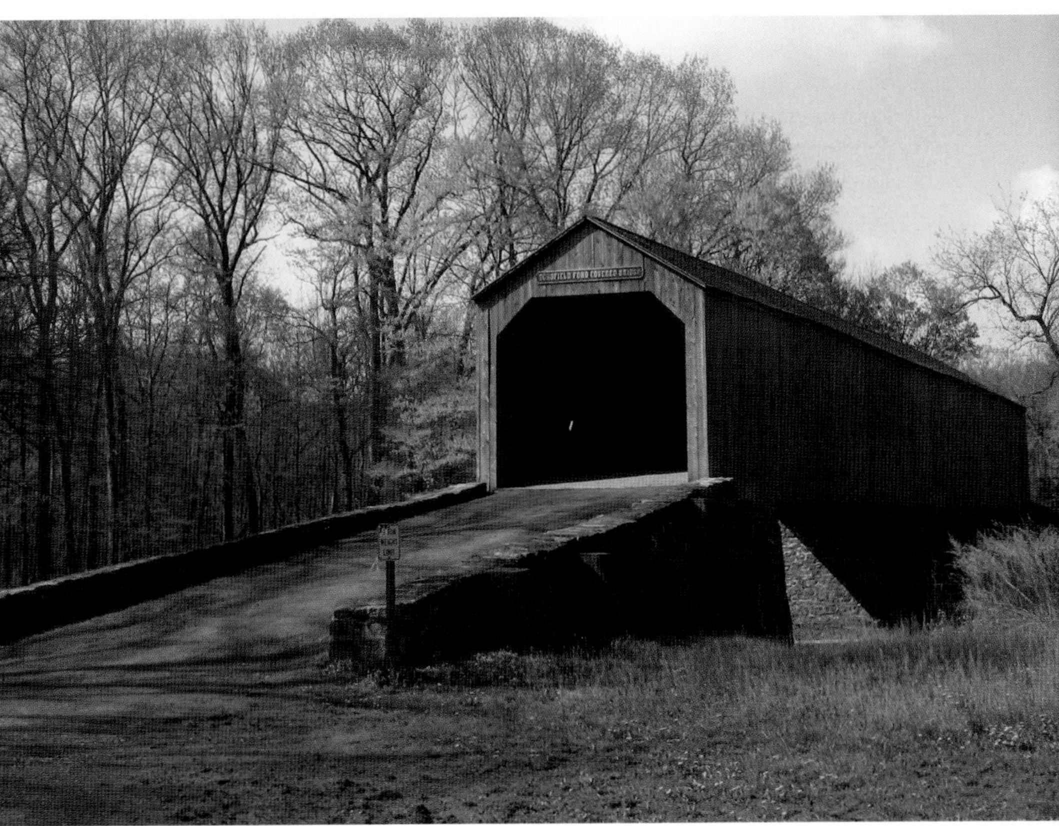

The Schofield Ford Covered Bridge

Trail and start encountering some of the hills in the park as you slowly climb up from the creek. You will be traveling mostly through some nice forests until you reach the top of the hill where the Dairy Hill Trail meets the Covered Bridge Trail. Here are some open fields and farm land that will allow you a good view of the surrounding area.

If you want to see the covered bridge, you will follow the Covered Bridge Trail down to Neshaminy Creek. This path will take you on a long downhill but be careful when you get close to the bottom because the paved trail ends here and you will have to ride on a few hundred feet of packed gravel to get to the bridge.

At 170 feet the Schofield Ford Covered Bridge is the longest covered bridge in Bucks County. It was originally built in 1874 but burned down in 1991. Fortunately a group of concerned citizens raised money, and the bridge was rebuilt using authentic materials and methods.

After your visit to the bridge, you will have to make your way back uphill on the Covered Bridge Trail then make a right onto the White Pine Trail. As the name implies, you will now be riding through a forested area populated with a number of white pine trees. But after you make a right at the next T, you will be riding through some farmland. When you see a residential area, you will have to make your next left and go through a gate to get on the College Park Trail.

College Park Trail will take you back into some nice woodland and past some small streams. The trails are fairly well marked, but at any time if you feel lost or want to shorten the ride, you can always follow signs to get back to the boathouse. At the next T you will make a right, which will take you away from the boathouse, onto the No 1 Lane Trail, which will take you to the parking area by CR 332. You are now on the opposite side of the park from where you started, making this a good alternate place to start.

A Park with a Past

Farming has been a tradition here for more than 300 years. The park was named for George F. Tyler, who purchased the land between 1919 and 1928 and turned it into one of the finest dairy herds in the county. About one quarter of the park is still under cultivation using modern conservation practices. The fields are still planted with crops like winter wheat, grains, corn, soybeans, and hay. This along with original stone dwellings in the park provides beautiful landscape views that serve to show people what this land must have looked like during the 18th century.

After passing the parking area, you will make a left onto the Stable Mill Trail, which you will follow until you make a left at the bottom of a nice long downhill onto the Mill Trail. From there you can either follow the Mill Trail back to the boathouse or bear right at the Woodfield Trail for an extra little loop.

Once back at the boathouse you will follow the Tyler Trail to the Quarry right to the parking lot where you started.

Bike Shops

Newtown Bicycle Shop, 30 N. State St., Newtown 18940; (215) 968-3200
Whether you need a child's bike, a mountain bike, beach cruiser, or a racing bike, this bike shop can meet all your needs.

MILES AND DIRECTIONS

0.0 From the parking lot head out the Main Park Road you came in on.

0.1 Turn right at intersection and follow the Main Park Road.

0.5 Turn right after parking lot onto the Tyler Park Trail.

1.6 Ride over the pedestrian causeway then make a right onto the Mill Dairy Trail.

2.1 Turn right at intersection and follow the Dairy Hill Trail.

3.1 Turn right onto the Covered Bridge Trail.

3.4 Paved path ends. Continue straight down packed gravel road to Schofield Ford Covered Bridge.

3.5 Arrive at Schofield Ford Covered Bridge.

3.5 Turn around and retrace your path up the Covered Bridge Trail.

4.0 Turn right onto the White Pine Trail.

4.5 Turn right at T onto Twining Ford Road.

5.0 Right after entering a residential neighborhood, turn left and go through a gate to get on the College Park Trail.

5.5 Turn right at T onto No 1 Lane Trail (away from boathouse)

5.8 Turn left after parking lot onto the Stable Mill Trail.

7.0 Turn left at bottom of hill onto the Mill Dairy Trail.

7.1 Turn right onto Woodfield Trail.

Tyler State Park
0
0.5
1 km.
0
0.5
1 mi.
N
Schofield Ford
Covered Bridge
Covered Bridge Trail
3.5
3.1/
4.0
Dairy Hill Trail
2.1
Neshaminy Creek
Swamp Road
413
Daisy Hill Trail
Worthington Mill Road
4.5
TYLER
STATE PARK
1.6
Main Park Road
Swamp
Road
Entry
0.0/
8.9
20
8.5
5.0
7.7
College Park Trail
Natural Area Trail
7.5
Mill Dairy Trail
Woodfield
Trail
0.5
7.1
Stable Mill Trail
5.5
7.0
413
No. 1 Lane Trail
5.8
332
Mill Pond Road
Newtown Richboro Road

7.5 Woodfield Trail merges back into the Mill Dairy Trail.

7.7 Turn right, go back over the pedestrian causeway, and follow the Tyler Park Trail.

8.5 Turn left to follow the Quarry Trail.

8.9 Arrive back at the parking lot where you started.

RIDE INFORMATION

Events/Attractions

Tyler State Park is a popular destination for people looking to spend some time outdoors. This wooded landscape along the Neshaminy Creek is a good place to enjoy fishing, canoeing, or some exercise on some of the hiking or

The pedestrian causeway over the Neshaminy Creek

biking trails through the park. For more information on the park, check out dcnr.state.pa.us/stateparks/findapark/tyler/index.htm.

Restaurants

Pineville Tavern, 1098 Durham Rd., Route 413, Buckingham Twp; (215) 598-3890; pinevilletavern.com: This old tavern has a great atmosphere and seves a wide variety of food. It is one of the better places in the area for a snack, some drinks, or a full meal.

The 18th-century stone farmhouse, located near the Schofield Ford Covered Bridge, is currently being used as a youth hostel.

Meglio Pizzeria, 25 Swamp Rd., Newtown 18940; (215) 860-4545: Great pizza from their wood-fired ovens and friendly service.

Restrooms

Mile 1.5: There is a bathroom near the boathouse before you cross the causeway.

Maps

Delorme Pennsylvania Atlas & Gazetteer: Page 73, G5

21

D&R Canal Towpath Trail

Back when the country was new, if you wanted to move a lot of goods quickly and cheaply from one point to another, you moved it by boat. If there wasn't a handy water route between the two points, often a water route was made by digging a canal. The D&R Canal is a great example of one of these canals and one of the few from this era that still holds water. Today, besides being used as a water supply, it also is a great recreation area with a great towpath that this ride will explore.

Start: D&R Canal Towpath parking lot on Lower Ferry Road, Ewing, NJ

Length: 27 miles one way (54 miles out and back)

Approximate riding time: 3.0 hours one way (6.0 hours out and back)

Best bike: Cross bike

Terrain and trail surface: Crushed rock, mostly flat

Traffic and hazards: This is an off-road trail with limited road crossings. The trail is heavily used by cyclists and pedestrians, particularly between Washington Crossing and Bulls Island. There are also a number of steep drop-offs on either side of the trail.

Getting there: By car: Drive north on I-95, cross the Delaware River, and take exit 1 in New Jersey to NJ 29 South. Drive 1.4 miles, then turn left at the River Road/Lower Ferry Road sign. Turn right onto River Road, drive 0.3 mile, then turn left onto Lower Ferry Road and drive 0.2 mile to the canal. There is parking available on the left side of the road. GPS: N40 15.49 / W74 48.94
By train: Take the train to 30th Street Station, and then transfer to the West Trenton Line. Take the West Trenton Line to West Trenton Station. From the station parking lot, turn left onto Grand Avenue and ride 0.7 mile to Lower Ferry Road (at the traffic light). Turn right onto Lower Ferry Road and ride 0.5 mile to the towpath.

THE RIDE

The Delaware and Raritan (D&R) Canal was built in the 1830s to provide a shortcut between Philadelphia and New York City. The main canal was built between Bordentown, NJ, and New Brunswick, NJ, and a feeder canal was built along the Delaware River to feed water into the canal. The feeder canal eventually became an important navigation channel as well, first as a water route, and then as the right-of-way for the Belvidere-Delaware Railroad. The D&R Canal is currently used as a water supply for much of central New Jersey and also provides many recreational opportunities.

The ride starts at the Lower Ferry Road access point. The trail will start out quiet but will get progressively busier the farther north you go, particularly after you pass the I-95 Bridge. There are several access points on the west side of NJ 29 north of I-95, and you pick up more cyclists and pedestrians with each access point.

The first interest point on the ride is at Washington Crossing State Park, where George Washington crossed the Delaware with his army before attacking and defeating the Hessians at the Battle of Trenton. There is a historic ferry house close to the trail. Water and toilets are also available here.

Bike Shops

Pure Energy Cycling and Java House, 99 South Main St. Lambertville, (609) 397-7008, pureenergycycling.com
Yes, you read correctly, it's a full-service bike shop and a coffee shop. Turn east on Mt. Hope Street on the south end of Lambertville; the shop is located on the northwest corner of Mt. Hope Street and Main Street.

Cycle Corner of Frenchtown, 52 Bridge St. # 2, Frenchtown, (908) 996-7712, thecyclecorner.com The only bike shop in Frenchtown, Cycle Corner sells, rents, and repairs bikes, and can also perform basic restoration of classic bikes. Turn east on Bridge Street in Frenchtown; the shop is located on the southeast corner of Bridge Street and NJ 29.

The next point of interest is the town of Lambertville. Lambertville is a popular destination for shopping and sightseeing, and is typically packed every weekend. Wells Falls, a particularly vigorous set of rapids, is visible from the towpath south of Lambertville.

A few miles north of Lambertville is the town of Stockton. Stockton is also busy every weekend and has shops and restaurants. Stockton is particularly popular with the cycling crowd, partly because of the towpath and partly because Stockton is the gateway to a large network of scenic but hilly country roads. On the north side of Stockton are the Prallsville Mills. In its heyday in the late 19th century, Prallsville Mills contained a gristmill, a sawmill, and a number of other businesses. Prallsville Mills currently hosts art exhibits and antiques shows, as well as historic exhibits about the time that Prallsville Mills was a major commercial center.

North of Stockton on the trail is Bulls Island, which contains a state park campground and a pedestrian bridge across the Delaware River, which is used on Ride 23. Bulls Island marks the end of the feeder canal. The remainder of the trail follows the railbed of the Belvidere-Delaware Railroad.

The final stop on the trail is Frenchtown. The trail extends a few miles north of Frenchtown.

There is also a towpath on the Pennsylvania side of the river (Delaware Canal State Park), which you could use for a part of your return trip.

MILES AND DIRECTIONS

0.0 From the parking lot head north on the trail (i.e., keep the river on your left).

4.7 Ride through Washington Crossing State Park.

11.4 Enter the town of Lambertville.

14.7 Ride through the town of Stockton.

View of the Delaware River from the D&R Canal path

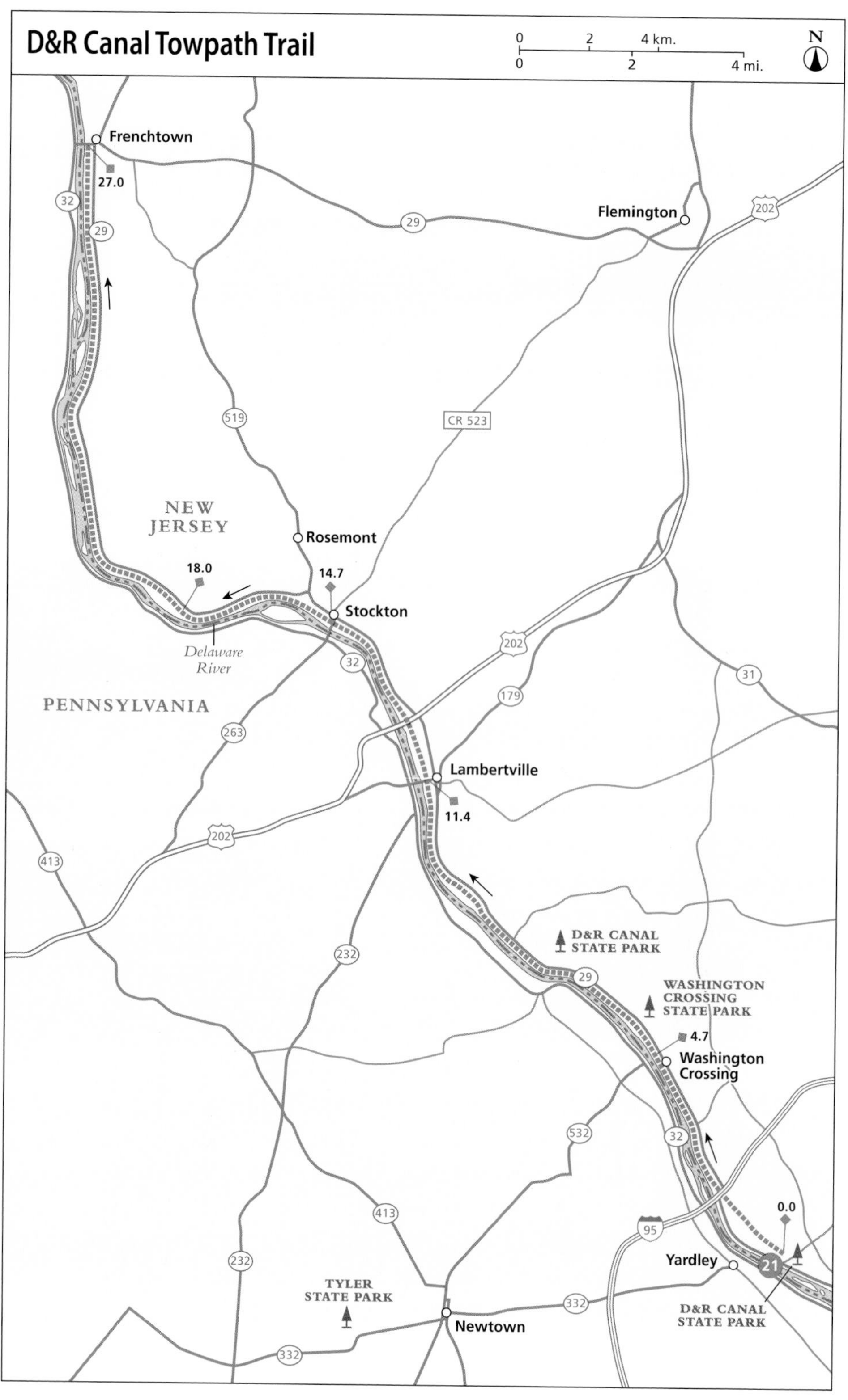
D&R Canal Towpath Trail
0 2 4 km.
0 2 4 mi.
N
Frenchtown
27.0
Flemington
NEW JERSEY
Rosemont
18.0
14.7
Stockton
Delaware River
PENNSYLVANIA
Lambertville
11.4
CR 523
D&R CANAL STATE PARK
WASHINGTON CROSSING STATE PARK
4.7
Washington Crossing
0.0
Yardley
D&R CANAL STATE PARK
TYLER STATE PARK
Newtown

15.2 Ride past Prallsville Mills.

18.0 Ride through Bulls Island State Park.

27.0 Enter Frenchtown. If you are doing an out-and-back ride, this is the turnaround point.

RIDE INFORMATION

Events/Attractions

Washington Crossing State Park has a historic ferry house, picnic areas, and an excellent view of the place where the Continental Army crossed the Delaware on their way to the Battle of Trenton. (609) 737-0623 or state.nj.us/dep/parksandforests/parks/washcros.html

Lambertville is a river town with many shops and restaurants.

Stockton is a local center for bicycling and also contains more shops and restaurants.

Prallsville Mills consists of a restored gristmill and its associated buildings. The mill complex hosts many arts and cultural events, and some facilities are available for meetings and private parties. The mill complex is operated by the Delaware River Mill Society at (609) 397-3586 or drms-stockton.org

Bulls Island State Recreation Area has a pedestrian bridge over the Delaware River and a state park campground. (609) 397-2949 or state.nj.us/dep/parksandforests/parks/bull.html

Frenchtown contains more restaurants and shops.

The Famous River Hot Dog Man

If you ride along the towpath near Frenchtown on a hot summer day, you will undoubtedly see people tubing down the Delaware River as this is a popular summertime activity. So many people tube down the river that one man, Greg Crance, decided to set up a hot dog stand in the middle of the river. He started in 1987 with a few tables and coolers filled with sodas and snacks. His small hot dog stand has been so successful that today he is now known as "The Famous River Hot Dog Man," and his full-service menu includes burgers, chicken, many different snacks and types of drinks, and of course hot dogs. He is now an actual attraction on the river. From June until Labor Day each year you can find his hot dog stand on a small rock-strewn island 5 miles south of Frenchtown. It's become so popular that he has his own website (riverhotdogman.com), and the temporary restaurant can be found on Google Maps.

The D&R Canal path

Restrooms

Mile 4.7: Washington Crossing State Park has toilets and water.

Mile 15.2: Prallsville Mills has toilets.

Mile 18.0: Bulls Island State Park has toilets and water.

Mile 26.0: Kingswood Fishing Access has seasonal portable toilets.

Maps

Delorme New Jersey Atlas & Gazetteer: Page 41, I26

Besides being a water supply and recreation area, the D&R Canal also serves as a major migration path for American shad and many waterfowl. This man-made canal has now become a key part of the New Jersey ecological system.

22

Green Lane

As you head out the Northeast Extension of the Pennsylvania Turnpike toward the Lehigh Valley, you will notice the land becoming more rural and slightly hillier. There are a lot of quiet roads and trails out this way that you can enjoy as long as you don't mind a few ups and downs. This ride will take you on a hilly ride in and around Green Lane Park.

Start: Green Lane Park, Green Lane

Length: 25.2-mile loop

Approximate riding time: 2.5 hours

Best bike: Road or hybrid bike

Terrain and trail surface: Paved roads, rolling hills with a couple of climbs. The hills should not be a problem for most recreational riders.

Traffic and hazards: Because you will be riding on public roads, you will see traffic along the way. Although there will be a couple of busy spots along the way, most of the roads will have light to moderate traffic.

Things to see: Green Lane Park

Getting there: From Center City Philadelphia take the Vine Street Expressway I-676 to I-76 west to I-476 north. Take I-476 north to exit 31. Take PA 63 north for 9.5 miles, then make a left turn onto PA 29 and follow that for 0.8 mile before making a right onto Snyder Road, which will bring you into the parking lot for Green Lane Park, just ahead on your left. GPS: N40 19.88 / W75 29.06

THE RIDE

Green Lane Park is a nice place to spend a warm summer day. Whether you want to relax on the beach, do a little fishing, or enjoy the biking or hiking trails, this park has enough variety to keep you busy. During the colder months people use this park for ice skating, cross-country skiing, sledding, and ice fishing. Green Lane Park is at one end of the Perkiomen Trail, which is described in Ride 25. For this ride we are going to explore some of the roads around the park and climb a few hills to get a view of the rural landscape. There are no places to stop for food or water along the way, so make sure you have enough water for the ride.

To start the ride, head down Snyder Road to its intersection with Old Gravel Pike/Deep Creek Road and make a right at the intersection to follow Deep Creek Road away from the park. Deep Creek Road is a quiet road through a forest; you will be slowly climbing up and down some rolling hills. Watch out for loose gravel on the road as it is washed out and beat up in a few spots.

As you get close to CR 663, you will be headed mostly uphill as you climb out of the valley. Once you cross Hill Road, you will have some nice downhills to enjoy. You will be traveling on rural roads with very light traffic through forest and farmland. There aren't any major sights here but the scenery is enjoyable. When you cross CR 663, you will be on Knight Road, which will take you across

The starting point of the ride at Green Lane Park

Green Lane Reservoir. The reservoir started in 1954 with construction of the dam across the Perkiomen Creek. The reservoir was completed in 1957, and in 1959 it was opened to the public for recreational use.

When you make the left onto Geryville Pike, you will begin a long, slow climb. This will end when you hit Upper Ridge Road. This will be followed by a quick downhill before making the right onto Swamp Creek Road; be careful not to miss the turn as you speed down the hill. Swamp Creek Road, as its name implies, will have you riding along a creek in a beautifully forested area. This road will bring you most of the way back to Green Lane Park. Be careful on the short stretch of SR 63 and SR 29 as there can be moderate traffic here at times. If you enjoyed the roads in this area, check out the Suburban Cyclists' website (suburbancyclists.org), as they have a couple other routes in this area.

Bike Shops

Tailwind Bicycles, 160 Main St., Schwenksville 19473; (610) 287-7870; tailwindbicycles.com A friendly full-service bike shop right on the Perkiomen Trail.

MILES AND DIRECTIONS

0.0 Leave the park by heading south on Snyder Road toward Deep Creek Road.

0.1 Turn right onto Deep Creek Road.

5.4 Cross Hill Road. Name changes to Parestis Road.

6.1 Turn left onto Wild Run Road.

6.9 Turn right onto West Branch Road.

7.9 Turn right onto Schwoyer Road (Congo Road).

8.2 Turn left onto Kutztown Road.

8.4 Turn right onto Mack Road.

8.7 Turn right onto Hock Road.

9.4 Turn right onto Church Road.

10.0 Turn left onto Kutztown Road.

10.3 Kutztown Road becomes Knight Road.

11.6 Turn left onto Markley Road.

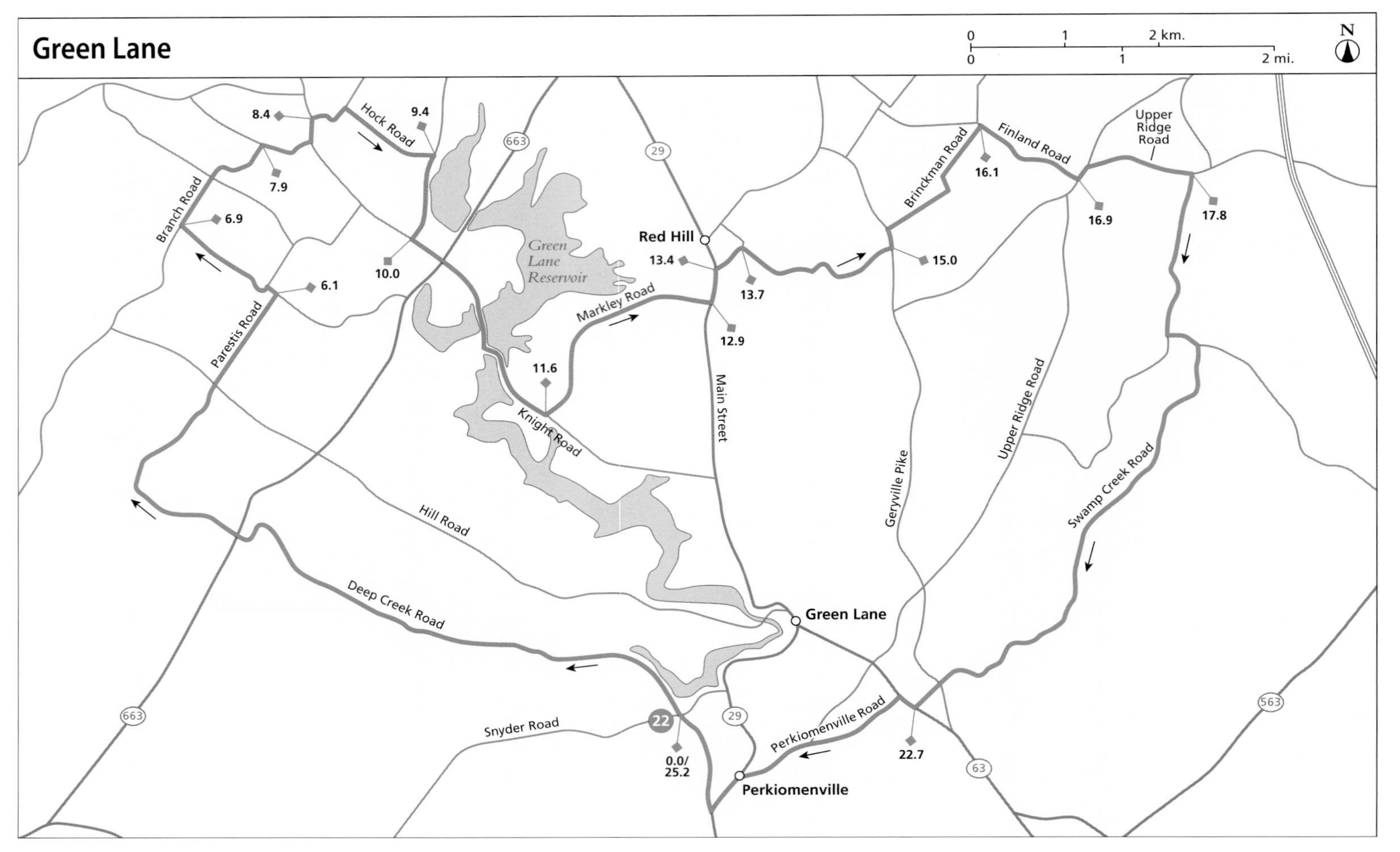

Green Lane
0
1
2 km.
0
1
2 mi.
N
Hock Road
Branch Road
Parestis Road
Green Lane Reservoir
Markley Road
Knight Road
Main Street
Red Hill
Brinckman Road
Finland Road
Upper Ridge Road
Geryville Pike
Upper Ridge Road
Swamp Creek Road
Hill Road
Deep Creek Road
Green Lane
Snyder Road
Perkiomenville Road
Perkiomenville
663
29
22
63
563
8.4
9.4
7.9
6.9
10.0
6.1
11.6
13.4
13.7
12.9
15.0
16.1
16.9
17.8
22.7
0.0/
25.2

12.9 Becomes West 3rd Street.

13.2 Turn left onto State Route 29 (Main Street/Gravel Pike).

13.4 Turn right onto East 4th Street.

13.7 Turn right onto Hendricks Road.

15.0 Turn left onto Geryville Pike.

15.1 Turn right onto Brinckman Road.

16.1 Turn right onto Finland Road.

16.9 Turn left onto Upper Ridge Road.

17.0 Bear right to stay on Upper Ridge Road.

17.8 Turn right onto Swamp Creek Road.

18.9 Turn left to stay on Swamp Creek Road.

22.2 Swamp Creek Road becomes Magazine Road.

22.7 Turn right onto State Route 63 (Sumneytown Pike/Main Street).

Land of the Lenni-Lenape

As with most of eastern Pennsylvania, the area in and around Green Lane was originally inhabited by the Lenni-Lenape Indians. Although some Lenape lived in large villages of 200 to 300 people, most of them lived in small bands of 25 to 50 people. The Lenape had three clans, Wolf, Turtle, and Turkey, which traced their descent through the female line.

The Lenape were a sedentary society and got a lot of their food by farming the land. Although the men were responsible for clearing the land, the women did most of the planting and harvesting of the crops as well as gathering of wild foods. Women were also responsible for making clay pots and preparing animal skins for use as cloths or shelters. The men were responsible for building shelters, making tools, and hunting for food. The Lenape used a number of different techniques to hunt animals including bow and arrow, herding them into pens, or trapping them with snares.

Although the Lenape no longer inhabit this area, a lot of the names and legends have survived and are still part of the character of this area.

22.8 Turn left onto Perkiomenville Road.

23.6 Keep left to merge onto Upper Ridge Road.

24.1 Turn left onto State Route 29 (Gravel Pike).

24.4 Hard right turn onto Deep Creek Road.

25.2 Turn right onto Snyder Road.

25.2 Finish at parking lot.

RIDE INFORMATION

Events/Attractions

Green Lane Park is in northwestern Montgomery County and offers a variety of year-round, outdoor activities including fishing, boating, camping, picnicking, horseback riding, mountain biking, and hiking. The park also offers summer concerts and movies. For more details see www2.montcopa.org/parks.

Green Lane Park is Montgomery County's largest county park, at approximately 3,400 acres.

Restrooms

Start/end: There are bathrooms near the parking lot.
Mile 13.2: There is a deli at the corner of 3rd and Gravel Pike that may let you use their bathroom.

Maps

Delorme Pennsylvania Atlas & Gazetteer: Page 71, E8

23

Bucks County Covered Bridges

At one time Bucks County had over fifty-four covered bridges. Although many of them have fallen into disrepair and have been replaced, there are still twelve of them in the county that have been preserved. Throughout the year a number of festivals and bike rides celebrate the unique beauty and history of these bridges and help fund their upkeep so they will be around to be enjoyed for many years to come. This ride will lead you through this area by a few covered bridges and show you some countryside that will take you back in time.

Start: Hansell Park, Doylestown

Length: 33.1-mile loop

Approximate riding time: 3 hours

Best bike: Road bike

Terrain and trail surface: The ride will be on paved roads with mostly light traffic. The area you will be riding in is hilly so there is no way to avoid a few climbs. Make sure you have done some hill training before you do this ride. The toughest hill will be on the start of Wismer Road, where you will have two short but steep climbs. After that most of the rest of the ride is rolling hills.

Traffic and hazards: You will encounter light traffic on most roads. The area in and around Frenchtown can be very busy on weekends, so there may be some heavy traffic here at times.

Things to see: Loux, Frankenfield and Erwinna Covered Bridges, Frenchtown, the Delaware River, and Bulls Island Park

Getting there: From Center City Philadelphia take I-95 north to exit 49. Take CR 332 (Newtown Bypass) west around Newtown to CR 413. Take CR 413 for just over 11 miles past Newtown then make a left onto Hansell Road. The entrance to the park is on the left in 0.25 mile. GPS: N40 20.99 / W75 5.06

THE RIDE

Bucks County is an easy ride from Philadelphia and provides a nice rural and scenic area in which to ride and is only complemented by the presence of the

different covered bridges. Each bridge has a unique design and history that gives you a view into the past.

The ride starts in Hansell Park; make a right out of the parking lot and head out toward SR 413. For the first couple of miles you will be heading downhill toward the Delaware. Be careful at the end of Stovers Mill Road where it meets Carversville as this is a very steep downhill.

The toughest climb of the ride will be just after you make the left onto Wismer Road. There are two short, steep climbs here that will have you working hard in your lowest gear. After you make it to the top of the second climb, the hills will be much easier and more rolling. You are now riding along the ridge and will have nice views of the Delaware River valley on your right.

After you cross Stump Road, you will soon start heading downhill and run into the Loux Mill Covered Bridge. This bridge was constructed in 1874 after the

The Loux Mill Covered Bridge

drowning of a popular young man named Reed Myers as he tried to ford Cabin Run Creek at this spot. This is a beautiful, well-maintained bridge; just be careful and yield to oncoming traffic as you ride through it.

As you continue you will be riding through some nice forested land with a few gentle downhill stretches mixed in with some uphill sections. You will see the Frankenfield Covered Bridge just after Cafferty Road meets Hollow Horn Road. The Frankenfield Covered Bridge was built to allow people, horses, and wagons a dry passage across the Tinicum Creek and was named after the Frankenfield family, who lived near the bridge.

From here you will continue to head down toward the Delaware. If you're interested in seeing another covered bridge, you can make a left onto Geigel Road instead of the right to continue on Headquarters Road. The Erwinna Covered Bridge is just 0.25 mile up Geigel Road. At 56 feet long it is the smallest covered bridge in Bucks County and not the most picturesque bridge.

When you make the left at the end of Headquarters Road, you will have to ride on SR 32, which can have moderate to heavy traffic so stay as far right as you can. After 1.7 miles you will make a right and cross over a bridge to get to Frenchtown. Bikes are not allowed to ride the main road across the bridge so use the sidewalk on the left-hand side.

Bike Shops

High Road Cycles, 73 Old Dublin Pike, Suite 4, Doylestown 18901; (215) 348-8015 A good bike shop with a friendly and knowledgeable staff to help you with all your biking needs.

Once on the other side of the bridge, you will be in Frenchtown, NJ, one of the more charming small towns along the river. This is a good place for a break. The best place to get a drink and some good snacks is the Bridge Cafe, which is right next to the bridge you just crossed. They have some outdoor tables that are a good place to relax and take in the view of the river and town.

After you have refueled, you will head away from the river and turn right onto PA 29. PA 29 starts off a little narrow, but after 0.75 mile it gets wider and has a nice shoulder to ride on. Although the road has some gentle inclines and declines, it is a relatively flat and easy ride. You will have some nice views of the river and the surrounding area as you ride along.

Nine miles from Frenchtown you will make a right into Bull's Island Recreation Area, which is a small, forested island surrounded by the Delaware River and the Delaware and Raritan Canal. You will follow the main road across a small bridge over the canal and then walk over the large pedestrian bridge over the river. Trying to ride over the bridge may get you a ticket as the officer told me when I forgot to dismount in the first few feet.

Once on the other side, you will make a right onto River Road followed by a left onto Fleecy Dale Road for your climb back to Doylestown. The climb up Fleecy Dale is very shallow so it's not a hard climb. There is a small stream to your left and some hills to your right, which makes for a scenic and enjoyable ride up the hill and back to Hansell Park where you started.

If you are hungry after the ride you can head to downtown Doylestown or a little further down the hill into New Hope. Both places have a number of good place to relax and recover.

MILES AND DIRECTIONS

0.0 Make right out of the parking lot onto Hansell Road.

0.1 Turn left onto SR 413 (Durham Road).

0.5 Turn right onto Long Lane.

1.7 Road turns left, becomes Street Road

2.0 Turn right onto Stovers Mill Road.

3.1 Merge onto Carversville Road (be careful of steep downhill before merge).

3.1 Quick left onto Wismer Road.

8.0 Turn right onto Dark Hollow Road.

10.0 Turn left onto Red Hill Road.

11.1 Turn right onto Hollow Horn Road.

13.4 Turn right to stay on Hollow Horn Road.

14.7 Turn right onto Headquarters Road.

15.7 Turn right on Headquarters Road (Erwinna Covered Bridge is to your left 0.25 mile).

16.0 Turn left onto State Route 32 (River Road)

17.7 Turn right onto PA 12 (Bridge Street). You need to walk your bike over the bridge on the walkway on the left.

17.9 Bridge Street Cafe on your right on the other side of bridge. Continue straight on Bridge Street.

18.0 Turn right onto PA 29.

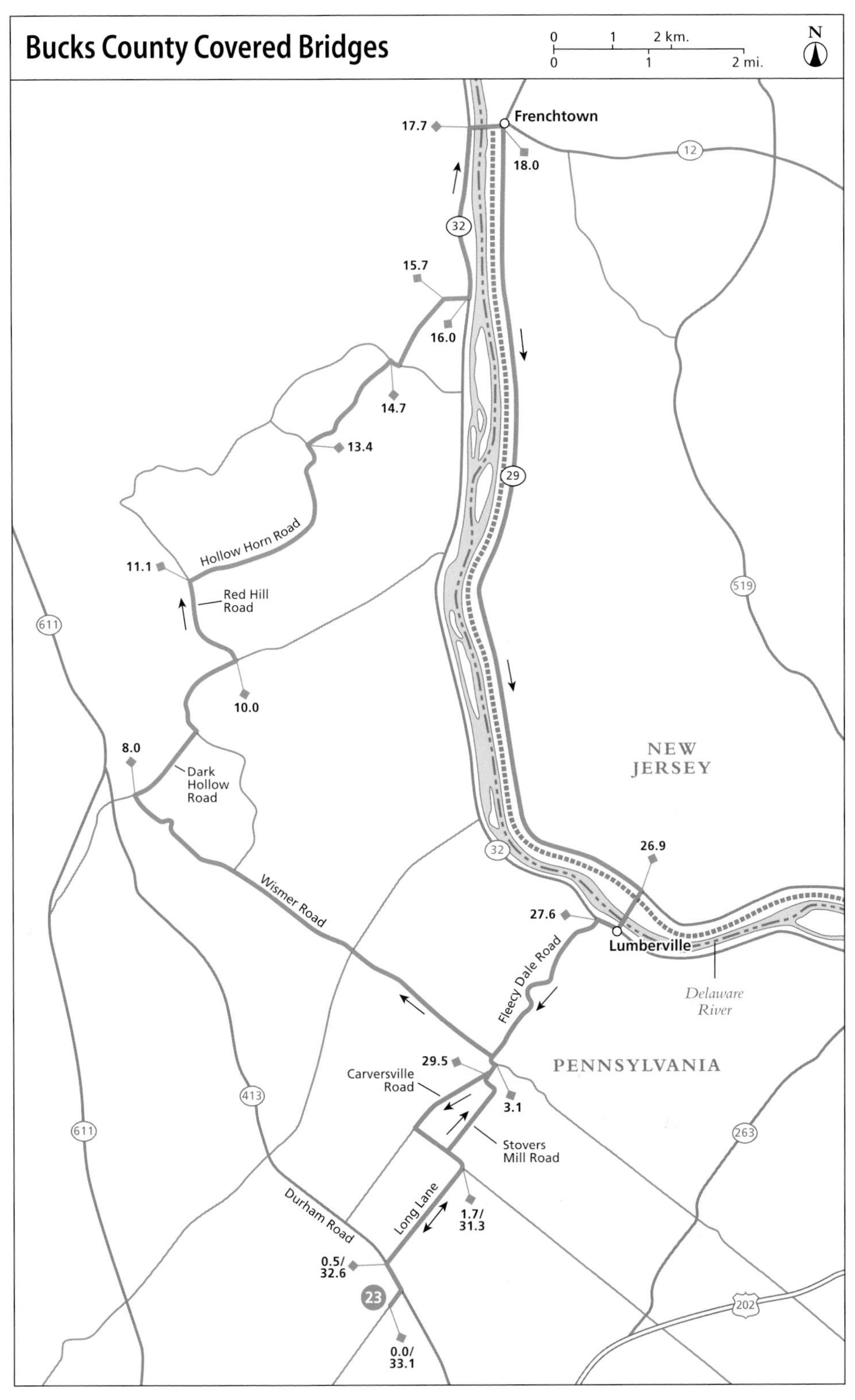
Bucks County Covered Bridges
0 1 2 km.
0 1 2 mi.
N
Frenchtown
17.7
18.0
12
32
15.7
16.0
14.7
13.4
29
Hollow Horn Road
11.1
Red Hill Road
611
519
10.0
8.0
Dark Hollow Road
NEW JERSEY
32
26.9
Wismer Road
27.6
Lumberville
Fleecy Dale Road
Delaware River
29.5
PENNSYLVANIA
Carversville Road
3.1
413
611
Stovers Mill Road
263
Long Lane
Durham Road
1.7/ 31.3
0.5/ 32.6
23
202
0.0/ 33.1

26.9 Turn right into the parking lot at Bull's Island. Continue over a small canal then through another parking lot toward the river. Walk your bike over the bridge over the Delaware River.

27.3 Turn right on the other side of the river onto State Route 32 (River Road)

27.5 Turn left onto Fleecy Dale Road.

29.6 Turn right onto Carversville Road.

30.7 Turn left onto Street Road.

31.3 Road curves to the left and becomes Long Lane.

32.6 Turn left onto State Route 413 (Durham Road).

32.9 Turn right onto Hansell Road.

33.1 Turn left back to the parking lot where you started.

RIDE INFORMATION

Events/Attractions

If you are interested in more information about the covered bridges of Bucks County, check out the Scenic Bucks County website (scenicbuckscounty.com/CoveredBridges/CoveredBridges.html), which contains details on all the bridges as well as a map showing where they all are.

Covered Bridges—Not Just Pretty

Although covered bridges today are considered nostalgic historic structures, their development had a more practical origin. Early bridge builders realized that wood exposed to rain, snow, and sun tended to decay much faster than wood that was shielded from the elements. The life of the trusses of a wooden bridge that was not covered was about 8 years whereas a covered bridge could last much longer. Some covered bridges have lasted as long as 80 to 100 years with good maintenance.

The other advantage of the covered bridge design was that the walls and roof of the covered bridge added strength to the structure so it could better handle the stresses exerted on the bridge by heavy snow and strong winds. So covered bridges are not only beautiful but also intelligently engineered structures.

Doylestown is a quaint historic town with some unique shopping and nice restaurants as well as the world-class James A. Michener Art Museum. For more information check out the town's official website at doylestownborough.net.

Restrooms

Mile 17.9: The Bridge Street Cafe has a bathroom that patrons can use.

Maps

Delorme Pennsylvania Atlas & Gazetteer: Page 72, E3

The 44-mile-long D&R Canal that you cross over at Bulls Island was built in the early 1830s to provide an efficient and safe route for transporting freight between Philadelphia and New York.

Farm to Farm Ride

As the city has grown, suburbs and exurbs have taken root in what was once a broad expanse of farmland. Much of this farmland has been developed, but there are still some plots here and there that have been preserved and adapted to their new suburban setting.

Start: Norristown Farm Park, Whitehall lot

Length: 22.6 miles out and back

Approximate riding time: 2.5 hours

Best bike: Road bike

Terrain and trail surface: Paved, rolling terrain, with two long climbs.

Traffic and hazards: The route has light to moderate traffic. Traffic can be heavy around the farms at times on the weekends. Most of the busier roads will have paved shoulders, but some will not, so use caution.

Getting there: Drive north on I-76 from Center City, and take exit 331B to I-476 North. After 3.1 miles, take exit 18B to Norristown. At the end of the ramp, turn right onto Chemical Road, drive 1.0 mile, and turn right onto Ridge Pike. Drive 3.7 miles on Ridge Pike (Main Street in Norristown) through downtown Norristown, and turn right onto Whitehall Road. Drive 1.3 miles to Norristown Farm Park. The Whitehall lot is on your right opposite the school complex. GPS: N40 8.38 / W75 21 26

THE RIDE

The ride will take you on a nice loop around this suburban area with an optional stop at one of the farms that have been preserved. The starting point of the ride, Norristown Farm Park, is an example of a historic farm that has been preserved and is still farmed but also provides a recreational area. To start the ride, leave the Whitehall lot to your left. You will ride south to Marshall Street, and then turn right (west). For the next 2 miles, you will weave westward through residential areas in suburban West Norriton. By the time the route reaches Ridge Pike, the road will have a paved shoulder that you can use to go the rest of the way out of town. You will have about a 100-foot climb to complete before you make a right turn onto Grange Avenue.

Grange Avenue borders Evansburg State Park on its east side, so the traffic will be light. You'll cross some busy roads on your way north, and there will be a few rolling hills, but for the most part it will be pleasant and shady. After you pass the golf course at about 8.7 miles, you'll descend a hill and pass an old mill by a creek. Turn left to cross the creek and climb up the other bank. The road ends in a T intersection at Skippack Pike, a highway with a paved shoulder. Turn left here, and then turn right at the next stoplight at Bustard Road.

Continue on Bustard Road until you pass Fischers Park on your left and come to a fork. Continue left on Bustard Road. Bustard Road will climb about 140 feet for 1 mile and cross the Northeast Extension of the Pennsylvania Turnpike. Turn right at the first stoplight after crossing the turnpike (Sumneytown Road). This road will take you to the next farm on the route: Freddy Hill Farms. This dairy farm sells ice cream and has a nice ice cream parlor—a good place to stop and get yourself a cone as a reward for climbing the hill.

When you leave Freddy Hill Farms, you will continue only 0.2 mile on Sumneytown Road before turning right onto Kriebel Road for the return

Freddy Hill Farms

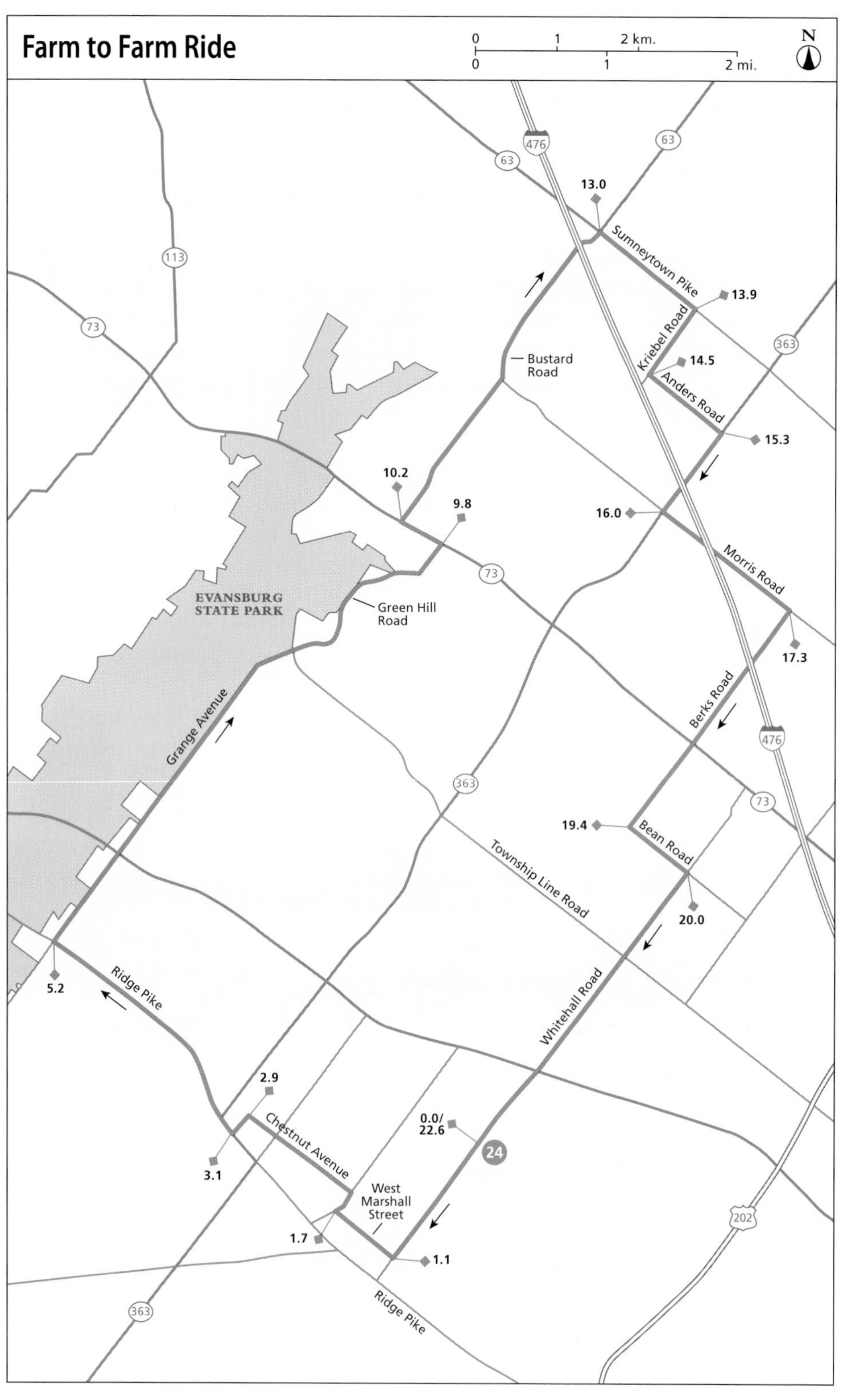
Farm to Farm Ride
0
1
2 km.
0
1
2 mi.
N
EVANSBURG STATE PARK
Grange Avenue
Green Hill Road
Bustard Road
Sumneytown Pike
Kriebel Road
Anders Road
Morris Road
Berks Road
Bean Road
Township Line Road
Whitehall Road
Ridge Pike
Chestnut Avenue
West Marshall Street
Ridge Pike
476
63
63
113
73
73
73
363
363
363
476
202
24
0.0/22.6
1.1
1.7
2.9
3.1
5.2
9.8
10.2
13.0
13.9
14.5
15.3
16.0
17.3
19.4
20.0

trip. Bike 0.6 mile farther, and turn left onto Anders Road (just before Kriebel Road crosses the turnpike). Bike another 0.7 mile, and turn right onto Valley Forge Road (a highway with a paved shoulder). Another mile will take you to the next farm: Merrymead Farm, where you can get another cone to tide you over.

Continue south for another 0.4 mile, and then turn left onto Shearer Road (opposite the Central Schwenkfelder Church). Bike another 0.3 mile, turn right to stay on Shearer Road, and before long you will come to the last farm on our route (before getting back to Norristown Farm Park, anyway). There's no ice cream available at the Peter Wentz Farmstead, but you can see here how farms were run in the late 18th and early 19th centuries. The Peter Wentz Farmstead Society maintains the farm and gives demonstrations throughout the year (such as Sheep Shearing Day in the spring).

Continue south until Shearer Road ends in a T intersection at Skippack Pike; turn left and bike on the paved shoulder until you reach Berks Road. Turn right onto Berks, and bike 0.8 mile. When you see Berks Road curving to the right, turn left onto Bean Road, and then turn right at Whitehall Road and follow Whitehall Road back to the Whitehall lot.

Bike Shops

Bike n Blade, 3823 Skippack Pike, Skippack; (610) 222-0560, bnbbikes.com Bike n Blade features lifetime free service on all adult bikes and multispeed children's bikes. This bike shop is located 1.3 miles west of the intersection of Skippack Pike and Bustard Road at mile 10.2 of the route.

MILES AND DIRECTIONS

0.0 Start at Norristown Farm Park, Whitehall lot; head southwest on North Whitehall Road.

1.1 Turn right onto West Marshall Street.

1.7 Turn right onto Burnside Avenue.

1.9 Turn left onto Chestnut Avenue.

2.6 Turn left onto North Trooper Road, then turn right onto Mann Road.

2.9 Turn left onto Wayne Avenue.

3.1 Turn right onto Ridge Pike.

5.2 Turn right onto North Grange Avenue. Grange Avenue turns into Green Hill Road.

9.5 Turn left to stay on Green Hill Road.

A Balm for Body and Mind

From the beginning of European settlement, the area's farms were of vital importance to the growth and vitality of Philadelphia. The reasons were simple: just as was the case with the first settlers of Jamestown and Plymouth, the residents of Philadelphia could not get a substantial and reliable supply of food from elsewhere. In fact, William Penn's original plan for Philadelphia was to keep houses and businesses far apart, so that gardens and orchards could be maintained within the city itself. Fortunately for the development of the early city, the extensive network of rivers in the area soon allowed the city to draw food from farms in the Delaware and Schuylkill River valleys. Residents were able to trade for food that the farmers brought into the city, which allowed the residents to fill in the spaces and allowed the city to grow.

As the population of the area grew, towns and cities started to grow together and to encroach on the farmland that once sustained the area. In time, many farms turned from growing grains (which could be produced more abundantly and cheaply elsewhere) to producing goods that could not be transported as easily, such as fruits, vegetables, and fresh dairy products. Other farms were bought by powerful and influential people and developed as country estates.

And then there was Norristown Farm, which was purchased by the commonwealth of Pennsylvania in 1876 and was the site of a state psychiatric hospital. The institution itself was built on one part of the property, and the remainder was farmed by the inmates to provide milk and vegetables to the institution (and to provide employment to the patients who worked the grounds). At the time, it was believed that the work improved the mental health of the inmates. In time, however, the officials who ran the hospital no longer thought that farmwork did the inmates any good, and that it was less expensive to buy food than to have inmates grow food. The state therefore turned the farm property over to the state Department of Conservation and Natural Resources, which converted the property into a park for all to enjoy. So, in a way, the farm is continuing to improve the mental health of the state's citizens by providing them with a place to fish, hike, bike, and enjoy nature.

9.8 Turn left onto West Skippack Pike.

10.2 Turn right onto Bustard Road.

11.6 Fischers Park on your left. Turn left to stay on Bustard Road.

13.0 Turn right onto Sumneytown Pike.

13.8 Freddy Hill Farms will be on your right.

14.0 Turn right onto Kriebel Road.

14.6 Turn left onto Anders Road (just before the turnpike overpass).

15.3 Turn right onto South Valley Forge Road.

16.4 Merrymead Farm will be on your left.

16.8 Turn left onto Shearer Road.

17.1 Turn right to stay on Shearer Road. The Peter Wentz Farmstead will be on your left.

17.6 Turn left onto West Skippack Pike.

18.6 Turn right onto Berks Road.

19.4 Turn left onto Bean Road.

A barn on the Peter Wentz Farmstead

20.0 Turn right onto Whitehall Road.

22.6 Finish at Norristown Farm Park, Whitehall lot.

RIDE INFORMATION

Events/Attractions

Freddy Hill Farms, 1440 Sumneytown Pike, Lansdale; (215) 855-1205; freddyhill.com: A dairy farm that processes, packages, and sells their own dairy products. Known for its ice cream parlor, which sells cones by weight. The farms also feature a driving range, a miniature golf course, and a fall festival.

Merrymead Farm, 2222 Valley Forge Rd., Lansdale; (610) 584-4410; merrymead.com: A farm that processes, packages, and sells milk and milk products, and sells pies and baked goods that are baked on the farm. The farm also holds an annual fall festival.

Washington's headquarters were located at the Peter Wentz Farmstead in the fall of 1777 (after Washington's defeat at Brandywine). On October 18, 1777, messengers arrived with the news that British General John Burgoyne surrendered at Saratoga. The troops that were stationed there fired a salute so close to the farmhouse that the shots shattered some of the windows.

Peter Wentz Farmstead, 2100 Schultz Rd., Worcester; (610) 584-5104; peterwentzfarmsteadsociety.org: A historic farmstead with exhibits and demonstrations through the year.

Norristown Farm Park, 2500 Upper Farm Rd., Norristown; (610) 270-0215; parks.montcopa.org: Parts of this park are still farmed actively. Contains a historic dairy barn, a stocked trout stream, and 8 miles of trails for hiking and biking.

Restrooms

Start/end: There are portable toilets at the Whitehall Lot. Water and toilets are available at the park office (which can be accessed by driving north 0.7 mile from Whitehall Lot, turning right onto Germantown Pike, driving 0.8 mile farther, and turning right on Upper Farm Road).

Mile 11.6: There are toilets and water available at Fischers Park.

Mile 13.8: There are toilets and water available at Freddy Hill Farms.

Mile 15.3: There are toilets and water available at Merrymead Farm.

Maps

Delorme Pennsylvania Atlas & Gazetteer: Page 86, A1

25

Perkiomen Trail Ride

The Perkiomen Trail extends the Schuylkill River Trail system northward into the Perkiomen Creek Valley. The trail connects the many parks in the valley, from Lower Perkiomen Valley Park in the south to Green Lane Park in the north. If you cared to do so, you could load camping equipment on your bike in Center City, stay overnight at the campground in Green Lane Park, and return the next day as many bikers do during the summer months.

Start: Junction of Perkiomen Trail and Schuylkill River Trail in Lower Perkiomen Valley Park, Oaks

Length: 18.3 miles one way (36.6 miles round-trip)

Approximate riding time: 2.5 hours one way (5.0 hours round-trip)

Best bike: Cross bike or mountain bike

Terrain and trail surface: The first 2 miles are paved and flat. The last 0.8 mile is on-road, paved, and flat. The remainder of the trail is on a crushed rock or gravel surface. Much of the trail was built on a railroad right-of-way, but there are frequent detours off the right-of-way, and there are a few steep climbs on the detours.

Traffic and hazards: The few on-road segments of this ride are on low-traffic roads. The main hazard is that the trail crosses a number of busy roads at grade, and the safe crossing route is sometimes not entirely obvious.

Getting there: From Center City, drive north on I-76, and take the ramp for exits 328B-A /327 to 422 West. Keep left on the ramp to exit 328A to US 422 West toward Pottstown. In 7.0 miles, take the exit to Oaks (Egypt Road). At the light at the end of the ramp, turn right onto Egypt Road and then almost immediately turn right again onto New Mill Road. Drive 0.2 mile to the parking lot that adjoins the trail, and then bike to the south end of the trail from there (about 1.1 miles). If you prefer, you can park in the picnic area that's closer to the south end of the trail. GPS: N 40 07.93 / W75 26.78

THE RIDE

The ride starts at the junction of the Perkiomen Trail and the Schuylkill River Trail at the south end of Lower Perkiomen Valley Park in Oaks. The first 2 miles of the trail are paved and flat. At the north end of the park, the paved trail ends at Upper Indian Head Road. For most of the rest of the way, the trail will be gravel or crushed rock. From this point into Collegeville, it's not such a problem, since the trail follows the railroad right-of-way and is therefore flat. There are a few tricky road crossings in this area, but this is the best area of the trail for scenery, as the trail goes through cuts in the rocky bluff.

There are a couple of tricky intersections in Collegeville itself. There's another tricky intersection just north of Collegeville where the trail meets PA 29 at a shallow angle. Ride alongside the highway to the indicated crossing point, watch for traffic, and then carefully cross the highway at a right angle.

Between Collegeville and Schwenksville, the trail starts to make detours away from the railroad right-of-way, so the trail isn't as level and straight as it

One of the river crossings along the trail

was south of Collegeville. Descending on gravel can be tricky, so be sure to keep your bike under control. The trail crosses the Perkiomen twice between Collegeville and Schwenksville, which gives you a good opportunity for some nice photographs.

The steepest part of the trail is just north of Schwenksville. The trail crosses to the east side of the Perkiomen, climbs 100 feet in elevation at a 10 percent grade, and then descends 120 feet in elevation at a 12 percent grade. When that's done, just cross back to the west side of the Perkiomen, and the trail is back on the railroad right-of-way. The right-of-way crosses back to the east side of the Perkiomen and runs all the way to Perkiomenville.

Bike Shops

Tailwind Bicycles, 160 Main St., Schwenksville; (610) 287-7870, tailwindbicycles.com Tailwind Bicycles offers lifetime free brake and gear adjustments with every bike purchase and rents bicycles to those who are not ready to buy. Located in the former Schwenksville Auditorium and Bakery building on the west side of the Perikomen Trail in downtown Schwenksville, 11.3 miles from the south end of the trail.

When you get to Perkiomenville, you will leave the railroad right-of-way for the last time. There's a short on-road segment, and then the trail crosses an old highway bridge over to the west side of the Perkiomen. The official trail follows Deep Creek Road for a short distance before cutting cross-country into Green Lane Park. At this point, you might decide to stay on Deep Creek Road for the duration. Deep Creek Road is a quiet, level, paved road, and the segment of the Perkiomen Trail that lies in Green Lane Park isn't very well cared for.

If you wish to continue on to Green Lane borough, continue on Deep Creek Road to Green Lane Road, turn right onto Green Lane Road, and then rejoin the Perkiomen Trail when it runs alongside Green Lane Road.

Green Lane Park is a nice place to spend a day and offers a variety of year-round activities including fishing, boating, picnicking, horseback riding, and more. If you want to camp overnight, you can stay at Deep Creek Campground. There are a lot of nice roads around the park; if you are interested in checking them out, Ride 22 will give you a nice 25-mile loop around this area.

MILES AND DIRECTIONS

0.0 Start at the junction of the Perkiomen Trail and the Schuylkill River Trail; start biking north on the Perkiomen Trail.

2.0 Turn left onto Upper Indian Head Road.

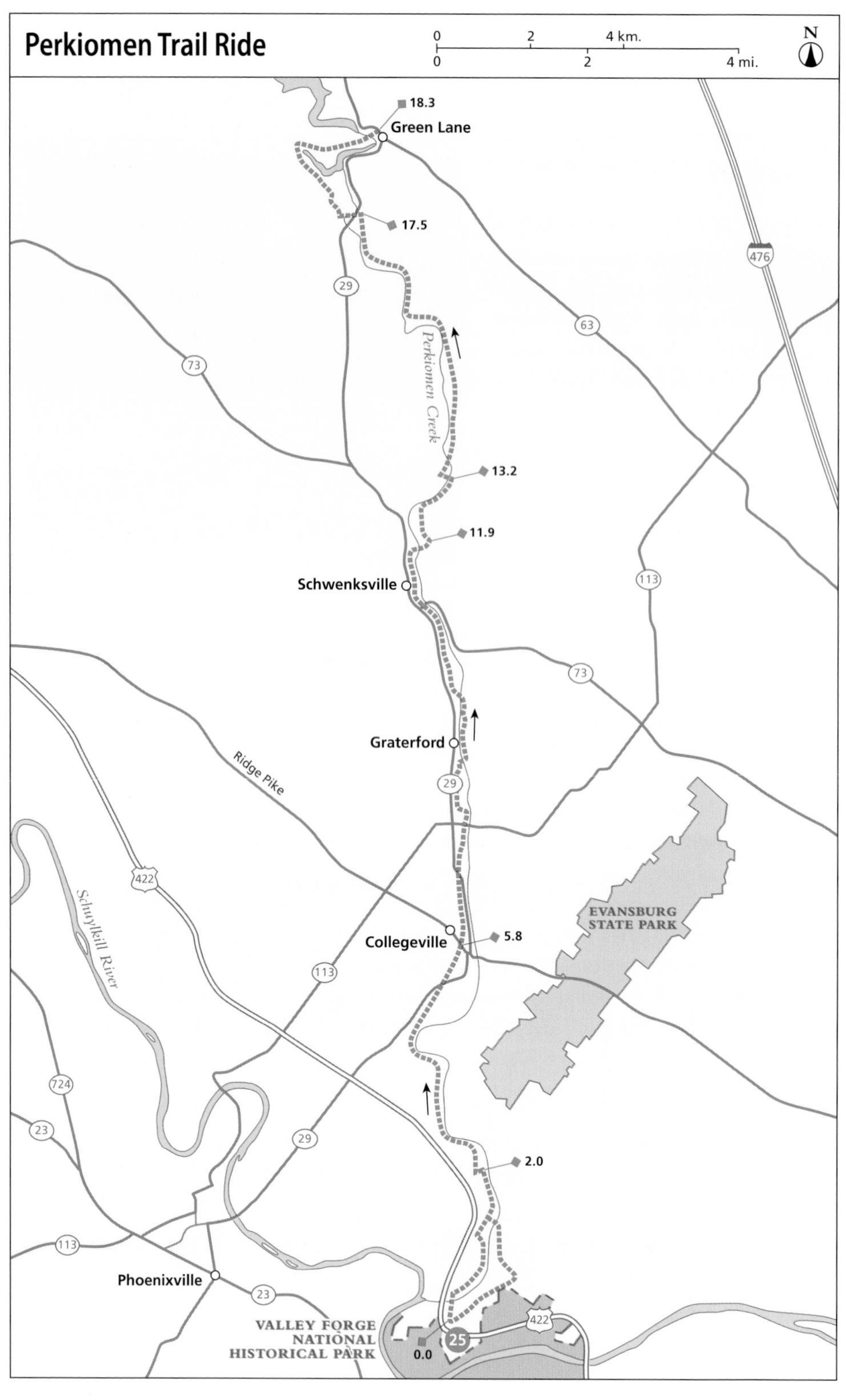

Perkiomen Trail Ride
0
2
4 km.
0
2
4 mi.
N
18.3
Green Lane
17.5
476
29
63
Perkiomen Creek
73
13.2
11.9
Schwenksville
113
73
Graterford
Ridge Pike
29
422
Schuylkill River
EVANSBURG
STATE PARK
Collegeville
5.8
113
724
23
29
2.0
113
Phoenixville
23
VALLEY FORGE
NATIONAL
HISTORICAL PARK
422
25
0.0

2.1 Turn right onto the Perkiomen Trail (unpaved).

5.2 Carefully cross 2nd Avenue in Collegeville and continue on the trail.

5.8 Carefully cross Main Street in Collegeville and continue on the trail.

6.9 Carefully cross PA 29 at the crosswalk and continue on the trail.

11.9 Carefully cross Schwenksville Road, turn right, and follow the signs across the bridge.

12.1 Continue straight onto Park Avenue to the next segment of the trail.

13.2 Turn left onto Spring Mountain Road, cross the bridge, and turn right onto the next segment of the trail.

17.5 Turn left onto Upper Ridge Road and follow the signs across the bridge.

17.8 Turn right onto Deep Creek Road and follow it into Perkiomen Park.

18.3 Finish at Snyder Road in Perkiomen Park.

RIDE INFORMATION

Events/Attractions

Deep Creek Campground at Green Lane Park (parks.montcopa.org) has 30 campsites with showers and toilets available for a fee.

Pennypacker Mills Historic Site (historicsites.montcopa.org) showcases the country estate of Samuel W. Pennypacker, governor of Pennsylvania from 1903 to 1907. To access the site, turn east onto West Skippack Pike (PA 73) at

Perkiomen Creek

Perkiomen Creek was the source of power for a number of mills on its banks. The mills were needed from the earliest times of settlement to grind grain into flour and saw lumber, and many were in use into the early years of the 20th century.

For example, in 1767, the mill that was to be known as Sunrise Mill was built on Swamp Creek, a tributary of Perkiomen Creek. By 1774, a gristmill and a sawmill were in operation at the site. Over the years, the mills and the mill dam were expanded and rebuilt. Turbines were added later on, and the water from the mill dam was used to generate electricity for lights after the gristmill and sawmill were shut down.

The Perkiomen Trail

mile 11.2 (just south of Schwenksville), bike 0.1 mile, and turn left onto Haldeman Road. The driveway is immediately to your left.

Restrooms

Mile 0.7: The picnic area of Lower Perkiomen Valley Park has toilets and water.

Mile 10.2: The Central Perkiomen Valley Park has toilets and water.

Mile 13.3: There is a portable toilet in the municipal park.

Mile 18.3: Green Lane Park has toilets and water.

"Perkiomen" is derived from a Lenape word that means "place where cranberries grow" or "cloudy waters."

Maps

Delorme Pennsylvania Atlas & Gazetteer: Page 85, A8

Delaware and Chester Counties

A quick drive south or west of Philadelphia will get you to Delaware or Chester County. Here nestled among the many towns and parks you will find some nice places to ride that will get you away from the city onto some less-traveled roads.

There are many nice parks in this area and one of the more popular ones is Ridley Creek State Park, which not only has a well maintained bike trail but is surrounded by some good roads you can use to take a longer ride.

If you travel a little farther, you can get to the intersection of Pennsylvania and Delaware by the Brandywine River where there is a great combination of old-world history, rolling hills, and many scenic roads to ride.

Exploring new areas is part of the joy of riding a bike, and Delaware and Chester Counties are easy places to find some new roads.

The Jeffords Mansion. See Ride 26.

26

Ridley Creek State Park

The suburbs that surround Philadelphia contain a number of parks worth visiting. Just 16 miles south of the city is a beautiful rural oasis called Ridley Creek State Park. Riding along the creek and through the forest, you will forget that you are anywhere near a major metropolitan area. This ride will start with a tour around the 5-mile paved multiuse trail within the park then head out for a loop of the suburban area around the park.

Start: The entrance of Ridley Creek State Park (intersection of Bishop Hollow, Chapel Hill, and Ridley Creek Roads)

Length: 23.1-mile loop

Approximate riding time: 3 hours

Best bike: Road or hybrid bike

Terrain and trail surface: This will be a rolling to hilly ride on the paved trail in the park and on the paved roads in the surrounding suburbs. This ride has a lot of ups and downs. There will be a few climbs of around 200 feet along with a couple of 100-foot climbs. None of these are very steep or hard, but you just should be aware that this ride will require a little hard work in some of your lower gears.

Traffic and hazards: This ride will be on the roads with moderate traffic. The roads in Havertown, especially Eagle Road, may have heavy traffic depending on the time of day.

Things to see: Ridley Creek, Hunting Mansion, Tyler Arboretum

Getting there: From Center City Philadelphia take Market Street west to State Street then take State Street to US 1. Take US 1 south to PA 252 north. After 0.4 mile on PA 252, make a left onto Providence Road. Take Providence Road 1.2 miles then make a left onto Chapel Hill Road, which will take you to the entrance to the park. There are dirt parking spaces along the road by the park entrance. GPS: N39 56.76 / W75 25.34

THE RIDE

If you are looking for a peaceful setting for a walk, run, or bike ride, it's hard to beat Ridley Creek State Park. This is a popular place and on a nice weekend

The trail in Ridley Creek Park

day it can sometimes be hard to find a parking spot close to the entrance of the park, so start out early if you can. Once you park, get your bike ready and head through the entrance to the park and on to the multiuse trail. This paved trail is one big loop of just under 5 miles that will take you through the main areas of the park. Although the trail can be a little rough in spots, it is wide and well maintained; just watch out for other runners, pedestrians, and bikers on the trail.

After 0.3 mile the trail splits. As you bear left here, you will encounter a hill that will take you up in altitude about 200 feet in 0.75 mile. It is a tough way to start the ride, but the result is the end of the loop will be a nice long downhill. At the top of the hill just outside the border of the park you will see Tyler Arboretum. This arboretum is a 650-acre horticultural park that contains rare plant specimens, ancient trees, historic buildings, and a number of hiking trails.

After you pass the arboretum, you have to bear to the right to stay on the trail. There are two paths that lead to the right here. Take the second one as the first one leads to a parking lot. The right turn will take you past a meadow then back into the forest as you slowly work your way downhill back to the entrance to the park. At mile 3.0 you will see a path to your left with a sign pointing to the park office, which is worth a quick visit if you have not seen it before. The park office is actually an old stone house built in 1914 by the Jeffords family around a 1789 farm house. It's surrounded by formal gardens and is a popular place for weddings and other formal events.

Bike Shops

Bike Line, 26 S. Sproul Rd., Broomall 19008; (610) 356-3022; bikeline.com
Bike Line is a full-service chain store with friendly people to fill all your biking needs.

Once you check out the mansion, you will head back to the trail where you continue back to the entrance of the park. At this point you're back to where you parked so you can either end the ride here or head out for a loop of the suburbs.

If you continue the ride, you will start out with another climb up Ridley Creek Road, then you will parallel US 1 as you head through Media and Havertown. There will be a few more climbs here that will slow you down a little. As you go through Manoa and Havertown on Eagle Road and Glendale Road, you may hit some heavy traffic so stay to the right here.

If you want to stop and grab some food, there is a shopping center on your left when you cross PA 3 (Chester Pike) or a 7-Eleven when you make the left onto Lawrence Road. Be careful not to miss the turn onto Darby Creek Road as it is on a downhill and a little hidden.

After a nice ride along the creek, you will cross over I-476 (the Blue Route) then travel on PA 320 through Broomall. PA 320 can be a busy road so use caution here. After you make the right onto Cedar Grove Road, you should only encounter light to moderate traffic the rest of the way back to the park. Be careful as you approach the park entrance as there can be cars pulling into and out of the parking spots near the entrance.

MILES AND DIRECTIONS

0.0 Start at the gate at the entrance to the park.

0.2 Bear left where trail splits (marked on some maps as East Forge Road).

1.2 Pass Tyler Arboretum on your left.

1.5 Take second path to the right to stay on the trail.

2.3 Bear right to stay on trail (marked on some maps as Sycamore Mills Road).

3.0 Turn left at bridge where sign points to park office.

3.2 Where path ends make left onto park road.

3.4 Turn left into parking lot of park office. Office is straight ahead on the left. To return to the path make a right out of the park office parking lot.

3.6 Turn right onto path to head back to multiuse trail.

3.7 Turn left to get back on multiuse trail.

5.4 Arrive back at entrance to the park.

5.4 To start the suburban loop, make a left out of the park onto Chapel Hill Road.

5.5 Turn right onto Ridley Creek Road.

6.4 Ridley Creek Road becomes Sycamore Mills Road.

7.3 Turn left onto Rose Tree Road.

8.5 Turn left onto State Road.

9.1 State Road becomes Old Marple Road.

10.0 Turn left onto Springfield Road.

10.1 Turn right onto Eagle Road.

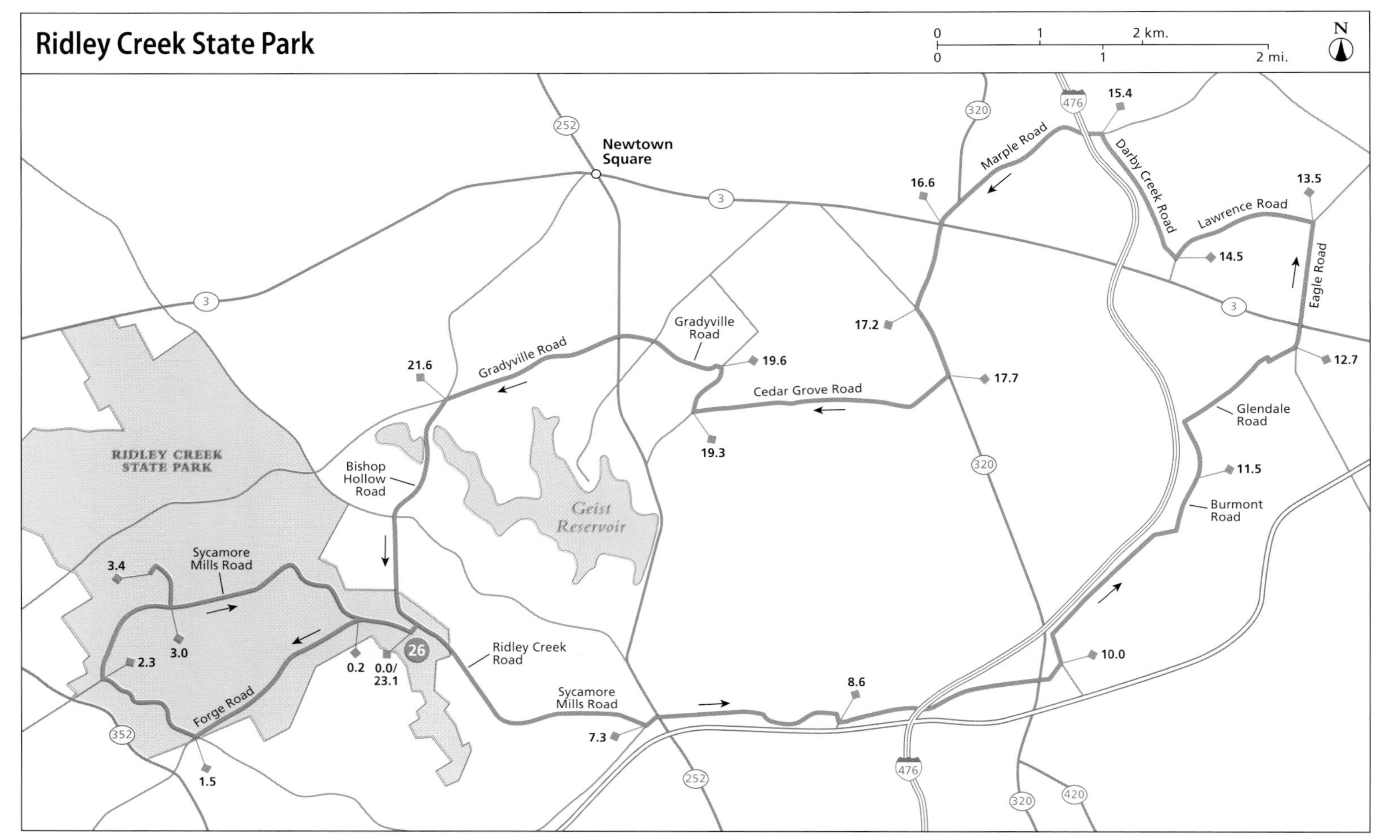
Ridley Creek State Park
0
1
2 km.
0
1
2 mi.
N
Newtown Square
252
3
320
476
420
352
Marple Road
Darby Creek Road
Lawrence Road
Eagle Road
Glendale Road
Burmont Road
Gradyville Road
Cedar Grove Road
Bishop Hollow Road
Geist Reservoir
RIDLEY CREEK STATE PARK
Sycamore Mills Road
Ridley Creek Road
Forge Road
26
0.0/ 23.1
0.2
1.5
2.3
3.0
3.4
7.3
8.6
10.0
11.5
12.7
13.5
14.5
15.4
16.6
17.2
17.7
19.3
19.6
21.6

11.1 Eagle Road becomes Burmont Road.

11.5 Bear left onto Glendale Road.

12.5 Turn right onto Oak Way. Quick left onto Wyndmoor Road.

12.7 Turn left onto Eagle Road.

12.9 Cross PA 3, Chester Pike (shopping mall on left if you want some food).

13.5 Turn left onto Lawrence Road (7-Eleven on far corner).

14.5 Turn right onto Darby Creek Road.

15.4 Turn right onto Marple Road.

16.4 Marple Road becomes PA 320 (North Sproul Road).

16.6 Turn left to stay on PA 320 (North Sproul Road).

17.2 Turn left to stay on PA 320 (Sproul Road).

17.7 Turn right onto Cedar Grove Road.

19.3 Turn right onto Old Cedar Grove Road.

19.6 Turn left onto Gradyville Road.

21.6 Turn left onto Bishop Hollow Road.

23.1 Turn right onto Chapel Hill Road.

23.1 Arrive back at entrance to the park.

A Colonial Plantation Lives On

The Colonial Pennsylvania Plantation in Ridley Creek State Park is a working farm that operates with the methods and tools of colonial America. The people and activities of the plantation represent the way of life that existed in the mid to late 1700s. The plantation offers a broader view of early American life and authentic demonstrations of how most people in this area lived during colonial times.

The plantation has been a working farm for over 300 years. Since 1974 it has operated as a farm museum and offers a number of events, tours, and workshops that allow people to understand and experience early American life on a farm. You can find more details on the plantation at colonialplantation.org/index.html.

RIDE INFORMATION

Event/Attractions

Ridley Creek State Park is a 2,606-acre park along Ridley Creek. It has a nice 4-mile-plus multiuse path and is a great place for many recreational activities, such as hiking, biking, fishing, and picnicking. For more information about the park, check out the website, dcnr.state.pa.us/stateparks/findapark/ridleycreek/index.htm.

Restaurants

Cut Above Deli, 3523 W. Chester Pike, Newtown Square 19073: Premium breads, meats, and toppings make this one of the favorite places to get a great sandwich.

Hot Spot Diner, 3604 W. Chester Pike, Newtown Square 19073: Friendly staff, quick service, and a large selection of food make this a good place for breakfast, lunch, or dinner.

Part of M. Night Shyamalan's movie *The Happening* was filmed on Sycamore Mills Road in Ridley Creek State Park.

Restrooms

Mile 5.4: Portable toilets can be found at the entrance to the park.

Maps

Delorme Pennsylvania Atlas & Gazetteer: Page 85, D8

Devon Ramble

The area around Devon has historically been associated with the Philadelphia elite, who would commute between their homes in the city and their estates in the western countryside. The estates are somewhat more subdivided now, but you don't need to go far off the beaten path to see horse farms and country clubs.

Start: Parking lot of Friendship Park, Tredyffrin Township

Length: 10.9 miles out and back

Approximate riding time: 1.3 hours

Best bike: Road bike

Terrain and trail surface: The terrain is paved and slightly rolling.

Traffic and hazards: Most of the route has light to moderate traffic. There are a couple of segments on a state highway with paved shoulders.

Getting there: By car: Drive north from Center City on I-76, and take the ramp for exits 328B-A /327 to 422 West. Keep left on this ramp for exit 328A to US 202 south toward West Chester. Drive 4.0 miles, then take the PA 252 South exit toward Paoli. Continue on PA 252 South for 2.3 miles. Friendship Park is on your left, just after the traffic light at Friendship Drive and Central Avenue. GPS: N 40 02.65 / W75 28.55
By train: Take the train to 30th Street Station, and then transfer to the Paoli/Thorndale Line. Take the Paoli/Thorndale Line train to Devon Station. The route passes by the station on Waterloo Road. The route also passes 1 block north of Daylesford Station.

THE RIDE

From the Friendship Park driveway, turn left onto Bear Hill Road (PA 252). Cross carefully, because the highway is busy at this point. After 0.1 mile, turn left onto Maple Avenue, and after another 0.1 mile turn right onto Russell Road. This part of the ride travels through a residential neighborhood about a block north of the railroad line. When Russell Road ends in a T intersection, turn left onto Old Lancaster Road, bike another 0.4 mile, and then turn left onto West Conestoga Road. West Conestoga Road shortly turns to the east and parallels the railroad line. Stay on West Conestoga Road for another 1.5 miles, and then turn right onto Devon State Road. Devon State Road even-

Historic Waynesborough

tually turns into Waterloo Road, passes under the railroad line, crosses US 30, and heads south out of town.

Continue on Waterloo Road for about 3 miles until you reach Darby Paoli Road. Along the way, you will pass the Waterloo Mills Preserve (brandywineconservancy.org/waterlooMills.html). Waterloo Mills is a private preserve owned by the Brandywine Conservancy (the same group that operates the Brandywine River Museum in Chadds Ford). The property itself is open only to members of Brandywine Conservancy, but the open space makes Waterloo Road pleasant to ride.

When you reach Darby Paoli Road (PA 252), turn right and bike on the shoulder for 1.2 miles. Your next turn is onto Grubbs Mill Road, on your left. When you make your turn, carefully look behind you, signal, and take the lane when you see a gap in traffic. Grubbs Mill Road

Bike Shops

Performance Bicycle, 1740 E. Lancaster Ave., Paoli; (610) 644-8522
Performance Bicycle is a chain store that specializes in discount bikes, parts, and accessories. Performance Bicycle also provides repair services for all makes. From Friendship Park, turn left onto Bear Hill Road and drive 0.1 mile to Lancaster Avenue (on the other side of the tracks). Turn left and drive 0.2 mile to Fairway Road. The shop is on the corner of Lancaster and Fairway on the right side of the street.

will travel west, and then curve to the south at a stop sign. Continue straight west from that stop sign onto South Valley Road. This will take you past estates with rail fences and stone fences. After about a mile, South Valley Road curves to the north. Continue following South Valley Road until you reach Waynesborough Road at about 9.4 miles cumulative. This turn is easy to miss, so watch for it.

The railroad that you cross during this ride was once part of the Main Line of the Pennsylvania Railroad, which was one of the busiest and most important transportation routes in the country. The Main Line was one of the two main routes between New York City and points to the west. The first transcontinental road, the Lincoln Highway, also passes through this area.

After about 0.5 mile on Waynesborough Road, you will pass by the Waynesborough Historic House on your left, just across from the golf course at the Waynesborough Country Club. Bike 0.2 mile farther, turn left onto Darby Paoli Road, and finish the final 0.8 mile of biking back to the park.

MILES AND DIRECTIONS

0.0 Start in the parking lot at Friendship Park, Tredyffrin Township; turn left onto PA 252 North/Bear Hill Road. This is a busy highway, so take care when turning.

0.1 Turn left onto Maple Avenue.

0.2 Turn right onto Russell Road.

0.9 Turn left onto Old Lancaster Road. Daylesford Station on the SEPTA Paoli/Thorndale Line is 1 block south of this intersection.

1.3 Turn left onto West Conestoga Road.

2.9 Turn right onto Devon State Road/Waterloo Spur Road.

3.0 Turn left onto Old Lancaster Road, then turn right onto North Waterloo Road. Devon Station on the SEPTA Paoli/Thorndale Line is 1 block south of this intersection.

6.1 Turn right onto PA 252 North/Darby Paoli Road.

7.3 Turn left onto Grubbs Mill Road.

7.8 Continue onto South Valley Road at stop sign.

9.4 Turn right onto Waynesborough Road.

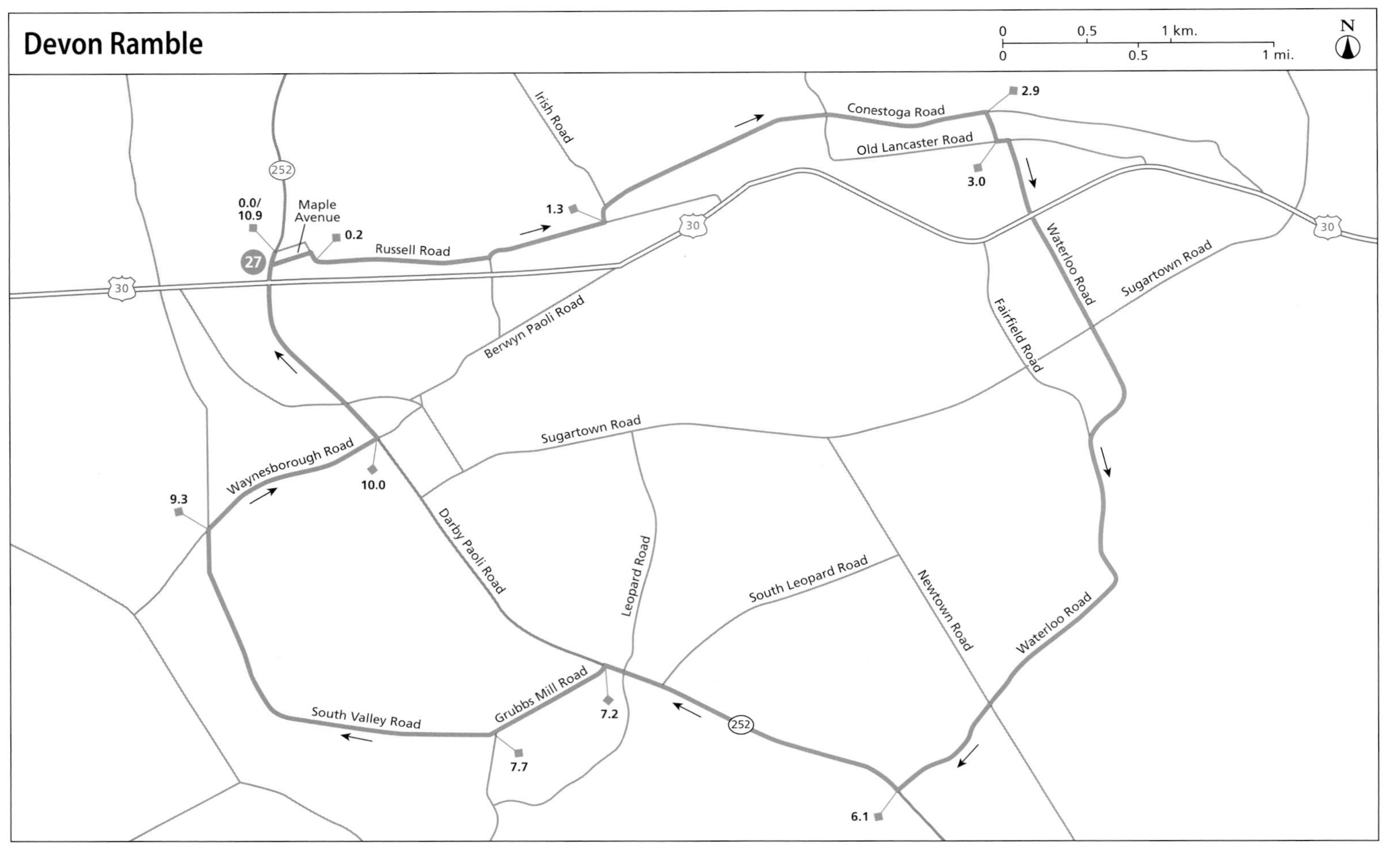
Devon Ramble
0
0.5
1 km.
0
0.5
1 mi.
N
Conestoga Road
2.9
Old Lancaster Road
3.0
Irish Road
1.3
252
0.0/
10.9
Maple
Avenue
0.2
Russell Road
27
30
30
30
Berwyn Paoli Road
Waterloo Road
Sugartown Road
Fairfield Road
Sugartown Road
Waynesborough Road
10.0
9.3
Darby Paoli Road
Leopard Road
South Leopard Road
Newtown Road
Waterloo Road
Grubbs Mill Road
7.2
South Valley Road
7.7
252
6.1

9.9 Waynesborough Historic House is on your left.

10.1 Turn left onto PA 252 North/Darby Paoli Road.

10.9 Finish at Friendship Park, Tredyffrin Township.

RIDE INFORMATION

Events/Attractions

Wayesborough Historic House, 2049 Waynesborough Rd., Paoli; (610) 647-1779; philalandmarks.org: Waynesborough is the birthplace and historic residence of General Anthony Wayne. The house was subsequently used by seven generations of the Wayne family before being restored as a museum in the general's memory.

Restrooms

Start/end: Friendship Park has a portable toilet and water.

Maps

Delorme Pennsylvania Atlas & Gazetteer: Page 85, B8

Mad Anthony

During this ride, you will pass by Waynesborough, which is the birthplace and historic residence of Anthony Wayne, who was an officer in the Continental Army during the Revolutionary War. During the war, Wayne earned the nickname "Mad Anthony" because of his impetuousness and fearlessness in battle.

After serving initially in the north (and leading a successful rear-guard action toward the end of the Canadian campaign), Wayne was commissioned to lead the Pennsylvania Line in George Washington's army. Wayne fought in all of the major battles of the Philadelphia campaign and distinguished himself at the Battle of Monmouth, where he commanded a forward position and drove back three attacks by British regulars before being forced to retreat. Wayne's most noteworthy battle was the Battle of Stony Point, in which he and his men made a surprise night attack on a British stronghold and took the position and over 400 prisoners in 30 minutes.

After the war, Wayne was granted land in Georgia and settled there temporarily. However, Wayne was soon recalled by Washington to lead an expedition against the Native Americans in the Northwest Territory. Wayne reorganized the army and defeated the Western Confederacy at the Battle of Fallen Timbers. He died two years later of complications from gout while returning to Pennsylvania from the west.

28

Longwood Gardens

One of the major attractions in the Brandywine area of Pennsylvania is Longwood Gardens, one of the premier botanical gardens in the United States. Its 1,000 acres of gardens, woodlands, and meadows are filled with beautifully maintained native and exotic plants that are always a treat for the eyes. Besides Longwood Gardens, this area has some quiet roads and scenic areas that are fun to explore by bike. This ride will show you some of the sights in the area.

Start: Delacy Soccer Park, West Chester

Length: 25.2-mile loop

Approximate riding time: 2 hours

Best bike: Road or hybrid bike

Terrain and trail surface: The ride will be on the paved roads. This is an area of rolling hills, so you will have a lot of ups and downs and not a lot of flat riding, but there is nothing very steep or long.

Traffic and hazards: This ride will be on paved roads with light to moderate traffic. Creek Road can have heavy traffic at times, and you will have to be careful when crossing US 1.

Things to see: Brandywine Creek

Getting there: From Center City Philadelphia take I-95 south to US 322 south to US 1 south. After getting onto US 1, go 2.6 miles then make a right onto Creek Road (SR 926). In 1.3 miles you will pass Brandywine Picnic Park on your left after you pass Lenape Road. Make the next left to stay on Creek Road and then make a left into the parking lot of the soccer fields. GPS: N39 55.21 / W75 38.10

THE RIDE

This corner of Pennsylvania where it meets Delaware has a number of attractions, including Brandywine Battlefield Park, Longwood Gardens, and Winterthur to name a few. This makes it a popular area for day trips not only to see these attractions but to bike on the quiet rural roads in the area. This ride will lead you around this area and show some of the better roads.

To start this ride, make a right out of the parking lot and head back the way you came in. This will take you back down Creek Road toward US 1. This road can be a little busy at times so watch out for cars and stay to the right. In 4.5 miles you will come to a light at US 1. At the light you will have to make a left turn and ride on the shoulder of US 1 for about 100 feet before making a right back onto Creek Road. Just watch the traffic here.

Once on Creek Road you will again be riding next to Brandywine Creek and will cross it a couple miles after crossing US 1. At 6.8 miles you will make a right on Cossart Road. There is no street sign here, so you will just have to rely on watching your mileage to know when to turn; since it is the only road for miles, it is hard to miss.

Halfway down Cossart you will start to slowly climb uphill until you reach the middle of Fairville Road; then it will be mostly rolling hills. There are no major sights here—just some quiet roads through the woods and farmlands of the area—but you will see some old stone houses mixed in with the newer homes. After you cross Rosedale Road and get onto Hillendale Road, you will be close to Longwood Gardens. In fact, if you make a left at Greenwood Road, you would get to the overpass that brings you into Longwood Gardens, but it would require a small stretch of riding on busy US 1.

As you continue on Hillendale, you will have a nice downhill stretch. Toward the bottom of the stretch you will see Virginia Place on your left. You will then cross a set of train tracks and there will then be an unmarked road on your right that you will turn onto. This is Fairville Road and will lead you back to Cossart Road from which you will retrace your path back to US 1. The only difference is that you will make a turn about 0.1 mile from US 1 onto Mill Road then a quick right on to Station Way Road, which will get you back to the light at US 1 directly across from Creek Road. A small strip mall here contains a deli that makes a good place to stop for a snack and a drink.

Bike Shops

Cycle Sports, 801 N. Providence Rd., Media 19063; (610) 565-9535; cyclesportmedia.com A full-service bike shop that sells and services most major brands of road and mountain bikes.

Once you cross US 1, you will just follow Creek Road back to your starting point. There are a lot of good roads around this area, so if you like this ride, you should also try out Ride 29, which shows you the northern section of this area. You can even combine the two rides if you want a longer ride since they start at the same location and share a few roads.

MILES AND DIRECTIONS

0.0 Make right out of parking lot onto Creek Road.

0.2 Turn right onto PA 52 (Creek Road).

4.5 Turn left at US Route 1 followed by a quick right onto Creek Road.

6.8 Turn right onto Cossart Road (unmarked).

8.5 Turn left onto Fairville Road.

8.9 Cross PA 52, staying on Fairville Road.

10.1 Turn right onto Spring Mill Road.

10.7 Turn right onto Norway Road.

11.5 Cross Rosedale Road on to Hillendale Road.

One of the many beautiful flowers you will see in Longwood Gardens

12.8 Cross PA 52.

15.0 Turn right onto Fairville Road.

16.0 Bear left onto Stockford Road.

16.7 Turn left onto Cossart Road.

18.3 Turn left onto Creek Road.

20.6 Turn left onto Mill Road.

20.6 Turn right onto Station Way Road.

20.7 Cross US 1; road becomes Creek Road.

25.0 Turn left to stay on Creek Road.

25.2 Turn right into parking lot of Delacy Soccer Park.

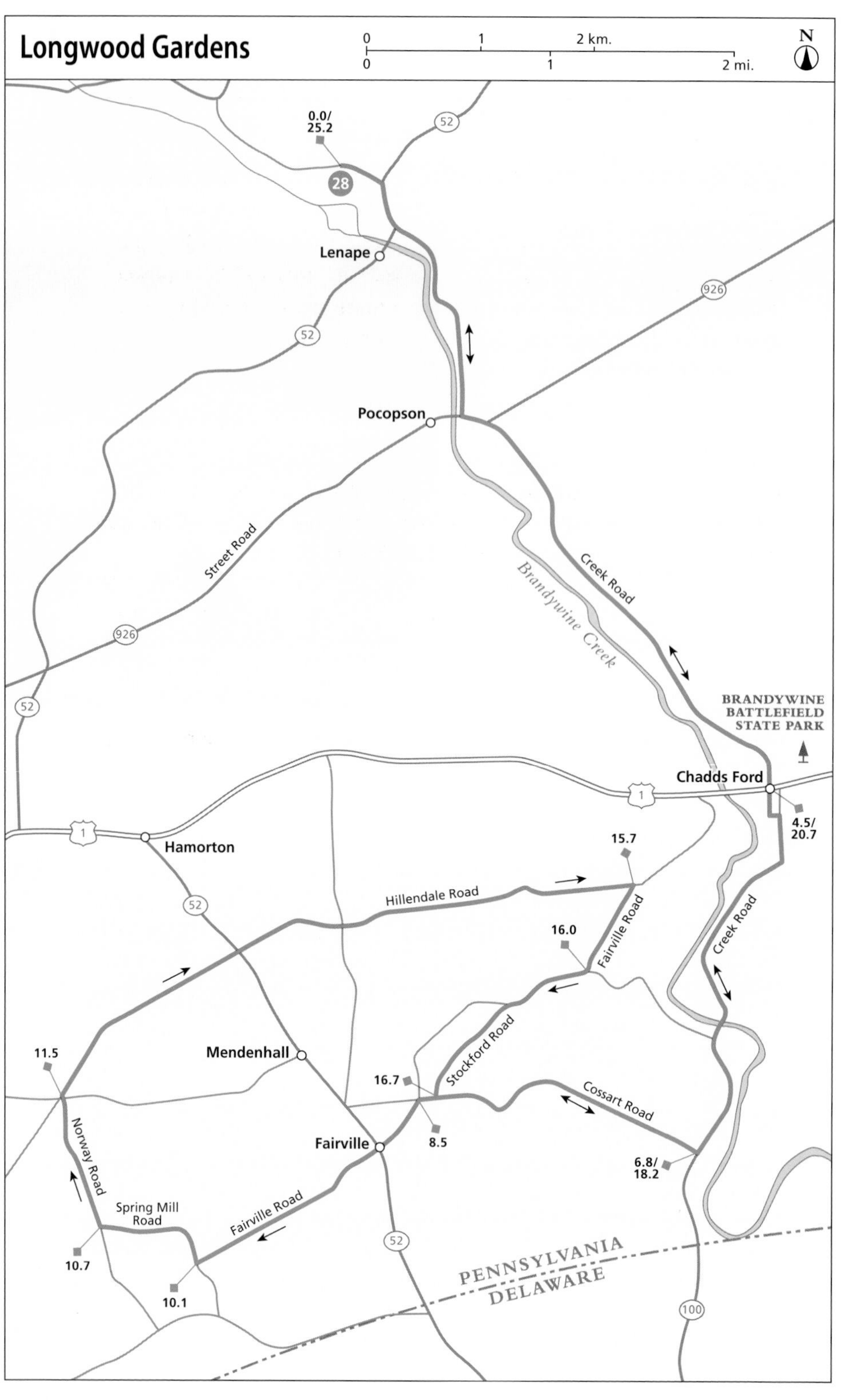
Longwood Gardens
0 1 2 km.
0 1 2 mi.
N
0.0/
25.2
52
28
Lenape
926
52
Pocopson
Street Road
Creek Road
Brandywine Creek
926
52
BRANDYWINE
BATTLEFIELD
STATE PARK
Chadds Ford
1
4.5/
20.7
1
Hamorton
15.7
Hillendale Road
52
16.0
Fairville Road
Creek Road
Stockford Road
11.5
Mendenhall
16.7
Cossart Road
8.5
Fairville
6.8/
18.2
Norway Road
Spring Mill
Road
Fairville Road
52
10.7
10.1
PENNSYLVANIA
DELAWARE
100

RIDE INFORMATION

Events/Attractions

Longwood Gardens is 1,000 acres of extremely extensive and diverse horticulture displays. Its inside and outside displays are filled with beautiful and exotic plants, fountains, and statues that will take hours to fully explore. For more details check out their website at longwoodgardens.org.

The Longwood organ is one of the largest pipe organs in the world with over 10,000 pipes and requires a 72 horsepower blower motor to supply wind to the pipes.

Restaurants

The Gables at Chadds Ford, 423 Baltimore Pike, Chadds Ford 19317; (610) 388-7700; thegablesatchaddsford.com: A beautiful restaurant in an old 1800s farm house that is a relaxing place for a drink or full meal.

Shoo Mama's Farm Fresh Cafe, 66 E. Street Rd., West Chester 19382; (484) 315-8431; shoomamascafe.com: Nice family-run cafe that is perfect to grab a quick meal or get some takeout.

Restrooms

Start/end: There is a portable toilet at the parking lot where this ride starts.

Maps

DeLorme Pennsylvania Atlas & Gazetteer: Page 85, E 7

A Christmas Extravaganza

If you love Christmas displays, you owe it to yourself to check out Longwood Gardens during the Christmas holiday. The outdoor lawn and gardens are decorated with over a half million lights. The open-air theater has a dancing fountain show with colorful lights and holiday music that is always spectacular. The indoor conservatory is filled with Christmas trees, poinsettias, and many other holiday decorations. Besides all the indoor and outdoor displays there are also regular concerts and skating demonstrations. Even in the dark and cold weather of winter Longwood Gardens is a fun place to visit.

Brandywine South

The Brandywine area of Pennsylvania is nestled in the rolling hills of southern Delaware County close to where it meets Delaware. This is where the Battle of Brandywine was fought during the Revolution, where the du Ponts made their fortunes, and where three generations of Wyeths have lived and painted the landscapes. This is an area with a lot of history that has managed to maintain its rural charm despite the encroachment of modern society. This ride will take you along the creeks and farmlands so that you can enjoy part of this historic area.

Start: Delacy Soccer Park, West Chester

Length: 21-mile loop

Approximate riding time: 2 hours

Best bike: Road or hybrid bike

Terrain and trail surface: The ride will be on paved roads. Terrain will be mostly rolling hills along the way—nothing steep or long, but there aren't a lot of flat sections either.

Traffic and hazards: This ride will be on paved roads with light to moderate traffic. Creek Road can have heavy traffic at times so stay to the right here. Branford Avenue in West Chester can be busy at times so use extra caution there.

Things to see: Brandywine Creek, Brandywine Battlefield

Getting there: From Center City Philadelphia take I-95 south to US 322 south to US 1 south. After getting onto US 1, go 2.6 miles then make a right onto Creek Road (SR 926). In 1.3 miles you will pass Brandywine Picnic Park on your left after you pass Lenape Road. Make the next left to stay on Creek Road and then make a left into the parking lot of the soccer fields. GPS: N39 55.21 / W75 38.10

THE RIDE

This area has been part of the history of our country since before the Revolutionary War. The Brandywine Creek, which is nearby, was used in the past to power a number of industries including du Pont's original gunpowder mill.

Although a lot has changed over the years, this area still has a lot of open land and quiet roads, which is why it is a popular place for cyclists.

To start this ride make a right out of the parking lot and head back the way you came in. This will take you back down Creek Road toward US 1. This road can be a little busy at times so watch out for cars and stay to the right. Right after you pass Brandywine Picnic Park, you will make a right onto Lenape Road (PA 52), which will take you over a narrow bridge. After going over the bridge, you will make a left onto Pocopson Road and this will lead you to quieter roads and some nice open land.

When you make the right onto Parkerville Road, you will do a little climbing in the rolling hills of the area. This will give you some nice views of the land around you. The path you are currently following is very similar to the path that British General William Howe followed to outflank George Washington's army by marching north on the west side of Brandywine Creek and crossing it at Jef-

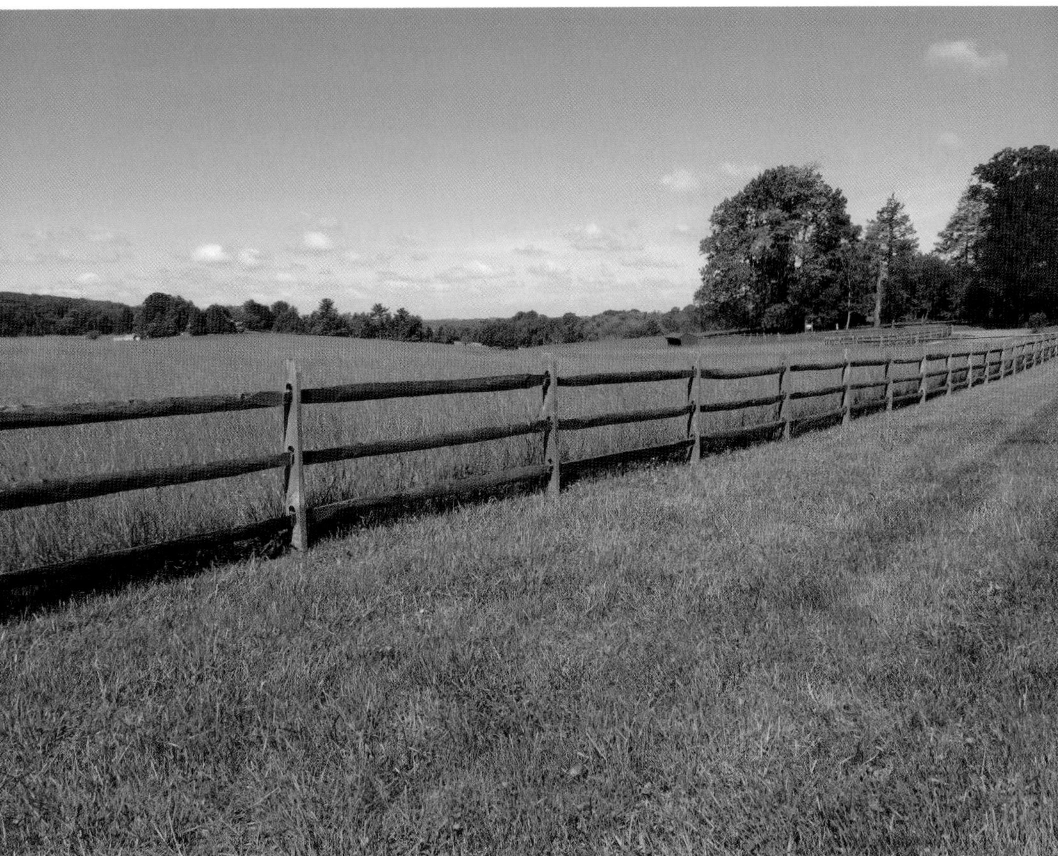

Part of the Brandywine Battlefield

feries Ford. The bridge you cross on Allerton Road across the east branch of Brandywine Creek is probably pretty close to where Howe's army crossed to attack Washington's army's right flank.

From here you will have some more rolling hills as you head to the town of West Chester. When you make the right onto Branford Avenue, you may encounter some moderate to heavy traffic depending on the time of day, so use a little extra caution here. If you need a break there is a gas station with a convenience store just after you cross Price Street (PA 52). As you are leaving town, you will have to make a hard left onto Rosedale Avenue. The angles of the roads limit visibility of oncoming traffic so be careful here.

Once you make a right onto New Road at a light, you will be back onto quieter roads and heading toward the main battlefield where the Battle of Brandywine was fought. In fact, when you come to a T at Birmingham Road, you will get a good view of the rolling hills of the battlefield. Eventually you will get back to Creek Road, which will take you back to your starting point. There are very few bad roads in this area; many of them can provide a lot of nice riding if you are willing to explore on your own.

Bike Shops

Cycle Sports, 801 N. Providence Rd., Media 19063; (610) 565-9535; cyclesportmedia.com A full-service bike shop that sells and services most major brands of road and mountain bikes.

MILES AND DIRECTIONS

0.0 Make right out of parking lot onto Creek Road.

0.2 Turn right onto PA 52 (Creek Road).

0.5 Turn right onto PA 52 (Lenape Road).

0.7 Turn left onto Pocopson Road.

3.5 Turn right onto Parkerville Road.

4.9 Turn right onto PA 52 (Lenape Road).

5.1 Turn left onto Wawaset Road.

5.6 Stay right to stay on Wawaset Road.

7.5 Turn right onto PA 842 (Bridge Road).

8.0 Turn left onto Allerton Road.

9.5 Turn left onto Creek Road.

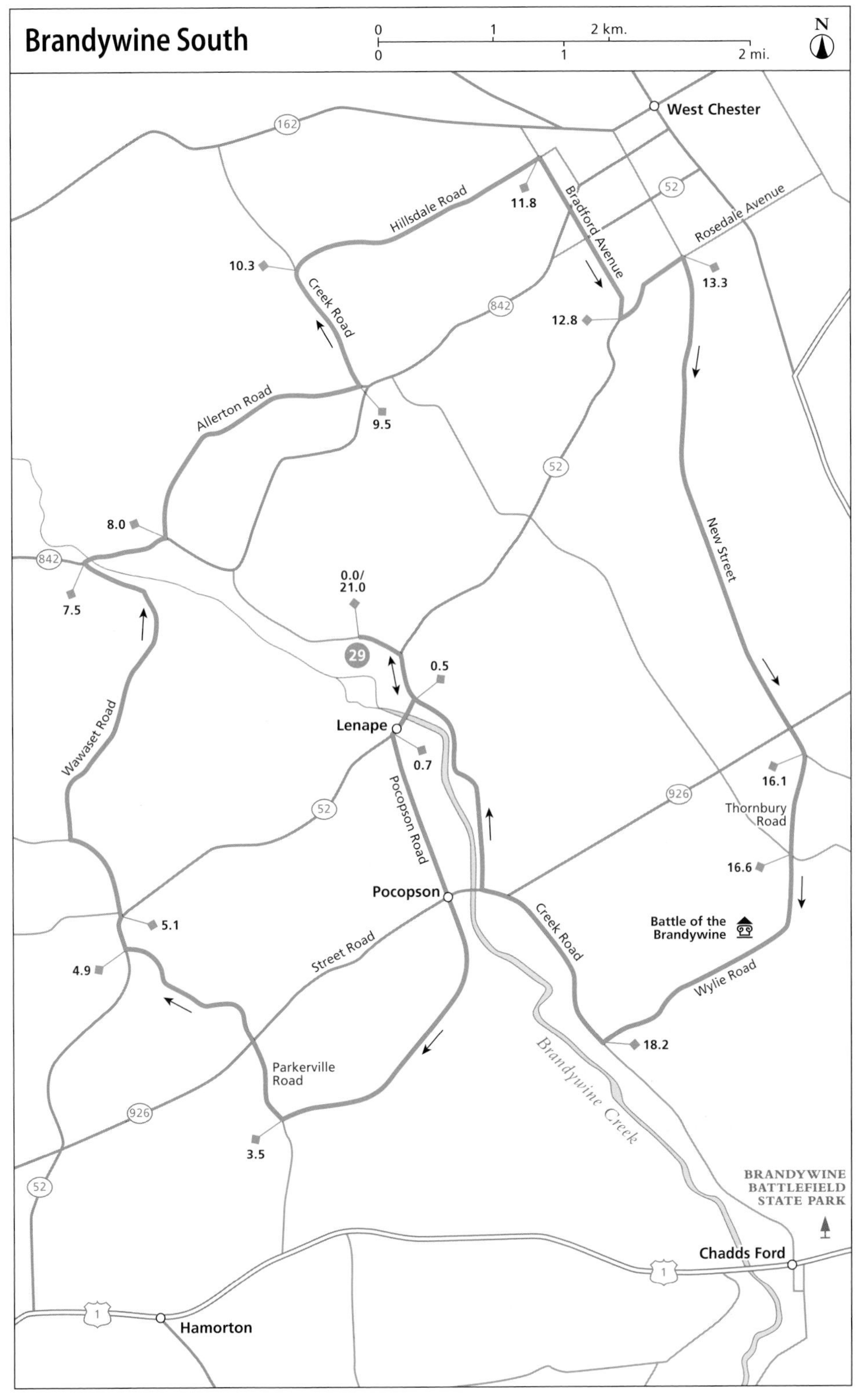

Brandywine South
0
1
2 km.
0
1
2 mi.
N
West Chester
162
52
Hillsdale Road
11.8
Bradford Avenue
Rosedale Avenue
10.3
Creek Road
13.3
842
12.8
Allerton Road
9.5
52
New Street
8.0
842
7.5
0.0/
21.0
29
0.5
Lenape
0.7
Wawaset Road
Pocopson Road
52
926
16.1
Thornbury
Road
16.6
Pocopson
5.1
Creek Road
Battle of the
Brandywine
Street Road
4.9
Wylie Road
18.2
Parkerville
Road
Brandywine Creek
926
3.5
BRANDYWINE
BATTLEFIELD
STATE PARK
52
Chadds Ford
1
1
Hamorton

10.3 Turn right onto Hillsdale Road.

11.8 Turn right onto Bradford Avenue.

12.8 Make a hard left turn onto Rosedale Avenue (watch the traffic here).

13.3 Turn right onto New Street.

16.1 Turn right onto Thornbury Road.

16.6 Turn left onto Birmingham Road.

16.6 Quick right onto Wylie Road.

18.2 Turn right onto Creek Road.

20.7 Turn left to stay on Creek Road.

21.0 Make left back into parking lot where you started.

RIDE INFORMATION

Event/Attractions

If you are interested in learning more about the Battle of Brandywine, check out the Brandywine Battlefield Historic Site (ushistory.org/BRANDYWINE).

Battle at Chadds Ford

On September 11, 1777, one of the major battles of the Revolutionary War was fought. British troops had marched north on Baltimore Pike (now US 1) and needed to ford the Brandywine near Chadds Ford. The British Army wanted to seize control of Philadelphia to drive out the Congress and hopefully bring an end to the war. Brandywine Creek was a major military obstacle to getting to Philadelphia. George Washington realized this and had been tracking the British troops. He prepared a defense on the opposite side of the river that stretched 5 miles north and 3 miles south of the ford.

On the day of the battle only 5,000 of the 17,000-strong British troops engaged the American troops at Chadds Ford. The rest of the troops marched north 6 miles, crossed Trimble's and Jefferies Fords, and came back and outflanked the American troops, forcing them to retreat and eventually leading to the British taking Philadelphia. More information about this famous battle can be found in Brandywine Battlefield Park, which was created to preserve the history of this battle.

Restaurants

The Gables at Chadds Ford, 423 Baltimore Pike, Chadds Ford 19317; (610) 388-7700; thegablesatchaddsford.com: A beautiful restaurant in an old 1800s farm house that is a relaxing place for a drink or full meal.

Shoo Mama's Farm Fresh Cafe, 66 E. Street Rd., West Chester 19382; (484) 315-8431; shoomamascafe.com: Nice family-run cafe that is perfect to grab a quick meal or get some takeout.

During the Revolutionary War, the Brandywine River was the site of a number of paper mills. These paper mills supplied Benjamin Franklin's print shop as well as the paper to print Continental currency and the Declaration of Independence.

Restrooms

Start/end: There is a portable toilet at the parking lot.

Maps

DeLorme Pennsylvania Atlas & Gazetteer: Page 85, E7

South Jersey and Delaware

If you want flat, rural, and empty, head to South Jersey or Delaware. The Pine Barrens of New Jersey are only a half hour away with roads as flat as it gets. This area has lots of forested land, many small streams and rivers, and not much civilization. There are very few bad roads down here, which makes it a great place to ride; the only problem is finding a place to stop for some food. Besides nice roads this area also has some good mountain biking trails for all different abilities.

Another quick ride from Philadelphia is the tiny state of Delaware. From the rolling hills in the north part of the state to the flat sandy stretches along the coast to the great mountain biking in White Clay Park, this state has an amazingly wide variety of rides to offer.

All these reasons make South Jersey and Delaware a great place for a day trip or a nice weekend getaway.

Boats rowing past the yacht club on Cooper River

30

Cooper River Park Ride

Cooper River Park is a showcase park for Camden County. Built in 1936 by Works Progress Administration (WPA) workers, the park features a river that has been reclaimed from its industrial past and that regularly hosts sporting events such as rowing tournaments and triathlons.

Start: Parking lot of Cooper River Park

Length: 3.7 miles round-trip

Approximate riding time: 0.3 hour

Best bike: Road bike

Terrain and trail surface: The terrain is paved and flat.

Traffic and hazards: The trail can have heavy pedestrian usage, particularly from users of the adjoining park facilities.

Getting there: **By car:** From Center City, cross the Benjamin Franklin Bridge, and drive east on US 30 (Admiral Wilson Boulevard) for 2.3 miles. Follow the signs for PA 70 East to Cherry Hill. One mile after PA 70 East splits from PA 38 East, take the exit for East Cuthbert Boulevard. Keep right, make an immediate right turn off the ramp onto Park Boulevard, and drive for 0.5 mile. The parking lot will be on your left. GPS: N39 55.63 / W75 03.48
By train: Take the train to 30th Street Station, and then transfer to the NJ Transit Atlantic City Line. Take the NJ Transit Atlantic City Line to Cherry Hill Station. Bike south and then west around the grocery store to Cornell Avenue. Bike 0.4 mile south on Cornell Avenue, cross Marlton Pike, and continue 1 block to North Park Boulevard. Turn right onto North Park Boulevard and continue 0.4 mile to the bike path along Cuthbert Boulevard.

THE RIDE

Cooper River Park serves as a nice oasis to the urban landscape that surrounds it. It may only be 346 acres but there are a lot of things tucked into this park that make it a popular place. Besides the trail that you will be riding, the park also has a stadium, yacht club, dog park, miniature golf, and a sculpture garden. Rowing is very popular here, so on a nice day you will almost certainly see a few boats on the river.

The ride starts at the parking lot in the northeast corner of Cooper River Park. There are numerous places to park within the park and on the surrounding streets, but the parking lot in the northeast corner is the closest lot to the water hydrant. If you need a bathroom, they are available at Jack Curtis Stadium 0.3 mile to the west.

You will be following the trail that just makes a simple loop around the lake, so you can ride around the lake in whichever direction you prefer. To start the ride head east on the trail back toward Cuthbert Boulevard. If you want to make the ride a little longer, instead of turning right onto Cuthbert Boulevard you can actually cross it and take the trail to Grove Street and back.

After the right onto Cuthbert Boulevard, you will cross the river and continue along South Park Drive where you will pass the yacht club, which offers sailing lessons. You will eventually make a right onto Crescent Boulevard and cross the river again then ride along North Park Drive back to the starting point.

Currently the Cooper River Park trail is not well connected to other trails in the area, but this will change soon. Trails and bike lanes are currently being built that will connect Cooper River with the Camden waterfront and trails to the east that will make it easy to get from Philadelphia to the more rural parts to the east.

Bike Shops

Erlton Bike Shop, 1011 W. Rt. 70, Cherry Hill, NJ, (856) 428-2344, erltonbike.com A full-service bike shop, Erlton has more than 65 years combined experience in repairing bicycles. Drive 0.5 mile east on Park Boulevard, turn left onto Cuthbert Boulevard, take the ramp onto eastbound Marlton Pike, and drive 1.9 miles. The shop is on the right.

Keswick Cycle, 305 E. Rt. 70, Cherry Hill, NJ, (856) 795-0079, keswickcycle.com In business since 1933, Keswick Cycle has locations in Glenside, PA, and Cherry Hill, NJ. To reach the Cherry Hill store, drive 0.5 mile east on Park Boulevard, turn left onto Cuthbert Boulevard, take the ramp onto eastbound Marlton Pike, and drive 2.9 miles. The shop is on the right.

MILES AND DIRECTIONS

0.0 Start in the parking lot in the northeast corner of Cooper River Park.

0.0 Head east on the path along Park Boulevard toward Cuthbert Boulevard.

0.4 Turn right onto the path along Cuthbert Boulevard and cross the river.

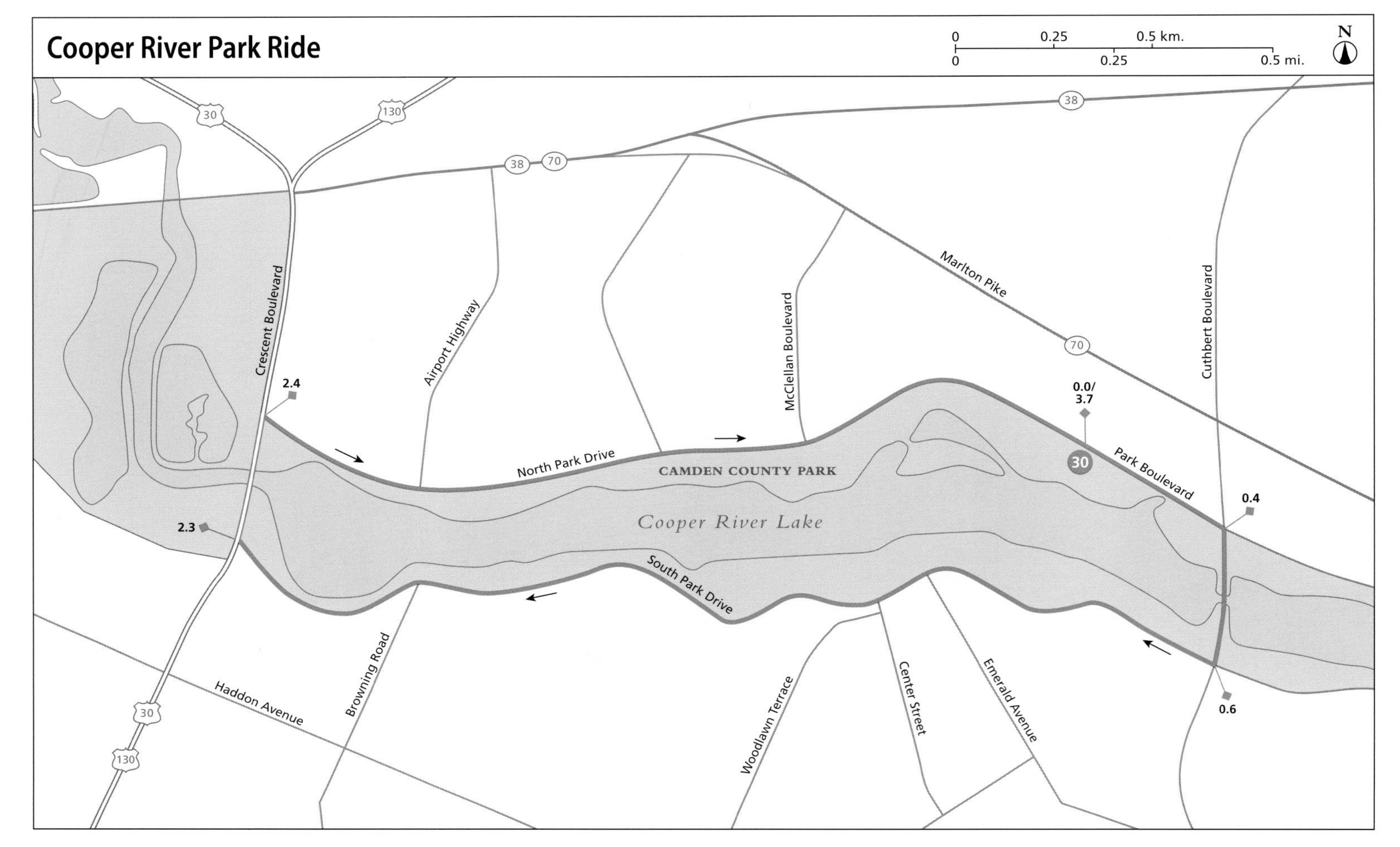
Cooper River Park Ride
0
0.25
0.5 km.
0
0.25
0.5 mi.
N
30
130
38
70
Crescent Boulevard
Airport Highway
McClellan Boulevard
Marlton Pike
Cuthbert Boulevard
2.4
2.3
0.0/
3.7
0.4
0.6
North Park Drive
CAMDEN COUNTY PARK
Park Boulevard
Cooper River Lake
South Park Drive
Haddon Avenue
Browning Road
Woodlawn Terrace
Center Street
Emerald Avenue

The trail in Cooper River Park

0.6 Turn right onto the path along South Park Drive.

2.3 Turn right onto the path along Crescent Boulevard. and cross the river.

2.4 Turn right onto the path along North Park Drive.

3.7 Arrive at the parking lot in the northeast corner of Cooper River Park.

RIDE INFORMATION

Events/Attractions

Cooper River Park is a 346-acre park in urban Camden and is a popular riverside destination throughout the year. Activities and facilities include running trails and tracks, recreational fields, pavilions, and sailing and sculling on a large open water area. Cooper River Park is home to many prestigious rowing events. There are also large grassland areas and waterside shrubberies that provide opportunities for bird watching.

Camden County Boathouse, 7050 North Park Dr., Pennsauken, NJ, is a 23,000-square-foot, 4-story structure with meeting rooms and a banquet room. The boathouse is available for weddings and other special events.

Cooper Family Settlement

The Cooper River is named after one of the first families to settle this area of New Jersey and eventually to found the city of Camden.

In the late 17th century, the east bank of the Delaware River was settled by Quaker immigrants from the British Isles. These immigrants soon began a brisk trade with the new town of Philadelphia across the river. To accommodate this trade, ferries were established between Philadelphia and various landings on the east side of the river. One of the earliest ferries was established by William Cooper at Coopers Point in 1689. In 1695, William's son, Daniel, assumed an already existing ferry at what is now Cooper Street in Camden. Many other ferries followed.

At first, the settlements around the ferry landings were very rudimentary: mainly taverns and inns to meet the needs of travelers. In the case of the Coopers, they owned the land around their ferry landings as their family estate, and were in no hurry to open up their land for development. It took until 1773 for Jacob Cooper, William Cooper's great-grandson, to lay out streets and lots and make the land available for development. Jacob chose to name the new settlement after the Earl of Camden, Charles Pratt, who was an advocate for the American colonies in the British Parliament.

Hopkins House Gallery of Contemporary Art, 250 South Park Dr., Haddon, NJ, hosts over 100 programs a year that feature the works of local artists.

The Cooper River is the site of the Intercollegiate Rowing Association's annual IRA Championship Regatta, which is considered to be the collegiate national championship of rowing in the United States.

Restrooms

Mile 0.3: There is a water hydrant.
Mile 3.4: There are toilets available at Jack Curtis Stadium.

Maps

DeLorme New Jersey Atlas & Gazetteer: Page 54, B10

31

Brendan Byrne State Forest

Brendan T. Byrne State Forest is one of the nicer state parks in South Jersey. It's a good place to get away from the city and take a relaxing ride in the woods. Brendan T. Byrne State Forest offers a lot of variety to explore from the pine forest to cranberry bogs to small lakes and streams. It also offers a lot of different terrain for riding from paved roads to sand paths to single track. Whatever type of riding you're looking for, you should be able to find something here to enjoy.

Start: Brendan T. Byrne State Forest, New Lisbon, NJ (formerly Lebanon State Forest)

Length: 12.8-mile loop

Approximate riding time: 2 hours

Best bike: Mountain bike

Terrain and trail surface: This ride will be on a combination of paved roads, sandy fire roads, and some dirt trails. There are some ups and downs but no real climbing. The sandy roads and dirt paths will have some bumpy spots and places where you will have to ride over some tree roots but nothing real technical or hard to ride on.

Traffic and hazards: All the roads and paths you will be riding will be in the park, although you need to watch out for the occasional car on the paved road and sand roads.

Things to see: Cranberry bogs, White Cedar Swamps, Pakim Lake, pine forests

Getting there: From Philadelphia head over the Ben Franklin Bridge and take Route 70 east until you come to the Four-Mile Circle where Route 70 and Route 72 meet. From the circle take Route 72 east; at mile marker 1 make a left. There is a forest entrance sign on your left as you turn in. Go past the ranger house on the left, then take the first right and the visitor center is just ahead; make a left into the parking lot. GPS: N39 53.74 / W74 34.53

THE RIDE

At 34,000 acres Brendan T. Byrne State Forest is New Jersey's second largest state forest. There are over 50 miles of trails for hiking, biking, and horseback riding. The forest has three main trails: the Red (Cranbury Trail), White (Mt. Misery Trail), and the Orange (Bike Trail). All these trails are well marked and easy to follow. The route for this ride will take you on parts of all three trails so you can get a sample of all the state forest has to offer. Before you start the ride, you should stop in the visitor center and pick up a trail map. If the visitor center is closed, there is usually a trail map in a bin just outside the office at the beginning of the Red Trail.

To start the ride, head toward the Red Trail, which is to the right side of the visitor center building as you are looking at it from the parking lot. From the visitor center you will take a small path that will take you across Four Mile Road and through a gate onto the main part of the Red Trail. Soon after you get on the Red Trail, you will see a Red Dotted trail going to the right. Stay straight here on the Red Trail. The Red Trail will take you along a wide path through the pine forest. The trail will run into a sand road. Take a left here and follow the road until the Red Trail veers off on the right side of the road.

One of the cranberry bogs you will see along the way

At 2.1 miles you will come down around a curve to where the Red and White Trails meet. The curve in the trail obscures the sign for the White Trail so be careful not to miss the turn.

From here take the White Trail, which will take you toward the cranberry bogs. Keep following the White Trail and at 3.2 miles you will ride past some of them. This is one of the more scenic places on the ride that allows you to see the many types of grasses, trees, and landscapes the state forest has to offer. There are a number of side paths here that will let you explore the other bogs in the area so feel free to explore the area on your own.

A tenth of a mile after reaching the end of the bogs, you will bear left to continue on the White Trail. This will take you through a narrower trail with some big roots crossing it, so the riding is a little more technical single-track trail. At 4.0 miles you will cross a paved road. Make a right onto the paved road. You are now riding the Orange Trail, whose markers are close in color to the Red Trail, and will be on paved roads for the next 5.3 miles. If you are enjoying the single track of the White Trail and want some more, you can continue on as this will eventually take you to Pakim Pond, where you can rejoin the route.

Bike Shops

Wheelies Bike Shop, 176 Route 70, Suite 6A, Medford, NJ; (609) 953-9383 A full-service bike shop that also has a mobile repair van that will come to you and make repairs.

You will eventually reach the parking lot at Pakim Pond. There is a bathroom here by the pond so it makes a good place to stop for a quick break and enjoy the view. When you are ready to continue, follow the signs to the Red Trail. This will take you along some wide sand and dirt trails through the forest and get you back to the visitor center where you started. Just follow the Red Trail and signs that direct you to the office. It's about 3.4 miles back to the office and an easy ride. With over 50 miles of networked sandy roads in the park, this is a place you can come back to many times before you experience all it has to offer.

MILES AND DIRECTIONS

0.0 From the visitor center follow the Red Trail.

0.1 Cross Four Mile Road and continue on the Red Trail.

0.3 Continue straight where the Red Dotted Trail goes off to the right.

1.2 Turn left onto Norlemon Road (unmarked dirt road).

Brendan Byrne State Forest

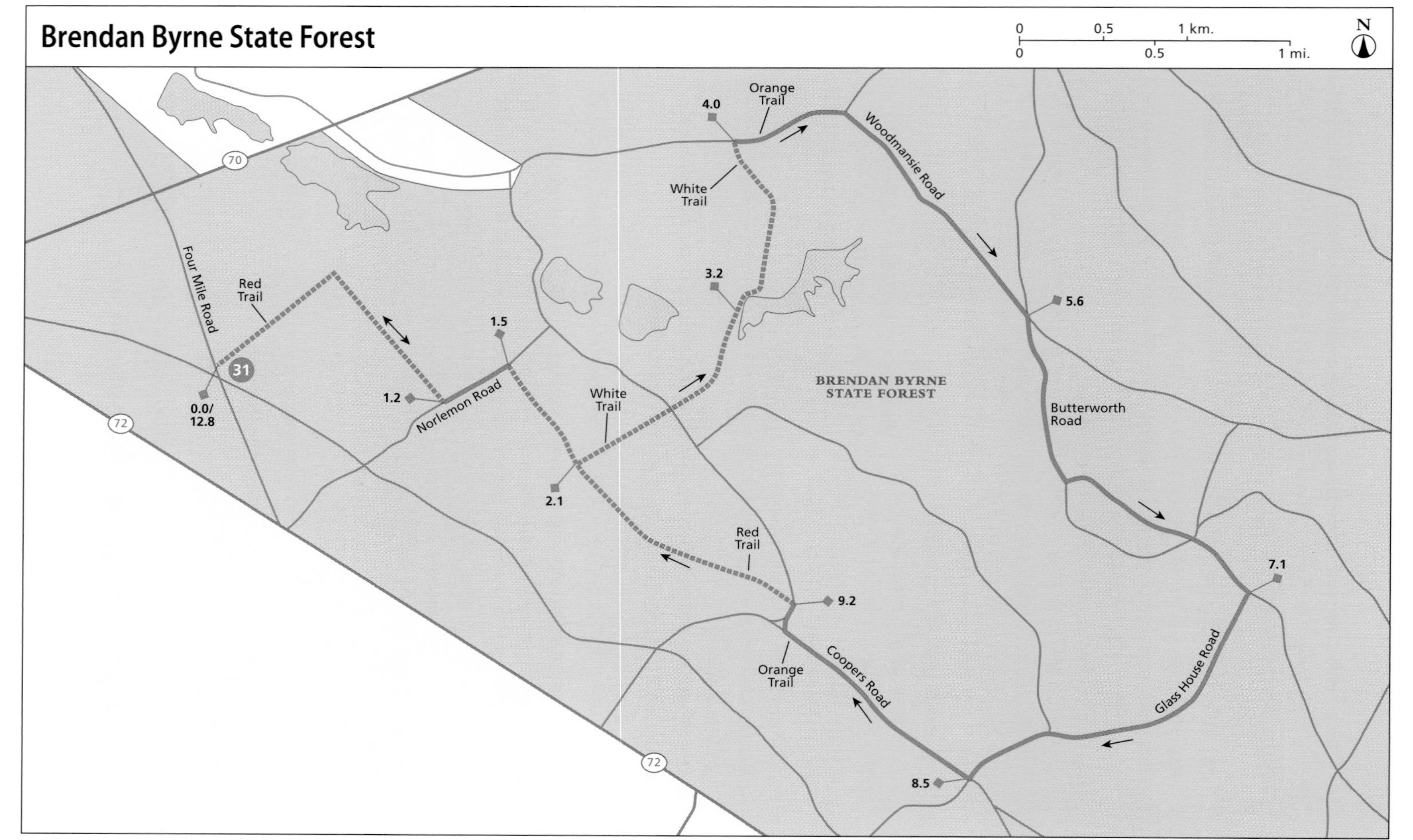

1.5 Turn right to continue on the Red Trail.

2.1 Turn left and start following the White Trail.

2.6 Cross Coopers Road (unmarked).

3.2 Ride past cranberry bogs (trail gets a little more technical after bog).

4.0 Turn right onto Woodmansie Road (unmarked paved road). Start following the Orange Trail.

5.6 Bear right onto Butterworth Road (unmarked paved road). Keep following paved road.

7.1 Turn right onto Glass House Road (unmarked paved road). Keep following paved road.

8.5 Turn right at stop sign onto Coopers Road (unmarked paved road).

9.3 Turn right into Parkim Pond parking lot and follow the Red Trail toward the office (visitor center).

12.8 Arrive back at visitor center.

RIDE INFORMATION

Events/Attractions

Brendan T. Byrne State Forest (formerly the Lebanon State Forest) is a 34,725-acre wilderness area in the New Jersey Pine Barrens. It is the state's second largest state forest (after Wharton State Forest). There are 50 miles

Myth of the Jersey Pinelands

The woods of the Jersey Pinelands are a beautiful place to ride, but it also can be a little scary at times. This vast isolated wilderness has given birth to a number of strange tales, the most famous of which is the birth of the Jersey Devil. According to the legend, during a raging storm in 1735 Mother Leeds, who was a suspected witch, gave birth to her thirteenth child. The baby was born completely normal. But soon before her terrified eyes, the child changed into a beast that resembled a dragon, with a head like a horse, a snake-like body, and bat's wings. It then vanished into the storm and is reported to still haunt the pines of New Jersey. Although nobody takes this myth too seriously, you can't ride around this area without at least thinking about it and wondering . . . was that an animal I just heard behind me or something else? . . .

of hiking and biking trails and a camping area. For more information check out the website, state.nj.us/dep/parksandforests/parks/byrne.html.

Restrooms

Mile 9.3: There are restrooms by Pakim Pond.

Maps

DeLorme New Jersey Atlas & Gazetteer: Page 56, D12

Mt. Misery is really not much of a mountain since it's only slightly higher than the surrounding area. It's more of a name of a place and the Methodist Retreat Camp that is in this area.

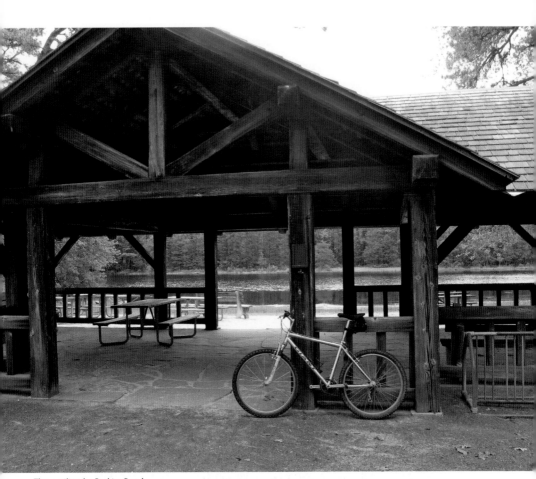

The pavilion by Parkim Pond

32

Wharton State Forest

Wharton State Forest is the largest single tract of land in the New Jersey park system. The 115,000 acres of the park contain over 500 miles of hiking trails and unpaved roads to explore. Although known for its large pinelands, this area has a very diverse and unique set of flora and fauna that can take years to fully appreciate. This ride will take you on one of the better mountain biking trails in the park and introduce you to the beauty of this area.

Start: Batsto Village, CR 542, Hammonton

Length: 9.8-mile loop

Approximate riding time: 2 hours

Best bike: Mountain bike

Terrain and trail surface: The ride will be on sandy single-track paths. The terrain is mostly flat with some rolling hills. The path is relatively clear of large debris and tree roots, but there are some small tree stumps you have to watch out for. The path is a little narrow in places so you will have to watch out for the tree branches and other things growing over or near the path.

Traffic and hazards: There will be no traffic since you will be on a dedicated mountain bike trail. The trail you are riding is well marked, but it is a good idea to have a good look at the map at the beginning of the trail or get a copy of the map from the office. The woods can be filled with bugs at times, so it's a good idea to wear some form of bug repellent. There will be no place to stop for water or food on this ride, so make sure you have enough supplies before you head out.

Things to see: Batsto Village

Getting there: From Center City Philadelphia take the Walt Whitman Bridge to North/South Freeway, Route 42, to Atlantic City Expressway. Continue to exit 28 (Hammonton). Exit to Route 54 and turn left. Go to the 5th traffic light and turn right onto Route 30 East (White Horse Pike). Go to the 2nd light and turn left. At the end of the road turn left at the T intersection onto Route 542. Batsto Village is 9 miles ahead on the left. There is a fee to park in the Batsto Village parking lot. If you want to avoid the fee, you can park in a sand parking lot 0.5 mile before Batsto Village that is used for people launching their canoes on Batsto Lake. GPS: N39 38.49 / W74 38.70

THE RIDE

Wharton State Forest has a large network of over 500 miles of hiking trails, sand roads, and other trails for horseback riding and mountain biking. With so many choices it's hard to decide where to start exploring. The best set of well-marked trails are in Batsto Village. Right off the parking lot is a set of 5 different trails that you can mix and match to do anything from an easy 6-mile ride to a long, tough 19-mile ride. If you study the trail map at the beginning of the trail, you will get a good idea where the different trails meet and overlap.

There are two main loops trails: the Green (Fire Tower) Trail, which is 6 miles, and the Orange (Penn Branch Trail), which is 19 miles. The Green Trail overlaps the lower part of the Orange Trail. The Blue (Huckleberry) Trail, the White (Oak Hill) Trail, and the Red (Teaberry) Trail are connector trails that link two parts of another trail together.

For this ride we will combine the Orange and Blue Trails to form a 9.8-mile loop that will take you around and past most of the trails and give you a good workout. To begin the ride head to the back side of the parking lot where all the trails begin.

The beginning of the path is marked with green and orange blazes (i.e., colored round reflectors). You will follow these markings as you head into the forest along a sandy single-track trail. After a windy 0.25 mile you will come up a small hill where the trail splits. This is where the loop starts. Take a left here and continue following the green and orange blazes. You will continue heading deeper into the forest, and after another 1.7 miles the Green Trail will split off and you will now follow the Orange and Blue Trail. After a little less than a mile the Orange Trail will split off and you will follow the Blue Trail. The Blue Trail seems a little narrower than the other trails, so you may encounter a few more branches and overgrowth impinging on the trail. It is well marked and fun to ride and will continue for 3.4 miles before rejoining the returning Orange Trail. Along the way you will pass the White and Red Trails, each of which give you an option to shorten the ride.

As you continue on, the Blue and Orange Trail will rejoin the Green Trail and you will follow that back to the start. You know you are getting close to the end when the trail emerges by a town next to a paved road. You bear right here to stay on the trail and in a little over 0.5 mile you will be back at the start. After the ride you will probably be looking for something to eat or drink. There is no

Bike Shops

Pro Pedals Bike Shop, 682 South White Horse Pike, Hammonton, NJ 08037; (609) 561-3030; propedalsbikeshop.com
A full-service bike shop that also offers Saturday and Sunday rides.

The intersection of the Blue and Orange Trails

food service here, but there are some vending machines with Gatorade, soda, and juices by the visitor center. In the summer there is usually a food truck in the parking lot on weekend days.

MILES AND DIRECTIONS

0.0 Start along the Green and Orange Trails.

0.3 Follow the Green and Orange Trails to the left. This is where the main loop starts.

2.0 The Green Trail splits off. Follow the Blue and Orange Trails.

2.9 The Orange Trail splits off. Follow the Blue Trail.

3.8 Pass the White Trail.

5.6 Pass the Red Trail.

6.3 Blue Trail merges with the returning Orange Trail. Follow the Blue and Orange Trails.

7.0 Green Trail merges with returning Orange Trail. Blue Trail ends. Follow the Green and Orange Trails.

The Pine Barrens Really Aren't

Although "Pine Barrens" may sound like the description of a desolate area, the truth is that the Pine Barrens is a very ecologically active and diverse area that was designated a US Biosphere Reserve by UNESCO, an agency of the United Nations, in 1983.

The Pine Barrens encompasses approximately 1.1 million acres which is 22 percent of New Jersey's land area. It is the largest body of open space on the Mid-Atlantic seaboard between Richmond and Boston and is underlain by The Cohansey-Kirkwood aquifer containing 17 trillion gallons of water. Most of the lakes and streams in the Pine Barrens are called brackish or "cedar water." The water is very acidic (4.4 mean pH) and looks like tea, but despite its color it is some of the purest water in the land.

The Pine Barrens are dominated by pitch pine trees because of the frequent fire in the area. Their ability to resist and recover from fire by resprouting directly through their bark allows them to dominate over oak trees, which are usually killed outright by a moderate or intense fire.

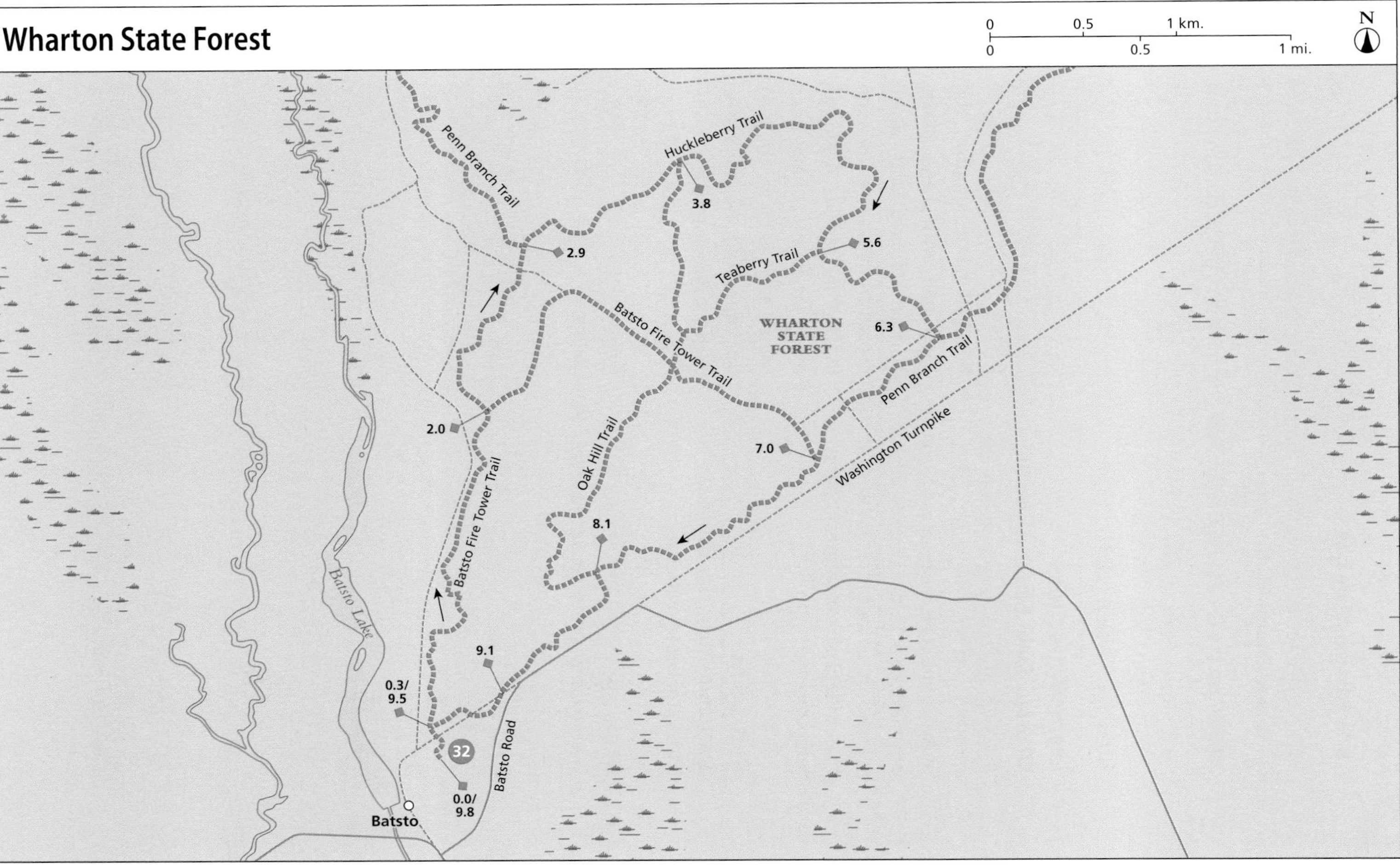
Wharton State Forest
0
0.5
1 km.
0
0.5
1 mi.
N
Penn Branch Trail
Huckleberry Trail
3.8
5.6
Teaberry Trail
2.9
Batsto Fire Tower Trail
WHARTON
STATE
FOREST
6.3
Penn Branch Trail
2.0
Oak Hill Trail
7.0
Washington Turnpike
8.1
Batsto Fire Tower Trail
Batsto Lake
9.1
0.3/
9.5
32
Batsto Road
0.0/
9.8
Batsto

8.1 Pass the White Trail.

9.1 Trail intersects paved road (Batsto Road). Bear right to stay on Green and Orange Trails.

9.5 Take the Green and Orange Trails on the left to get back to the start.

9.8 Arrive back at start.

RIDE INFORMATION

Events/Attractions

Wharton State Forest is the largest park in New Jersey. This large forested area with numerous lakes, streams, and trails is a great place for any outdoor activity. For more information check out the website at nj.gov/dep/parksandforests/parks/wharton.html.

Before each major league baseball game, umpires rub each ball with Lena Blackbourne Rubbing Mud, which comes from a secret location in the Pine Barrens. Although many other muds have been tried, Lena's is by far the best for improving the ball's grip without discoloring it.

Restrooms

Start/end: There is a bathroom in the visitor center of Batsto.

Maps

DeLorme New Jersey Atlas & Gazetteer: Page 64, E7

33

Nixon's General Store Ride

Just over 30 miles east of Philadelphia are the New Jersey Pine Barrens. This is a largely rural and undeveloped area of forested land that is mostly known for its pine trees. Life is a little slower in this region. This ride will take you on a loop through the Pine Barrens for a quiet ride with a great stop at a general store with some rocking chairs to relax on. This is a scenic area with no major sights but a lot of pleasant nothingness that makes this a peaceful area to ride.

Start: Brendan T. Byrne State Forest, New Lisbon, NJ (formerly Lebanon State Forest)

Length: 30.7-mile loop

Approximate riding time: 2.5 hours

Best bike: Road or hybrid bike

Terrain and trail surface: This ride is on paved roads that are as flat as it gets. There are some gradual inclines and declines but nothing that would be mistaken for a hill.

Traffic and hazards: Most of the roads will have light traffic. New Road may have moderate traffic depending on the time of day. Half of the roads on this ride have a dedicated bike lane, which makes riding easy. Just watch out for the Jersey Devil.

Things to see: Chatsworth Lake, Nixon's General Store, and lots and lots of pine trees

Getting there: From Center City Philadelphia head over the Ben Franklin Bridge and take Route 70 east until you come to the Four-Mile Circle where Route 70 and Route 72 meet. From the circle take Route 72 east; at mile marker 1 make a left. There is a forest entrance sign on your left as you turn in. Go past the ranger house on the left then take the first right and the visitor center is just ahead; make a left into the parking lot. GPS: N39 53.74 / W74 34.53

THE RIDE

The Pine Barrens is a slightly mysterious place that is the birthplace of some of New Jersey's stranger legends. A visit to this area seems like stepping back in time. The Pine Barrens is not really barren but just a large area of sandy, acidic,

nutrient-poor soil that is not good to grow crops in. This area does, however, support a unique and diverse spectrum of plant life, including orchids and carnivorous plants. The area is also notable for its population of some of the rarer species of pines and other plant species that depend on fire to reproduce (fire is very frequent in the Pine Barrens).

The ride starts at the visitor center in Brendan T. Byrne State Forest. To start the ride exit the parking lot and make a left onto Shinns Road. The roads are not marked real well here. Shinns Road is on your left as you are facing the visitor center.

Shinns Road runs along the edge of the forest. It's a nice, quiet road with no traffic. After about 2 miles you will come to an intersection where Shinns Road changes to sand. Turn right here on an unmarked road and head west toward NJ 72. At the next T is NJ 72; make a left here and stay on the shoulder, then make a right onto CR 563. This road has a nice bike lane that you can ride on.

As you continue on CR 563, you will be heading south toward Chatsworth. In a little over 4 miles you will come to the center of Chatsworth. There really isn't much to this town so it's hard to know when you are in the center. Here you will make a right onto CR 532. The bike lane on CR 563 continues on CR 532.

Enjoying the rocking chairs at Nixon's

CR 532 will have light to moderate traffic depending on the time of day, but the bike lane makes the riding easy. You will continue on this road for a little over 9 miles. You will pass by Chatsworth Lake, some hunting lodges, and lots of pine trees. When you make the turn onto New Road, you will see Nixon's General Store. This general store has been here since 1850, and although it has evolved with the times and needs of the customers, the one constant has been great food and good service as this store has won "The Best in Burlington County" for the past 6 years. The rocking chairs at the front of the store are very inviting, so this is a great place to take a break.

New Road does not have a bike lane and has moderate traffic, so stay to the right. Once you make the right onto Foxchase Road, you will again be on quiet back roads with little traffic. When Powell Place becomes Sooy Place Road, you will have about 6 miles before the next turn. There's nothing much to see here, but it is a pleasant type of nothingness that makes the ride enjoyable.

At the end of Sooy Place you will make a left onto CR 563 and retrace your way back to the visitor center. This is a nice area for a lot of outdoor activities, so if you are interested in checking out some of the other outdoor activities like hiking or canoeing, you can get more information in the visitor center.

Bike Shops

Mount Holly Bicycles, 1645 Route 38, Mount Holly, NJ 08060; (609) 267-6620; mthollybicycles.com This bike shop has everything from beach cruisers to serious racing bikes. The owners are very friendly and glad to help out riders of any ability.

MILES AND DIRECTIONS

0.0 Start at the visitor center; make a left out of the west end of the parking lot onto Shinns Road.

2.0 Turn right at unmarked road where Shinns Road changes to sand onto Buzzard Hill Road.

2.5 Turn left onto NJ 72; stay on shoulder (beware of fast-moving traffic).

2.9 Bear right onto CR 563.

6.8 Turn right onto CR 532 (Tabernacle Chatsworth Road).

16.5 Turn right onto New Road (Nixon's General Store on the corner).

17.9 Turn right onto Foxchase Road.

18.8 Turn right onto Powell Place Road.

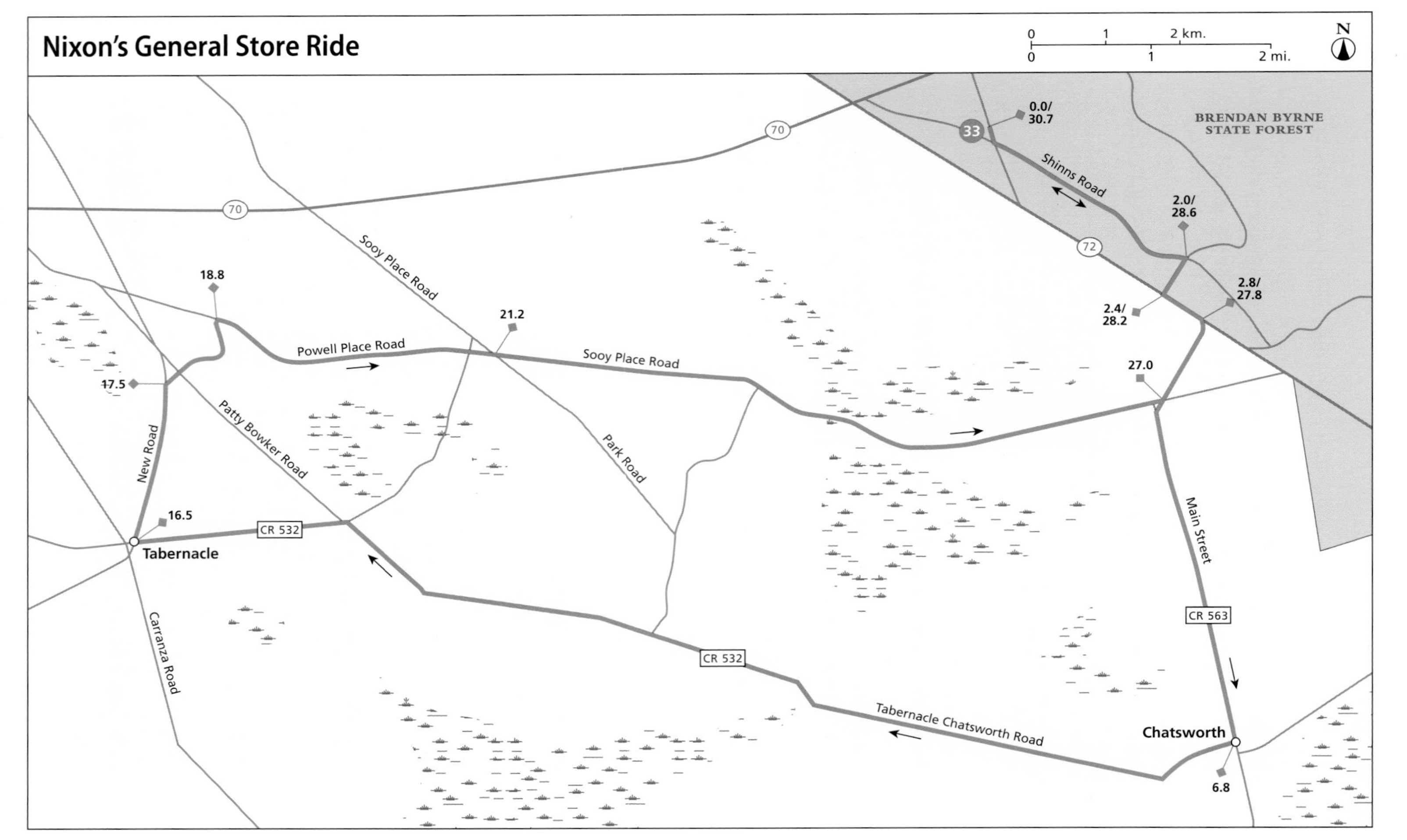
Nixon's General Store Ride
0
1
2 km.
0
1
2 mi.
N
BRENDAN BYRNE
STATE FOREST
33
0.0/
30.7
Shinns Road
2.0/
28.6
2.4/
28.2
2.8/
27.8
27.0
70
70
72
Sooy Place Road
18.8
21.2
Powell Place Road
Sooy Place Road
17.5
New Road
Patty Bowker Road
Park Road
Main Street
16.5
CR 532
Tabernacle
CR 532
CR 563
Carranza Road
Tabernacle Chatsworth Road
Chatsworth
6.8

21.2 Road becomes Sooy Place Road.

27.0 Turn left onto CR 563.

27.8 Turn left onto NJ 72; stay on shoulder (beware of fast-moving traffic).

28.2 Turn right onto Buzzard Hill Road.

28.6 Turn left onto Shinns Road.

30.7 Keep right. Arrive back at visitor center.

RIDE INFORMATION

Events/Attractions

Brendan T. Byrne State Forest (formerly the Lebanon State Forest) is a 34,725-acre wilderness area in the New Jersey Pine Barrens. It is the state's second largest state forest (after Wharton State Forest). There are 50 miles of hiking and biking trails and a camping area. For more information check out the website state.nj.us/dep/parksandforests/parks/byrne.html.

A person from this area is referred to as Piney (the New Jersey version of a hillbilly). It's sort of a tongue-in-cheek term most people of the area wear with pride as the "Piney Power" stickers attest to.

Restrooms

Mile 16.53: Nixon's General Store has a well-maintained portable toilet on the side of the building.

Maps

DeLorme New Jersey Atlas & Gazetteer: Page 56, D12

Lebanon Glass Works

In the 1800s this area was once home to the Lebanon Glass Works. The abundance of wood and sand made the Pine Barrens a perfect place to make glass. The Glass Works was established in 1851 and was successful until 1867, when it shut down after cutting down all the trees in the area and hence no longer had fuel for the furnaces to operate. Today's forested acres are a strong contrast to the barren, cleared land that existed in the 1800s.

Batsto Village

Beautiful Batsto Village, located in Wharton State Forest, is the site of a former bog-iron and glass-making community. The area around Batsto is surrounded by a number of preserved forests and some nice rivers. The flat land and empty roads make this a great place to ride. This cruise takes you around the area and shows you some of the nicer forests, rivers, and roads around.

Start: Batsto Village, CR 542, Hammonton

Length: 27.8-mile loop

Approximate riding time: 2 hours

Best bike: Road or hybrid bike

Terrain and trail surface: Very flat, paved roads. There are some gradual inclines and declines but nothing that could be mistaken for a hill.

Traffic and hazards: Most of the roads for this ride are through or around protected forest, so the roads have very little traffic although there will be a few spots of moderate traffic.

Things to see: Batsto Village, Mullica River

Getting there: From Center City Philadelphia take the Walt Whitman Bridge to North/South Freeway, Route 42, to Atlantic City Expressway. Continue to exit 28 (Hammonton). Exit to Route 54 and turn left. Go to the 5th traffic light and turn right onto Route 30 East (White Horse Pike). Go to the 2nd light and turn left. Go the end of the road and turn left at the T intersection onto Route 542. Batsto Village is 9 miles ahead on the left. There is a fee to park in the Batsto Village parking lot; if you want to avoid the fee, you can park in a sand parking lot 0.5 mile before Batsto Village that is used for people launching their canoes on Batsto Lake. GPS: N39 38.49 / W74 38.70

THE RIDE

Few areas around Philadelphia are easier to ride in than the area around Batsto. The roads here are the definition of flat. It's very rural so there is not much traffic to deal with, and between the forest, rivers, and small streams, it is very scenic. The only problem here is that there isn't a lot of civilization, so it is hard to find a place to stop for a break. Because of this, make sure you have enough food and water for the ride before starting out.

To start the ride head out of the parking lot and make a left onto Batsto Road. This road is not signed, and on maps it may be named Bulltown or Tylerville Road and look like there are many other intersecting roads to get lost on, but the truth is that Batsto, which eventually turns into Bulltown Road, is the only paved road here; all the others are sand roads. As long as you stay on the paved road, you will not get lost. Batsto Road is a nice, wide, traffic-free road that feels more like a wide bike path.

After a little over 5 miles you will have to make a left at a T followed by a right onto River then Green Bank Road. This will get you riding next to and over the Mullica River. This river is just over 50 miles long and is the principal river that drains the Pinelands into the Atlantic Ocean at Great Bay. This estuary is considered one of the least-disturbed marine wetlands habitats in the northeast.

Once past the Mullica River, you will make a few quick turns and then be on Clarks Landing Road and riding through some nice forested land. Watch your mileage and don't miss the turn onto Leipzig Avenue. If you pass under the Garden State Parkway. you went too far.

As you ride down Leipzig Avenue and the next few roads, you may notice there are a lot of German-sounding names here. That is because you are riding near the town of Egg Harbor City, which was founded by German immigrants in 1854.

When you make the turn onto Indian Cabin Road, you will begin about 5 miles of great riding. Although there is nothing spectacular or special about this road, it has some unidentifiable quality that makes it a good ride.

At the end of Indian Cabin Road, you will make a left onto CR 643 (Pleasant Mills Road). You are only about 1.5 miles from the end of the ride, but if you want to get something to eat, you can make a right and stop at a deli about a mile down the road.

The end of the ride doesn't have to be the end to your outdoor activities. The area around Batsto offers many other activities like hiking and canoeing. There are also a lot more roads to ride on out here, so if you liked this ride, you should get a good map and explore some more on your own.

Bike Shops

Pro Pedals Bike Shop, 682 S. White Horse Pike, Hammonton, NJ 08037; (609) 561-3030; propedalsbikeshop.com
A full-service bike shop that also offers Saturday and Sunday rides.

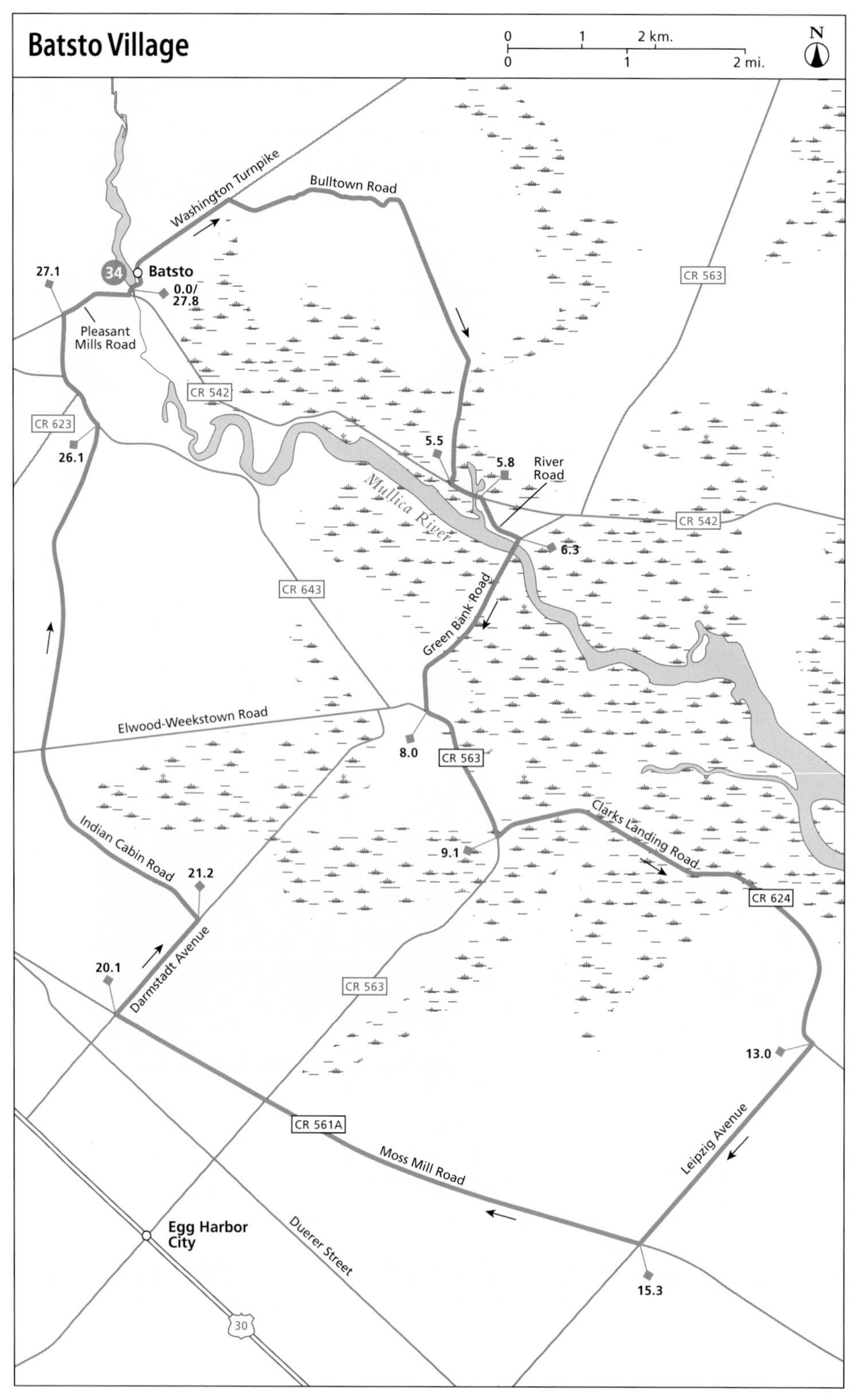
Batsto Village
0
1
2 km.
0
1
2 mi.
N
Washington Turnpike
Bulltown Road
34
Batsto
27.1
0.0/
27.8
Pleasant
Mills Road
CR 563
CR 542
CR 623
26.1
5.5
5.8
River
Road
Mullica River
CR 542
6.3
CR 643
Green Bank Road
Elwood-Weekstown Road
8.0
CR 563
Clarks Landing Road
9.1
Indian Cabin Road
21.2
CR 624
Darmstadt Avenue
20.1
CR 563
13.0
CR 561A
Leipzig Avenue
Moss Mill Road
Egg Harbor
City
Duerer Street
15.3
30

MILES AND DIRECTIONS

0.0 Turn left out of Batsto Village parking lot onto Batsto Road (also known as Bulltown or Tylerville Road).

5.5 Turn left onto CR 542 (Pleasant Mills Road).

5.8 Turn right onto SR 651 (River Road).

6.3 Turn right onto CR 563 (Green Bank Road).

8.0 Turn left at T to stay on CR 563 (Green Bank Road).

9.1 Turn left onto CR 624 (Clarks Landing Road).

13.0 Turn right onto Leipzig Avenue.

15.3 Turn right onto CR 561A (Moss Mill Road).

20.1 Turn right onto Darmstadt Avenue.

Historic Batsto

In 1766 Charles Read built the Batsto Iron Works along the Batsto River. The rivers and streams in the area had an abundance of bog ore that could be easily mined. The area's forests also provided wood that was made into charcoal for smelting the ore. The iron works made cooking pots, kettles, and other household items as well as manufacturing supplies for the Continental Army during the American Revolutionary War.

The iron works grew and prospered over the next 90 years, but in the mid-19th century demand for iron declined; Batsto turned to glassmaking but was not very successful and soon Batsto was in bankruptcy.

In 1876 Philadelphia businessman Joseph Wharton purchased Batsto along with a substantial number of other properties in the area. He improved the village buildings and turned the village from iron and glassmaking to more agricultural projects, including cranberry farming and a sawmill. Eventually in the mid-1950s New Jersey purchased all the properties and land that Joseph Wharton had bought and has preserved most of the history of Batsto.

Today there are more than forty sites and structures, including the Batsto mansion, a sawmill, a 19th-century ore boat, a charcoal kiln, ice and milk houses, a carriage house and stable, a blacksmith and wheelwright shop, a gristmill, and a general store. If you enjoy history, it's a fun place to explore.

Riding across the Mullica River

21.2 Turn left onto Indian Cabin Road.

26.1 Turn left onto CR 643 (Pleasant Mills Road).

27.1 Turn right onto Pleasant Mills Road.

27.7 Turn left onto Batsto Village Road.

27.8 Turn left into parking lot at Batsto.

RIDE INFORMATION

Events/Attractions

Batsto Historic Village is a historic site located in the south-central Pinelands of New Jersey. There are a number of historic buildings that have been preserved and can be explored. For more information check out the website at batstovillage.org.

Egg Harbor City was founded in 1854 by German Americans from Philadelphia. It remained an island of German language and culture in South Jersey for more than 50 years, which explains why there are so many roads with names like Frankfurt, Vienna, and Leipzig.

Restrooms

Start/end: There is a restroom in the visitor center of Batsto.

Maps

DeLorme New Jersey Atlas & Gazetteer: Page 64, E7

Philadelphia to Atlantic City

Atlantic City has long been a favorite getaway for the people of Philadelphia. Whether you want to lie on the beach, walk the boardwalk, or try your luck at gambling, Atlantic City is a fun place to visit. This ride will show you how to bike from Center City Philadelphia to Atlantic City and then ride back to Center City on the Atlantic City Line. You can even use the Atlantic City Line to bypass the city and ride the quieter country roads that make up the last two-thirds of this ride.

Start: South side of the 30th Street Station

Length: 63.2-mile straight line for the full ride. There are entry and exit points roughly every 15 miles along the route, which you can access from Atlantic City Line stations.

Approximate riding time: 5.0 hours (1.6 hours return by rail on Atlantic City Line)

Best bike: Road bike

Terrain and trail surface: The terrain is mostly flat, with occasional climbs. The biggest climb is the climb up the Benjamin Franklin Bridge. The route runs entirely on paved streets and roads.

Traffic and hazards: The first third of the ride uses normally busy roads in downtown Philadelphia and Camden. This section of the ride is best completed early on a weekend morning. Alternatively, you can use the Atlantic City Line to bypass the city. The last two-thirds of the ride uses suburban and rural roads and highways with paved shoulders.

Things to see: City Hall, Independence National Historic Park, Benjamin Franklin Bridge, New Jersey Pine Barrens, Atlantic City

Getting there: By car: From I-95, take I-676 west to the I-76 East exit on the right side. When the exit merges with a lane that comes from the right side, move to the right lane, and then take exit 345 to 30th Street/ Market Street. Turn right at the stoplight and follow the street around the north and west sides of 30th Street Station. When you reach Market Street, you can turn right to look for a parking space in University City. There are a number of metered on-street parking spaces in University City. Many of the on-street parking spaces in University City are free on Sunday. GPS: N39 57.17 / W75 11.00
By train: Take the train to 30th Street Station. The ride starts on Market Street south of the station.

THE RIDE

Ever since the Camden and Atlantic Railroad established the first rail line to Atlantic City in 1854, it has been very easy for Philadelphians to get to Atlantic City. Over the years, multiple railroads have connected Philadelphia with Atlantic City. Two of these railroads, the Pennsylvania Railroad and the Reading Railroad, are immortalized as properties in the board game Monopoly. Nowadays, most people drive to Atlantic City, but the city that's "Always Turned On" is still served by the NJ Transit Atlantic City Line, which you will pass a number of times during the ride.

The first 7.7 miles passes through downtown Philadelphia and Camden. These streets are typically packed with motor traffic on weekdays (and sometimes during the weekend). Early on weekend mornings, though, the traffic is much more manageable. Riding on Market Street toward City Hall on a nice summer day is a treat that's well worth getting up early for. If you are riding at a different time of day, you can optionally detour 1 block south and take Chestnut Street through town or follow the first 3.2 miles of Ride 4, which takes you on the bike lane on Pine Street then up 5th to the Ben Franklin Bridge.

Bike Shops

Pro Pedals Bike Shop, 682 S. White Horse Pike (US 30), Hammonton, NJ 08037; (609) 561-3030, propedalsbikeshop.com A family-owned shop that has been in business since 1984, this shop is on the east side of town, just 0.7 mile north of the route at Moss Mill Road.

After you pass Independence National Historic Park, turn left on 5th Street and bike over to the pedestrian walkway on the Benjamin Franklin Bridge. You then make your way through downtown Camden to Martin Luther King Boulevard, Haddon Avenue, and White Horse Pike.

At 7.8 miles, you reach Newton Avenue. This is the beginning of an urban escape route that runs along a train track for most of its length. The train track limits the number of vehicles that use the street and the number of side streets and driveways that cross your route. By the time you reach the end of this street at 16.4 miles, you will be done with most of the city riding. For the next 16 miles, you will be riding mostly on county roads past farms and housing developments.

At 32.4 miles, you reach the outskirts of Hammonton. Hammonton is the halfway point of the ride and is a good place to stop for a break. The road between Hammonton and Egg Harbor City is the least-traveled road on the route and is nicely sheltered by pine trees.

At 48.9 miles, the route starts to get busy again as the route turns onto CR 563 and goes past Atlantic City International Airport. At 53.4 miles, you turn onto Delilah Road, which takes you to US 30 and the causeway that crosses the salt marsh to Atlantic City. US 30 is the busiest road used by this route, but there is a paved shoulder for all but the last 0.3 mile (when you cross a drawbridge). You exit US 30 immediately after the bridge and ride down Ohio Avenue to Atlantic City Station. If you're not in a hurry to take the train back, you can head over to the boardwalk for some food or entertainment.

MILES AND DIRECTIONS

0.0 Start at the corner of 30th Street and Market Street; head east on Market Street.

0.9 Turn right onto South Penn Square at City Hall and follow around the south side of City Hall.

1.1 Turn right onto Market Street.

1.8 Turn left onto 5th Street. Benjamin Franklin's grave is in Christ Church Cemetery (to your right on Arch Street, at 1.9 miles).

2.1 At Race Street, pull onto the sidewalk, and follow the sidewalk to the pedestrian walkway on the Benjamin Franklin Bridge. Go slow; the pedestrian walkway ends in a stairway on the New Jersey side.

3.6 At the foot of the stairs, turn left onto Pearl Street.

3.7 Turn right onto North 5th Street.

4.2 Turn left onto Dr. Martin Luther King Boulevard.

4.5 Turn right onto Haddon Avenue.

6.4 Turn right onto White Horse Pike.

7.7 Turn right onto West Lakeview Drive. This is the first street after you cross the lake.

7.8 Turn left onto Newton Avenue. After about 0.5 mile, a railroad track will start to run to the right of the avenue. The railroad reduces the number of intersections that you must cross and makes the avenue safer for biking.

8.8 Newton Avenue becomes East Atlantic Ave.

14.3 The first entry/exit point is at the intersection of East Atlantic Avenue and East Laurel Road. You can exit by turning left on East Laurel Road and riding on East Laurel Road/White Horse Road to Lindenwold

Philadelphia to Atlantic City

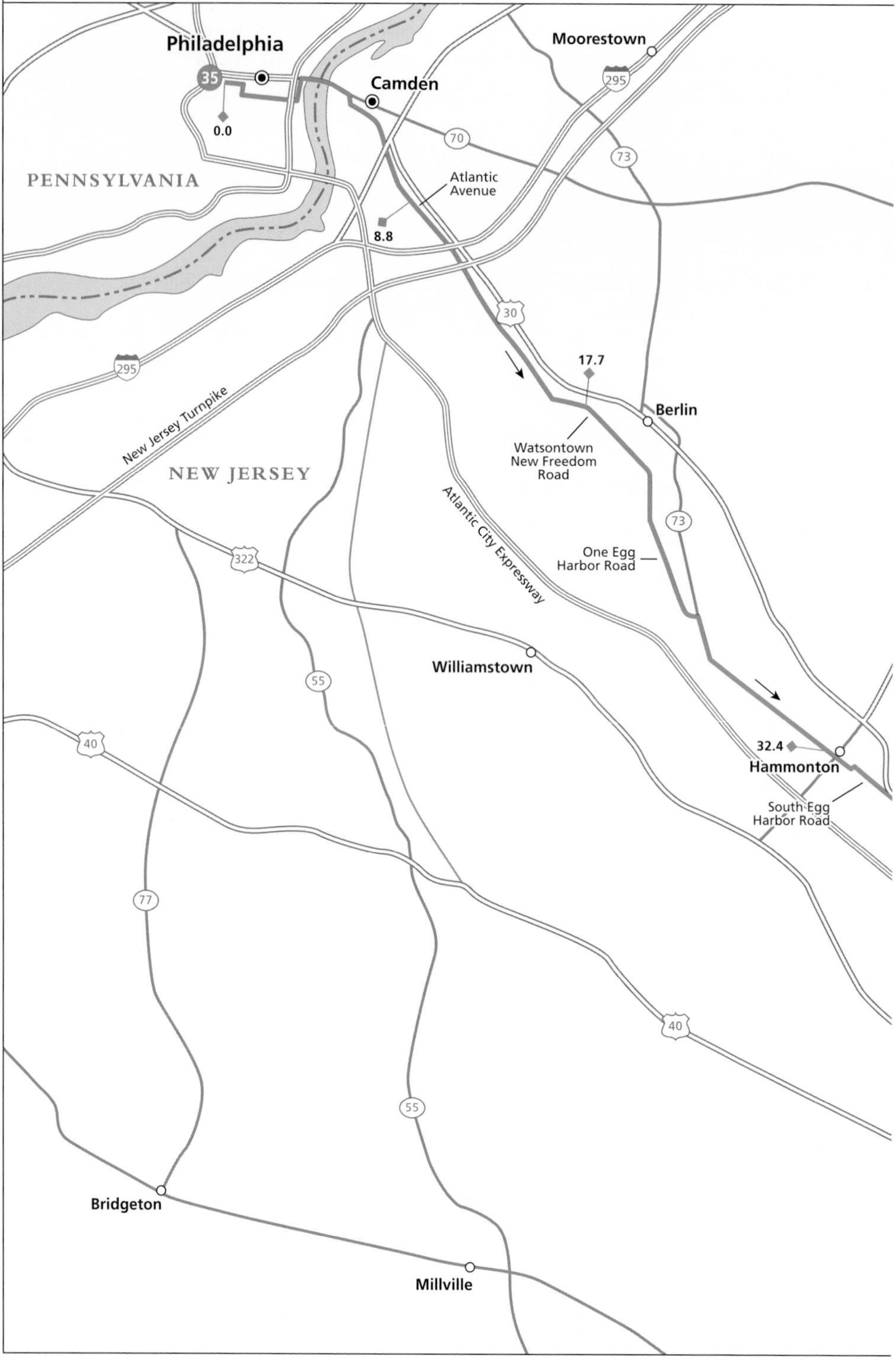

Philadelphia
35
0.0
Camden
Moorestown
295
70
73
PENNSYLVANIA
Atlantic
Avenue
8.8
30
17.7
295
Berlin
Watsontown
New Freedom
Road
New Jersey Turnpike
NEW JERSEY
Atlantic City Expressway
73
One Egg
Harbor Road
322
Williamstown
55
32.4
Hammonton
40
South Egg
Harbor Road
77
40
55
Bridgeton
Millville

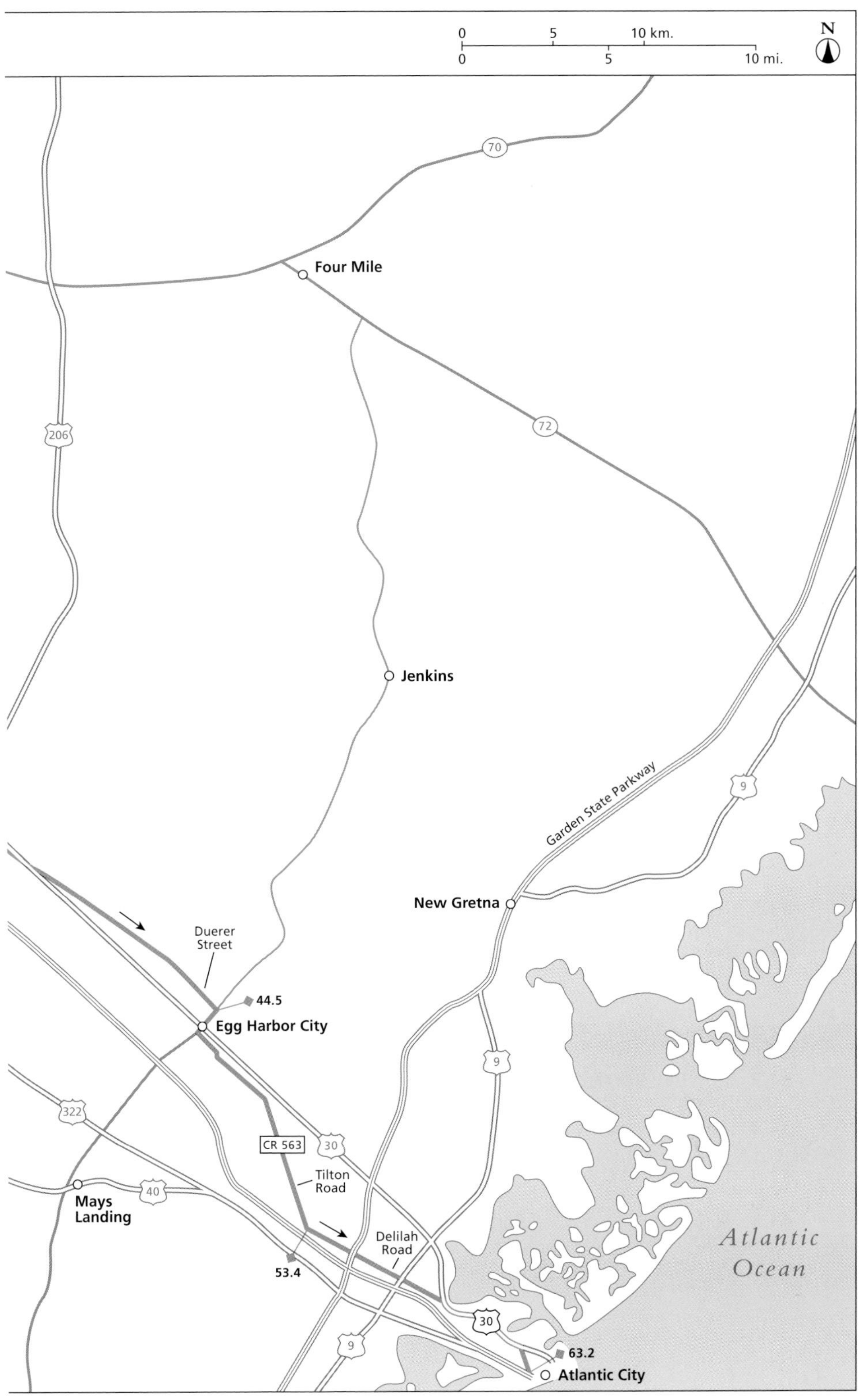
0
5
10 km.
0
5
10 mi.
N
70
Four Mile
206
72
Jenkins
Garden State Parkway
9
New Gretna
Duerer
Street
44.5
Egg Harbor City
9
322
CR 563
30
Tilton
Road
Mays
Landing
40
Delilah
Road
53.4
Atlantic
Ocean
30
9
63.2
Atlantic City

Station (0.9 mile). Alternatively, you can ride on White Horse Road/East Laurel Road from Lindenwold Station to the route at East Atlantic Avenue.

15.7 East Atlantic Ave becomes Garfield Avenue. The railroad starts to veer away from Garfield Avenue about 0.5 mile before you make your next turn onto Berlin Road.

16.4 Turn left onto Berlin Road at the T intersection.

17.7 Turn right onto CR 691/New Freedom Road.

20.6 Turn right onto Berlin New Freedom Road at the T intersection.

21.3 Turn right onto Taunton Road at the T intersection.

21.4 Turn left onto New Brooklyn Road.

22.2 Turn left onto North Grove Street. This is the street immediately after the railroad tracks.

26.4 Turn left onto Blue Anchor Road at the T intersection.

26.7 Turn right onto NJ 73 South and ride on the paved shoulder.

27.3 Turn left onto CR 561 to Hammonton. Be careful crossing the highway from the shoulder to the left-turn lane.

31.3 Turn left at the fork to stay on North Egg Harbor Road.

32.4 Turn right onto 13th Street.

32.5 Turn left onto Washington Street N.

33.5 Turn left onto 11th Street.

33.6 The second entry/exit point is Hammonton Station on the left side of 11th Street.

33.7 Turn right onto South Egg Harbor Road.

34.7 Turn left onto Lakeview Avenue.

34.8 Turn right onto Moss Mill Road.

41.9 Turn right at the fork onto Duerer Street.

44.5 Turn right onto Philadelphia Avenue.

45.5 Turn left onto Atlantic Avenue.

Passing City Hall on the way out of the city

45.6 The third entry/exit point is at Egg Harbor City Station on right side of Atlantic Avenue.

46.4 Turn right onto Bremen Avenue.

46.5 Turn left onto West Aloe Street.

48.9 Turn right onto CR 563. There are two stop signs that are close together on West Aloe Street, just south of an overpass over the railroad. CR 563 is at the second stop sign.

53.4 At the traffic circle, turn east onto Delilah Road (3rd exit).

58.5 Take the ramp onto US 30 East. There is a paved shoulder on US 30 for all but the last 0.3 mile, at the drawbridge. When you reach the bridge, pick a gap in traffic and cross on the right side.

61.5 Take the ramp immediately after the bridge (Absecon Boulevard).

Planes, Trains, and Automobiles

It can be said that Atlantic City was a creation of the railroads that served it. Certainly Atlantic City was chartered in the same year that the first railroad came to town (1854). The trains brought the people who filled the hotels, which meant more and larger hotels, which meant more trains, which meant more people, which meant more and larger hotels. Before long, one railroad was not enough to carry the people to Atlantic City. By 1880, Atlantic City was served by three railroad lines, two lines owned by the Pennsylvania Railroad and one line owned by the Reading Railroad. The competition between the lines was such that the trains would race each other to their destinations.

By the 1920s, though, the railroads (and Atlantic City itself) faced competition on a number of fronts. In 1926, the Benjamin Franklin Bridge opened over the Delaware River. Motorists were now able to drive their cars straight from Philadelphia to Atlantic City over the White Horse Pike (US 30) or the Black Horse Pike (US 40). Cars enabled people to go wherever they pleased within southern New Jersey, instead of spending all of their time in Atlantic City. Further, when air travel became more affordable, it expanded the number of places where people could spend their vacation time. The railroads were forced to consolidate operations and eliminate duplicate lines in the 1930s. However, ridership continued to decline until the railroad companies went bankrupt and were taken over by the federal government in the 1970s.

61.8 Turn right onto East Riverside Drive.

61.9 Turn left onto North Ohio Avenue.

62.9 Turn right onto Baltic Avenue.

63.0 Turn right onto North Michigan Avenue.

63.2 Arrive at Atlantic City Station (in the Atlantic City Convention Center).

RIDE INFORMATION

Events/Attractions

Atlantic City, New Jersey, is a beachside resort town. Here you can walk the boardwalk, enjoy the ocean and beach, or try your luck at one of the many casinos. There are also a lot of great attractions, entertainment, and food here. For more details check out the official website at atlanticcitynj.com.

The board game Monopoly was developed by Philadelphia resident Charles Darrow in 1934.

Restrooms

Mile 0.0: 30th Street Station has a bathroom that patrons can use.
Mile 21.2: There is a park on the left that has a seasonal portable toilet.
Mile 33.0: The WaWa in Hammonton has a bathroom that patrons can use.
Mile 45.4: There are a number of businesses in Egg Harbor City with bathrooms that patrons can use.
Mile 63.2: The Atlantic City Station has a bathroom.

Maps

Delorme Pennsylvania Atlas & Gazetteer: Page 86, D3 or *DeLorme New Jersey Atlas & Gazetteer:* Page 71, G21

Smith's Bridge

The lower Brandywine Creek is known for its rustic beauty, the artists and artisans who were drawn to the area, and the chemical company that was founded on its banks. Fortunately, the gunpowder mill that was built by Eleuthère Irénée du Pont in 1803 did not change the character of the area much. Over the years, concerned Delaware citizens have worked to ensure that the land along Brandywine Creek is preserved in its natural state for many generations to come.

Start: Woodlawn Trustees parking lot on Brandywine Creek

Length: 16.6 miles round-trip

Approximate riding time: 1.5 hours

Best bike: Road bike

Terrain and trail surface: Paved and hilly, with two long climbs toward the beginning and rolling hills toward the end.

Traffic and hazards: Most of the roads have moderate traffic, but this is a popular area for bicycling, so the motorists will be expecting bicycles. There is a short segment on US 1 and a longer segment on State Highway 52. There is a paved shoulder on both of these highways.

Getting there: Drive south on I-95 to Delaware. Immediately upon crossing the Delaware border, take exit 6 to Naamans Road (DE 92). Turn right onto Naamans Road and drive 5.1 miles. Turn left onto Ramsey Road (the next road after you cross US 202) and drive 0.4 mile, and then turn right to stay on Ramsey Road and drive 1.4 miles more. Ramsey Road turns right and becomes Brandywine Creek Road at Brandywine Creek. The parking lot will be on your left. GPS: N39 50.02 / W75 34.50

THE RIDE

The ride starts at the Woodlawn Trustees parking lot on Brandywine Creek. Head north from the parking lot to Smiths Bridge Road, turn right, and then turn north again on Ridge Road. This will be a long, slow climb. When you reach the top of the ridge, you turn left onto Ring Road to descend back to creek level.

Toward the bottom of the ridge, at the intersection with Bullock Road, is Archie's Corner. An octagonal schoolhouse was built here in 1838; it was sold in 1875 and became a church. The building was a favorite subject for Andrew Wyeth in the middle part of the 20th century. All that remains now are the walls of the building and an adjoining cemetery.

Continue on to US 1 and cross the highway at the light. Ride along US 1 on the shoulder until you cross the Brandywine at Chadds Ford. Turn left at the first light onto Fairville Road, which will take you to the top of the ridge on the west side of the Brandywine. Railroad tracks cross the road at a bad angle before you start climbing, so be careful.

When you reach the top of the ridge at Kennett Pike, turn left and continue back south into Delaware. Not long after crossing the border, you will enter Centreville, which features a number of shops and places to eat.

Continue south on Kennett Pike, past the Winterthur Museum, and turn left onto Kirk Road at the light. Turn left again onto Montchanin Road, which takes you back to Smiths Bridge Road. Turn right onto Smiths Bridge Road, descend the hill to the bridge, and turn right onto Brandywine Creek Road immediately after crossing the bridge.

The Smith's Covered Bridge

MILES AND DIRECTIONS

0.0 Start in the Woodlawn Trustees parking lot on Brandywine Creek; head northwest on Brandywine Creek Road toward Smiths Bridge Road.

0.3 Turn right onto Smiths Bridge Road.

0.4 Turn left onto Ridge Road. You will cross the Pennsylvania border immediately before this turn.

1.8 Turn left onto Ring Road.

3.2 Cross US 1 at the light, turn left, and ride on the shoulder.

4.3 Turn left onto Fairville Road (at the light just after you cross Brandywine Creek).

7.4 Turn left onto Kennett Pike (PA 52, which turns into DE 52 at the Delaware border).

11.5 Turn left onto Kirk Road.

12.3 Turn left onto Montchanin Road.

14.9 Turn right onto Smiths Bridge Road.

Bike Shops

Garrison's Cyclery of Centreville, 5801 Kennett Pike, Centreville, DE 19807; (302) 384-6827; garrisonscyclery.com Garrison's Cyclery is a full-service bike shop that offers personalized service. The shop is on the route, at the intersection of Kennett Pike and Twaddell Mill Road in Centreville, on the east (left) side of the road.

For the Public Enjoyment

The park from which you start this ride is owned and maintained by Woodlawn Trustees, a not-for-profit private corporation. Woodlawn Trustees was founded by William Bancroft in 1901 to preserve open space in the Wilmington area and to provide affordable housing to people of modest means. Woodlawn Trustees uses the earnings from the real estate that it owns and manages to maintain parkland for public enjoyment. Woodlawn Trustees currently owns and maintains 2,000 acres of land around Brandywine Creek and in Pennsylvania.

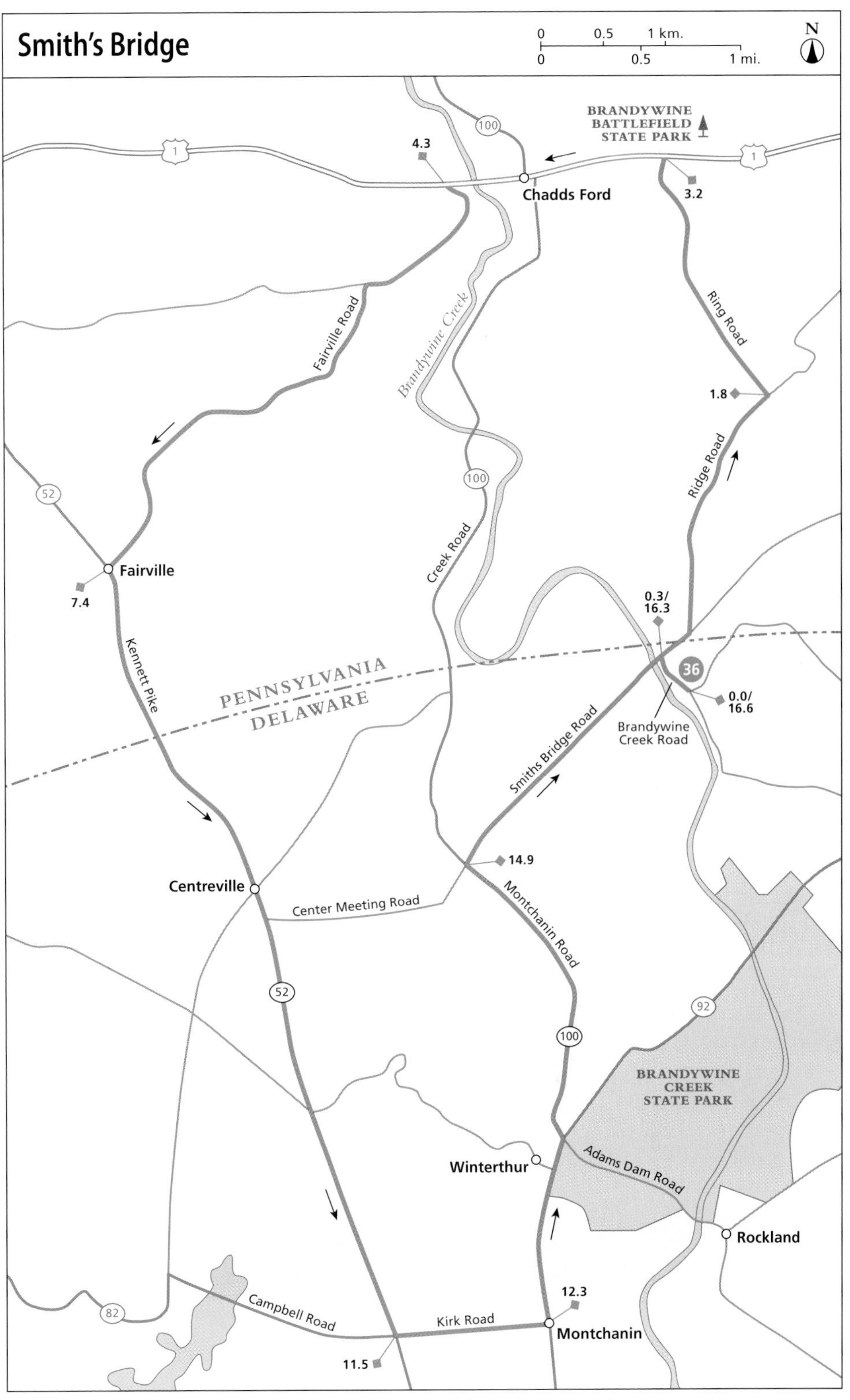

Smith's Bridge
0 0.5 1 km.
0 0.5 1 mi.
N
BRANDYWINE BATTLEFIELD STATE PARK
4.3
100
1
Chadds Ford
3.2
Brandywine Creek
Fairville Road
Ring Road
1.8
Ridge Road
52
Creek Road
Fairville
7.4
0.3/ 16.3
36
0.0/ 16.6
Kennett Pike
PENNSYLVANIA
DELAWARE
Smiths Bridge Road
Brandywine Creek Road
14.9
Centreville
Center Meeting Road
Montchanin Road
92
BRANDYWINE CREEK STATE PARK
Winterthur
Adams Dam Road
Rockland
82
Campbell Road
Kirk Road
12.3
Montchanin
11.5

16.3 Turn right onto Brandywine Creek Road.

16.6 Arrive at the Woodlawn Trustees parking lot on Brandywine Creek.

RIDE INFORMATION

Events/Attractions

The Brandywine River Museum (1 Hoffman Mill Rd., Chadds Ford, PA; (610) 388-2700, brandywinemuseum.org) owns a collection of paintings by Andrew Wyeth and other artists from the area. The museum also maintains the N.C. Wyeth House & Studio, which N.C. Wyeth purchased in 1911. An admission fee is charged.

Winterthur Museum (5105 Kennett Pike, Wilmington, DE; (800) 448-3883, winterthur.org) is a museum of decorative arts and antiques founded by Henry Francis du Pont. The museum is in the 175-room house in which du

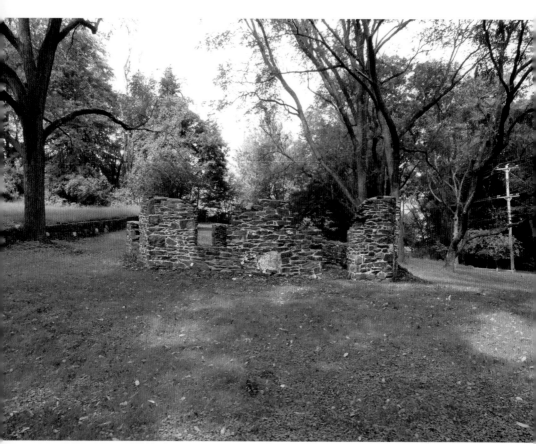

Archie's Corner (old octagonal schoolhouse)

Pont was born. There is also a decorative garden on the grounds. An admission fee is charged.

Restrooms

Mile 4.1: There are a number of businesses in Chadds Ford, PA with restrooms.

Mile 9.0: There are a number of businesses in Centreville, DE with restrooms.

Maps

Delorme Pennsylvania Atlas & Gazetteer: Page 85, F7

Smith's Bridge has gone through many changes since it was originally constructed in 1839. The bridge had to be rehabilitated in the 1950s to accommodate heavier traffic. The bridge was destroyed by fire in 1961 and was rebuilt without a cover in 1962. A cover was added to the bridge again in 2002.

Newark Ramble

Newark, Delaware , is the home of the University of Delaware. Newark is also the hub for an extensive network of highways with bicycle lanes and quiet country roads, which makes it a good place for a ride.

Start: Parking lot of Paper Mill Park, Newark, DE

Length: 20.3 miles out and back

Approximate riding time: 2.0 hours

Best bike: Road bike

Terrain and trail surface: The ride is on paved roads with some hills.

Traffic and hazards: Most of the route is either on quiet country roads or on highways with paved shoulders. Use caution when biking through Newark.

Getting there: Drive south on I-95 past Wilmington, DE, and take exit 3 to DE 273 West toward Newark. Drive 1.8 miles, then exit right to Red Mill Road. At the bottom of the ramp, turn left onto Red Mill Road and drive 4.3 miles. Red Mill Road turns into Polly Drummond Hill Road, and Paper Mill Park will be on your left. GPS: N 39 44.32 / W75 43.35

THE RIDE

To start the ride, head north from the parking lot of Paper Mill Park, turn left onto Polly Drummond Hill Road, and then turn left again onto Paper Mill Road. You will cross some rolling hills on Paper Mill Road and then gradually descend into Newark itself.

After you cross White Clay Creek in Newark, turn right at the light onto Cleveland Avenue. This is the trickiest part of the ride, since you're riding uphill in traffic. When you reach the top of the climb, get out of traffic by turning right onto Wilbur Street and left onto Prospect Avenue. You will then proceed westward through the outskirts of town until you reach DE 896. Turn right on DE 896 and climb the hill (about 1.3 miles long). Look for the water tower at the top of the hill, and then continue on the ridge to Hopkins Road.

Turn right onto Hopkins Road and descend the hill back to White Clay Creek. There will be a short, sharp climb on the opposite bank of the creek. Turn left onto Thompson Station Road. After 0.3 mile, the road will pass a parking lot and narrow considerably. On weekends, there will be a barrier across the road to block motor traffic. Walk your bike around the barrier if it is there and continue on. The road will gradually climb back up to ridge level. When you reach the top of the ridge at the stop sign, continue straight for 1.8 miles until you reach Little Baltimore Road. Turn right onto Little Baltimore Road and continue 0.8 mile farther to North Star Road. At this intersection, Woodside Farm Creamery should be within sight to your right. This would be a good time to take a break and enjoy an ice cream cone in season.

When you are done, continue south on North Star Road (left from the parking lot). There will be some rolling hills, but the general trend will be downhill. When you get south of Paper Mill Road, the road becomes Upper Pike Creek Road, and before long you will see the remains of some lime kilns to your left. Continue down the road until you reach New Linden Hill Road and then turn right and climb back up to ridge level. When New Linden Hill Road ends in a T intersection, turn right onto Polly Drummond Hill Road, which will take you back to the parking lot at Paper Mill Park.

Bike Shops

Bike Line, 212 E. Main St., Newark, DE; (302) 368-8779; bikeline.com Bike Line is the world's largest Trek bicycle retailer, with stores throughout the lower Delaware Valley. From Paper Mill Park, turn left onto Polly Drummond Hill Road, and then turn left at the light onto Paper Mill Road. Drive 4.4 miles on Paper Mill Road to East Main Street in Newark. Turn right onto Main Street and drive 0.1 mile. Bike Line is on the right side of Main Street.

Wooden Wheels, 141 E. Main St., Newark, DE; (302) 368-2453; woodenwheels.com Wooden Wheels is a family-owned bike shop that has been in business for over 30 years. From Paper Mill Park, turn left onto Polly Drummond Hill Road, and then turn left at the light onto Paper Mill Road. Drive 4.4 miles on Paper Mill Road to East Main Street in Newark. Turn right onto Main Street, drive 0.1 mile, and turn left onto Haines Street. Wooden Wheels is on the left side of Haines Street.

MILES AND DIRECTIONS

0.0 Start at Paper Mill Park; head north on Sunrise Drive toward Polly Drummond Hill Road.

0.1 Turn left onto Polly Drummond Hill Road.

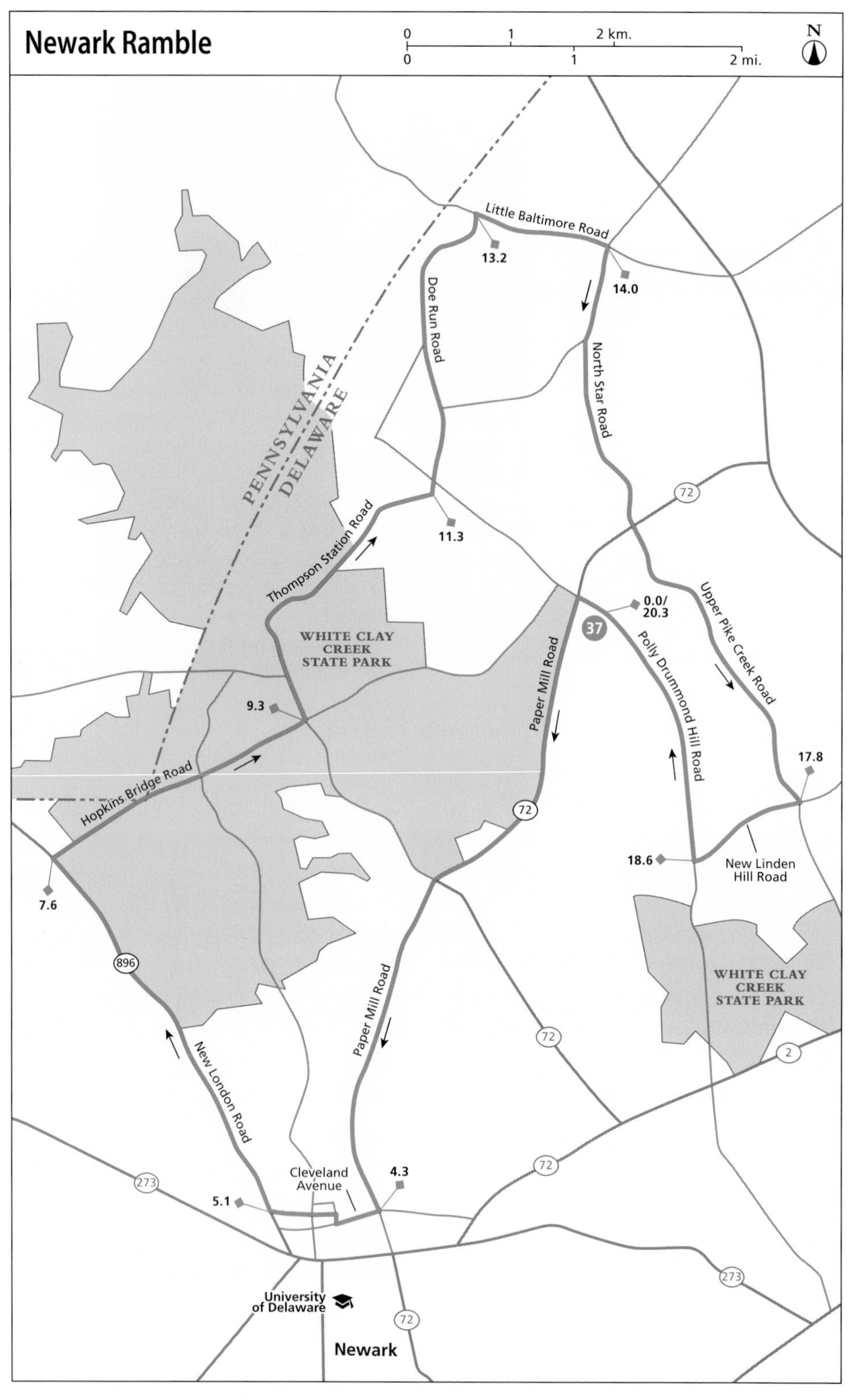
Newark Ramble
0
1
2 km.
0
1
2 mi.
N
Little Baltimore Road
13.2
14.0
Doe Run Road
North Star Road
PENNSYLVANIA
DELAWARE
Thompson Station Road
11.3
72
0.0/
20.3
37
Upper Pike Creek Road
Polly Drummond Hill Road
Paper Mill Road
WHITE CLAY
CREEK
STATE PARK
9.3
Hopkins Bridge Road
17.8
72
18.6
New Linden
Hill Road
7.6
896
WHITE CLAY
CREEK
STATE PARK
Paper Mill Road
72
2
New London Road
273
72
Cleveland
Avenue
4.3
5.1
273
University
of Delaware
72
Newark

0.2 Turn left onto Paper Mill Road.

4.3 Turn right onto East Cleveland Avenue.

4.6 Turn right onto Wilbur Street.

4.7 Turn left onto Prospect Avenue.

4.8 Turn right at North College Avenue, then left onto Ray Street.

5.1 Turn right onto DE 896.

7.6 Turn right onto Hopkins Road.

9.3 Turn left onto Thompson Station Road. There might be barriers across the road at 9.6 miles and 10.5 miles, because the road is closed to motor vehicles on the weekends. If the barriers are across the road, walk the bike around the barriers.

13.2 Turn right onto Little Baltimore Road.

Woodside Farm Creamery

14.0 Turn right onto North Star Road.

14.1 Woodside Farm Creamery.

17.8 Turn right onto New Linden Hill Road.

18.6 Turn right onto Polly Drummond Hill Road.

20.2 Turn left onto Sunrise Drive.

20.3 Arrive at Paper Mill Park.

The mascot of the University of Delaware is YoUDee, the fighting Blue Hen. In the Revolutionary War, troops from Delaware became known as Blue Hens, both for the chickens that they used in cockfighting and for their fighting prowess.

Old Eastburns-Jeanes Mining Complex

Lime Kilns

The lime kilns that you see on the ride are a product of the area's agricultural past. When a plot of land is farmed, the soil tends to become acidic over time. To maintain the fertility of the soil, farmers must occasionally neutralize this acidity, and the favored way to neutralize soil acidity is to spread lime (or calcium oxide) on the fields. To get lime, you must quarry limestone and then "burn" or heat the limestone to convert the limestone into lime that can be spread on fields. Through the 19th century, most lime in the United States was produced in the general area in which the lime was consumed, and this was the case with the lime that was produced by the Eastburn-Jeanes Mining Complex. At its peak, the business employed about forty people and produced limestone that was used as far away as southern Delaware. By the end of the 19th century, however, small operations such as Eastburn-Jeanes were driven out of business by larger companies that could produce lime much more inexpensively.

RIDE INFORMATION

Events/Attractions

Woodside Farm Creamery, 1310 Little Baltimore Rd., Hockessin, DE; (302) 239-9847; woodsidefarmcreamery.com: The creamery serves ice cream that is made on the premises from milk that is produced on the adjoining farm. Flavors range from Vanilla to Motor Oil (coffee with caramel swirls).

Restrooms

Start/end: Paper Mill Park has toilets and water.
Mile 14.1: Woodside Farm Creamery has toilets.

Maps

Delorme Pennsylvania Atlas & Gazetteer: Page 85, H5

Blackbird Loop

This ride travels through a mixture of farmland and shady woodland. Although there is some development visible along this route, much of the route travels through the Blackbird State Forest and is one of the quieter rides in the book.

Start: Parking lot of Smyrna Municipal Park, Smyrna, DE

Length: 29.6 miles round-trip

Approximate riding time: 2.5 hours

Best bike: Road bike

Terrain and trail surface: The ride is on paved roads and mostly flat.

Traffic and hazards: The roads are not very busy. There are not very many places to stop, so be sure to take water and snacks with you.

Getting there: Drive south on I-95 past Wilmington, DE, and take exit 4A to DE 1 South. Continue on DE 1 for 27.2 miles and take exit 119A to US 13 South. Continue on US 13 South for 2.3 miles and turn right onto East Glenwood Avenue. In 0.3 mile, turn right onto North Main Street. The park is on your right in 0.4 mile. GPS: N39 18.35 / W75 36.94

THE RIDE

The town of Smyrna was founded in 1716 on the southern bank of Duck Creek, near the fork of Green's Branch, which is very close to where this park is located. To start the ride turn right onto North Main Street from the parking lot, bike 0.3 mile, and turn left onto Duck Creek Parkway. The parkway runs past the school complex and along the northern edge of town, so traffic is generally light when school isn't in session. Bike 1.5 miles until you reach North Main Street in Clayton. Turn right, cross the railroad tracks, and then turn right again onto Clayton Avenue. Clayton Avenue ends in a T intersection at DE 15, which will take you out of town.

After 0.7 mile on DE 15, turn left onto Clayton Delaney Road. This road will take you in a westerly direction through farmland with occasional wooded areas. Continue westward until you pass into Maryland, where Clayton Delaney Road becomes Maryland Line Road. The route continues north on Black Bottom Road, which is 1.3 miles west of the Maryland border. You can make a side trip to the Massey Air Museum by riding 1.0 miles west of the intersection of Black Bottom Road and Maryland Line Road, and then ride back to continue the route.

After 2.6 miles, you will reach the small town of Golts, MD. There is not much in town apart from a railroad track and a tavern, and the tavern's closed on Sunday. Continue north on Golts Caldwell Road for about a mile, and then turn right onto Vandyke Road.

Vandyke Road turns back toward the railroad tracks. By the time the road runs alongside the tracks, you will be back in Delaware. When the road ends in a T intersection, turn right onto Vandyke Greenspring Road to recross the railroad tracks, and then turn left at the first opportunity onto Ebenezer Church Road. In a mile, the road will pass its namesake church, cross the tracks again, and intersect with DE 15. Continue straight north on DE 15 for 0.5 mile and turn right onto Caldwell Corner Road. From this point, it's pretty much open farmland and residential housing for 2 miles until you enter the town of Townsend.

Ebenezer Church

When you reach Townsend, turn right onto Commerce Road (just after crossing the train tracks) and continue south out of town (and over the train tracks again). In 2.0 miles, turn left onto Grears Corner Road, which will take you to Blackbird Station Road. Turn left onto Blackbird Station Road. The road will curve from east to southeast and become Massey Church Road. This road travels past woods, farms, marshland, and residential development. When the road ends in a T intersection at Vandyke-Greenspring Road, turn left, and then turn right when Vandyke-Greenspring Road ends in a T intersection at Duck Creek Road. Duck Creek Road becomes North Main Street in Smyrna and will take you directly back to the park.

Bike Shops

Bike Line, 486 Middletown Warwick Rd, Middletown, DE; (302) 285-0134; bikeline.com Bike Line is the world's largest Trek bicycle retailer, with stores throughout the lower Delaware Valley. From Smyrna Municipal Park, turn right onto North Main Street and drive 1.6 miles to US 13. Turn left onto US 13, drive 0.8 mile, and take the ramp on your left to DE 1. Drive on DE 1 for 8.9 miles, and take exit 136 to DE 299. Turn left at the end of the ramp and drive 2.7 miles through town. Cross the railroad tracks on the west side of town, drive past Peterson Road, and turn right into the Food Lion shopping center (just before you reach US 130). The shop is at the northern end of the shopping center.

MILES AND DIRECTIONS

0.0 Start in the parking lot of Smyrna Municipal Park, Smyrna, DE; head west on North Main Street.

0.3 Turn left onto Duck Creek Parkway.

1.8 Turn right onto Main Street in Clayton, DE.

1.9 Turn right onto Clayton Avenue.

2.1 Turn right onto SR 15.

2.8 Turn left onto Clayton Delaney Road.

8.4 Right at the fork to stay on Clayton Delaney Road.

8.7 Right onto Delaney Maryland Road. Delaney Maryland Road becomes Maryland Line Road when the road crosses into Maryland.

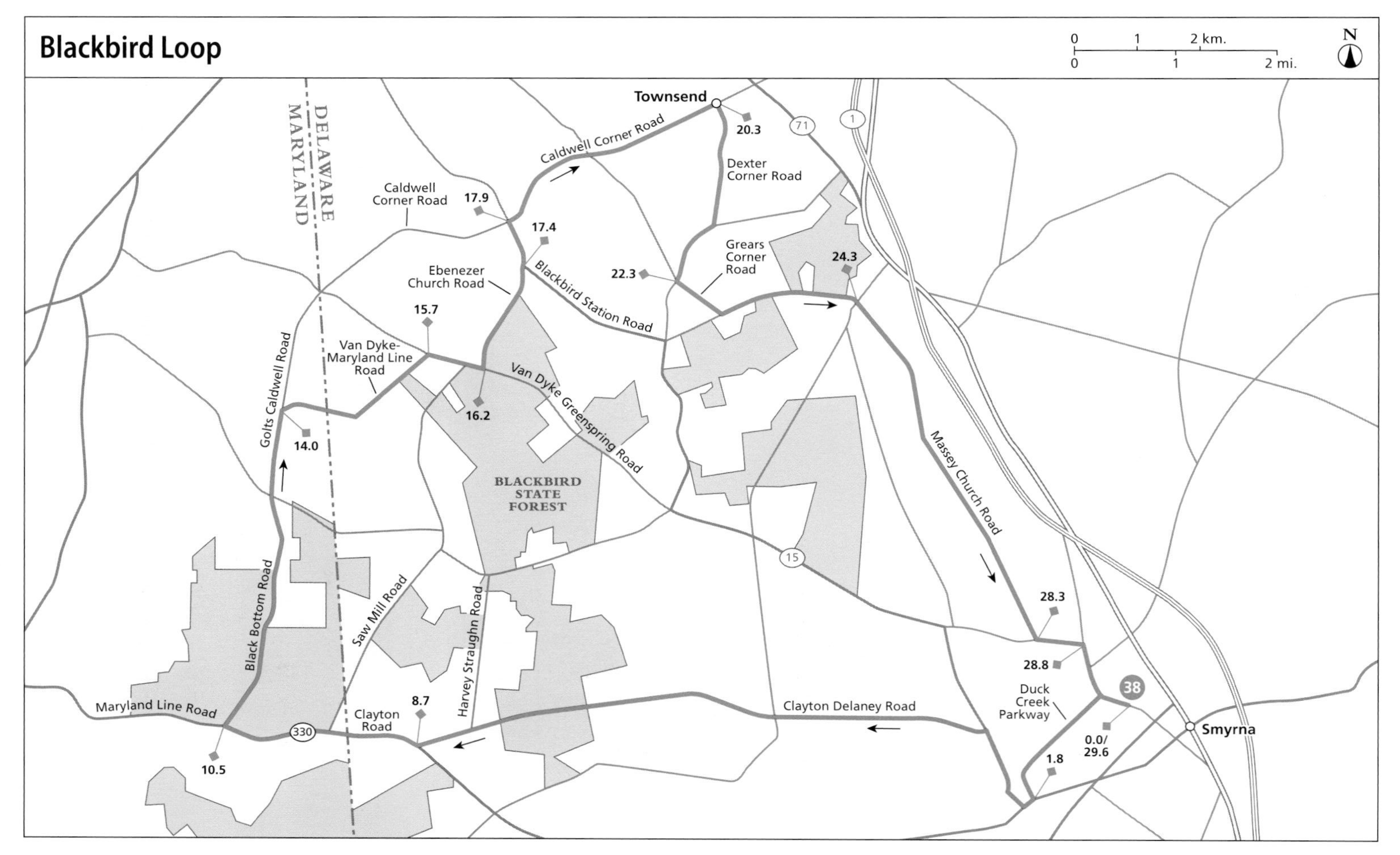
Blackbird Loop
0
1
2 km.
0
1
2 mi.
N
Townsend
Smyrna
DELAWARE
MARYLAND
BLACKBIRD STATE FOREST
Caldwell Corner Road
Dexter Corner Road
Grears Corner Road
Blackbird Station Road
Ebenezer Church Road
Van Dyke-Maryland Line Road
Van Dyke Greenspring Road
Golts Caldwell Road
Black Bottom Road
Maryland Line Road
Saw Mill Road
Harvey Straughn Road
Clayton Road
Clayton Delaney Road
Massey Church Road
Duck Creek Parkway
71
1
15
330
38
0.0/
29.6
1.8
8.7
10.5
14.0
15.7
16.2
17.4
17.9
20.3
22.3
24.3
28.3
28.8

10.5 Turn right onto Black Bottom Road. Massey Air Museum is 1.0 miles further west from this point on Maryland Line Road.

13.1 Turn slightly right onto Golts Caldwell Road (turn left to go to the tavern).

14.0 Turn right onto Vandyke Road, which becomes Van Dyke–Maryland Line Road when you cross into Delaware.

15.7 Turn right onto Vandyke Greenspring Road.

16.2 Turn left onto Ebenezer Church Road.

17.4 Continue straight onto SR 15.

17.9 Turn right onto Caldwell Corner Road.

Old World War II airplane

Settling Territorial Disputes

It is (relatively) well known that the Mason-Dixon Line defines the boundary between Pennsylvania and Maryland. It is much less well known that Mason and Dixon also surveyed and marked the western border of Delaware. In fact, the reason why the expert survey team of Mason and Dixon were commissioned to draw these boundaries was to settle once and for all the numerous territorial disputes between the Penn family (the proprietary governors of Pennsylvania and Delaware) and the Calvert family (the proprietary governors of Maryland). Curiously enough, the disputes were almost inevitably resolved in the favor of the Penns.

Maryland's original charter covered all the land between the Potomac and the 40th parallel. A problem arose in 1664, when the Duke of York (the future King James II of England) sent a fleet of ships to drive the Dutch from the area that is now known as Delaware. This area was subsequently claimed by the Duke of York as a part of the province of New York.

Another problem arose in 1681, when Charles II of England (the brother of the Duke of York) granted to William Penn a charter for Pennsylvania with the understanding that the proposed site of Philadelphia was north of the 40th parallel. It was soon discovered that this was not so. The situation was later complicated when the Duke of York leased his claim to Delaware to William Penn. It took several decades of disputes and sporadic violence before the Penns and Calverts signed a provisional agreement to divide their territories in 1732 (which was subsequently disowned by the Calverts). It wasn't until 1760, when King George II ordered the Calverts to accept the settlement, that Mason and Dixon were commissioned to fix the border once and for all.

20.3 Turn right onto Commerce Street.

22.3 Turn left onto Grears Corner Road.

22.9 Turn left onto Blackbird Station Road.

24.3 Continue straight onto Massey Church Road.

28.3 Turn left onto Vandyke Greenspring Road.

28.8 Turn right onto Duck Creek Road.

29.6 Finish at Smyrna Municipal Park, Smyrna, DE.

RIDE INFORMATION

Events/Attractions

Blackbird State Forest, 502 Blackbird Forest Rd., Smyrna, DE; (302) 653-6505; dda.delaware.gov/forestry/forest.shtml, consists of nine tracts in southwestern New Castle County and northwestern Kent County in Delaware. The forest is open for a variety of recreational activities, including hiking, mountain biking, and horseback riding on its trails and fire roads.

Massey Air Museum, 33541 Maryland Line Rd., Massey, MD, (410) 928-5270, masseyaero.org, is a living airport-museum reminiscent of rural airports of the early twentieth century. The museum features vintage airplanes and sponsors fly-ins and special events throughout the year. The museum is 1.0 miles west of the intersection of Maryland Line Road and Black Bottom Road at mile 10.5 of the route.

One of the disputes between the Calverts and the Penns was the location of the southern border of Delaware. Unfortunately for the Calverts, the map that the Calverts submitted to the court mistakenly used the border that was claimed by the Penns. The Calverts subsequently petitioned in vain to have the court reject their own map.

Restrooms

Start/end: Smyrna Municipal Park has toilets and water.

Mile 20.3: There are a number of businesses in Townsend with bathrooms.

Maps

Delorme Maryland Delaware Atlas & Gazetteer: Page 62

39

White Clay Creek State Park

White Clay Creek State Park contains the most extensive network of mountain bike trails in northern Delaware. The park is known for its fast single-track and its mixed landscape (woods and meadow). Note: White Clay Creek State Park charges a park admission fee for vehicles for most of the year.

Start: Possum Hill Trailhead, White Clay Creek State Park

Length: 8.6-mile out-and-back loop

Approximate riding time: 1.5 hours

Best bike: Mountain bike

Terrain and trail surface: The trails are mostly single track (that is, trail that is just wide enough for a single biker), though there are some wider sections available. The trails have the usual obstacles (rocks and roots, with the occasional washout). The loops tend to circle around local high points, and each loop features a cutoff across its middle that bikers can use to make a shorter loop. Even so, the maximum grade of these trails is over 20 percent.

Traffic and hazards: There are a couple of road crossings on the route that is designated here. Hiking is allowed on these trails, and there is no designated direction for mountain biking on all but the most technical trails, so be careful and alert.

Getting there: Drive south on I-95 past Wilmington, DE, and take exit 3 to DE 273 West toward Newark. Drive 1.8 miles, then exit right to Red Mill Road. At the bottom of the ramp, turn left onto Red Mill Road and drive 2.8 miles. Turn right onto Fox Den Road and drive 1.0 mile to Paper Mill Road. Turn right, and drive 0.3 mile to Smiths Mill Road. Turn left onto Smiths Mill Road and drive 0.3 mile farther. The parking lot will be on your left. GPS: N 39 43.68 / W75 44.12

THE RIDE

With its well-maintained trails, varied terrain, and miles and miles of interconnected loops, White Clay Creek is a great place to do some mountain biking. Most of the trails are not very technical, but you can find some man-made and natural features that offer challenges, so both novice and experienced moun-

tain bikers should be able to find a trail to meet their needs. Our chosen route uses the northernmost three loops on which mountain biking is allowed in White Clay Creek State Park. Our first loop will be on the Bryan's Field Trail, which is just south of the trailhead. When the trail forks, turn left to bike clockwise around the loop. The trail descends gradually and crosses cleared pasture and fields before heading into the woods. You will soon pass a sign that points to the cutoff and to the "Mason Dixon Marker." The trail then continues to descend until it crosses a stream. After you cross the stream, turn right to continue on the trail and climb back up to the ridge. There is an overlook on the stream where you can stop and rest if you like. After you reach the top of the ridge, there will be a skills trail to your left, which features a number of natural and man-made technical features that you can use to develop your

Single-track trail going past a house

mountain biking skills. After the skills trail entrance, the trail rolls a bit before passing the other end of the cutoff, and then climbs back up to the parking lot.

If you were OK with the Bryan's Field Trail, continue through the parking lot to the road on which you entered and turn left. This road is part of the Tri-Valley Connector trail that connects the mountain bike trails of White Clay Creek State Park with each other. When you reach the Whitley Farms Loop, turn left. The trail will run around the Nine Foot Road trailhead area and across a meadow before the trail reenters the woods and descends a long, steep hill.

When the trail reaches the bottom of the hill, it will run more or less parallel with a road until you reach the Tri-Valley Connector (which is the cutoff trail for the Whitley Farms Loop). Turn left to cross the road on the connector, and then turn left onto the David English Loop when you reach it. This section of the David English Loop roller-coasters a bit until it passes the park office (and the cutoff), and then gradually climbs back up to ridge level again. The other end of the cutoff is at the top of the hill. Past that point, the trail passes a pair of lakes before descending quickly to the Tri-Valley Connector.

Bike Shops

Bike Line, 212 E. Main St., Newark, DE; (302) 368-8779; bikeline.com
Bike Line is the world's largest Trek bicycle retailer, with stores throughout the lower Delaware Valley. From the parking lot, turn right onto Smiths Mill Road and drive 0.3 mile to Paper Mill Road. Turn right onto Paper Mill Road and drive 3.6 miles to East Main Street in Newark. Turn right and drive 0.1 mile. Bike Line is on the right side of Main Street.

Wooden Wheels, 141 E. Main St., Newark, DE; (302) 368-2453; woodenwheels.com Wooden Wheels is a family-owned bike shop that has been in business for over 30 years. From the parking lot, turn right onto Smiths Mill Road and drive 0.3 mile to Paper Mill Road. Turn right onto Paper Mill Road and drive 3.6 miles to East Main Street in Newark. Turn right, drive 0.1 mile, and turn left onto Haines Street. Wooden Wheels is on the left side of Haines Street.

From this point, turn left on the connector, cross the road back to the Whitley Farms Loop, and turn left. When the trail branches, turn left to continue on the loop (or turn right to take the cutoff back to the top of the ridge). The climb on the loop is steep at first and then becomes more gradual as it passes through woods and meadow. When you reach the top of the ridge, turn right on the Bryan's Field Connector to return to the Tri-Valley Connector and the Possum Hill trailhead.

There is a lot more to see here so if you enjoyed these loops, you can also try the loops in the Middle Run Valley Natural Area and the Judge Morris Estate

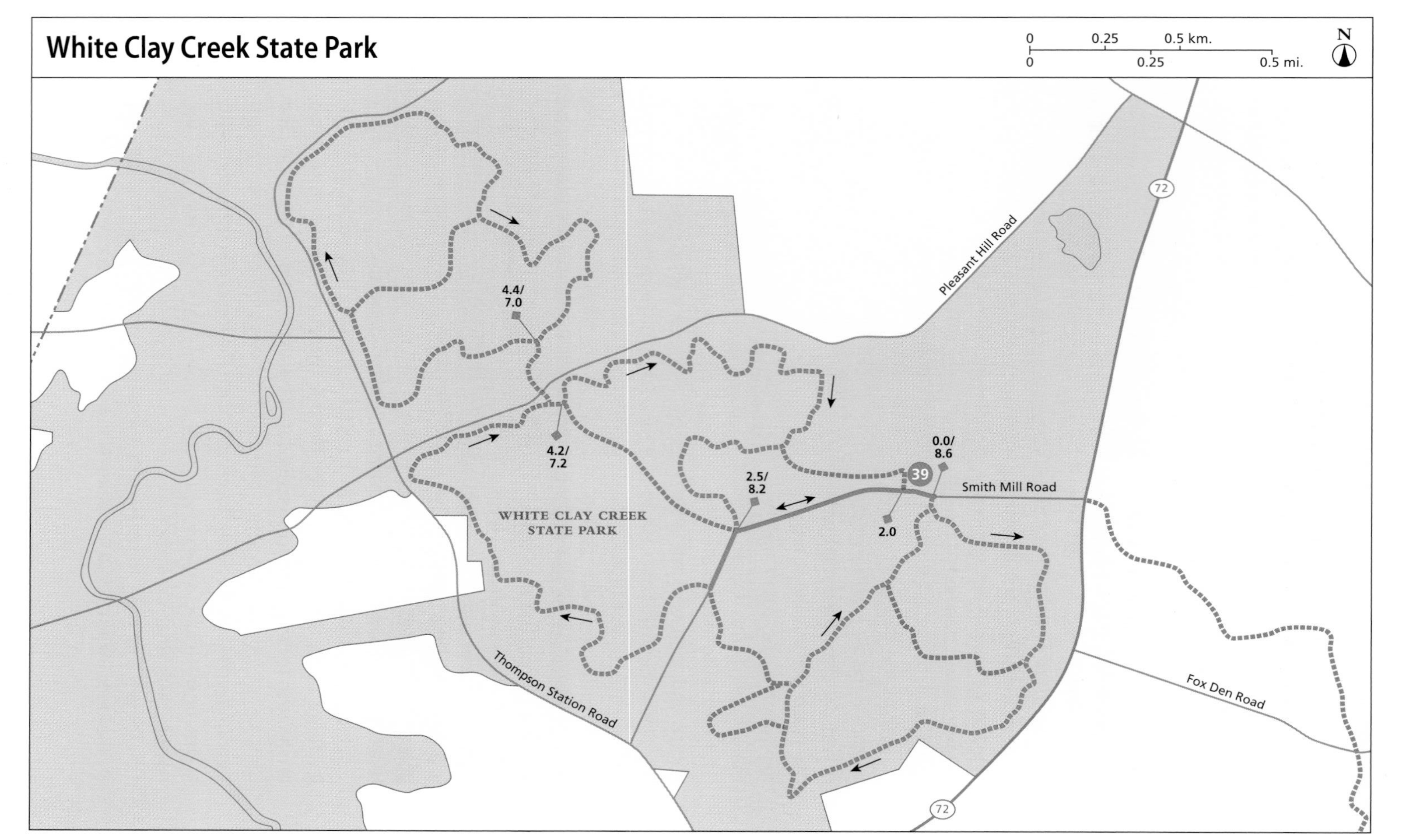
White Clay Creek State Park
0
0.25
0.5 km.
0
0.25
0.5 mi.
N
72
Pleasant Hill Road
4.4/
7.0
4.2/
7.2
2.5/
8.2
0.0/
8.6
39
2.0
Smith Mill Road
WHITE CLAY CREEK
STATE PARK
Thompson Station Road
Fox Den Road
72

unit to the southeast. Biking is not allowed on the trails in the Carpenter unit of White Clay Creek State Park except for the Pomeroy Trail that runs along White Clay Creek.

MILES AND DIRECTIONS

0.0 Start in the parking lot at the Possum Hill trailhead; ride south to Bryan's Field Trail, turn left, ride the trail clockwise, and return to the parking lot.

2.0 Ride north to the road (the Tri-Valley Connector), turn left, and ride to Whitley Farms Trail.

2.5 Turn left onto Whitley Farms Trail and ride the trail clockwise to its next intersection with the Tri-Valley Connector.

The Dam That Was Never Built

White Clay Creek State Park is an unusually extensive area of protected land for this area of the country. The size of the park can be attributed to the dam and reservoir that never came to be and to the efforts of the many concerned citizens who fought the dam.

In 1960 the Corps of Engineers proposed that a dam and reservoir be built on White Clay Creek to provide for the anticipated future water needs of the area. The DuPont Company in particular was concerned about having enough water for planned plant expansions and acquired land in the area to prevent residential development from interfering with the construction of a reservoir.

Opposition to the reservoir was not immediate, but when it came, it was widespread. Many opponents questioned the projections of population growth that were used to justify the project (which, in retrospect, had the population of New Castle County growing at twice the rate it actually increased). Pennsylvania residents were worried that the project would result in unsightly mudflats in their area, while Delaware businesses would be the main beneficiaries. Opponents also argued that future needs could be easily met by sharing existing water resources, rather than by developing new ones. By 1984, the DuPont Company realized that the opposition was too great, and DuPont generously donated the land to the states of Delaware and Pennsylvania to use as a preserve. So in the end, the existence of White Clay Creek State Park owes much to the dam that was never built.

Bridge over White Clay Creek

4.2 Turn left onto the Tri-Valley Connector and ride north to the David English Trail. There will be a road crossing between the Whitley Farms Trail and the David English Trail.

4.4 Turn left onto the David English Trail, ride the trail clockwise, and return to the Tri-Valley Connector.

The "Mason Dixon Marker" on the Bryan's Field Loop is a stone that marks the base point from which Mason and Dixon defined the boundary between Pennsylvania and Maryland. This stone is on the same latitude as the boundary.

7.0 Turn left onto the Tri-Valley Connector and ride south back to the Whitley Farms Trail.

7.2 Turn left onto the Whitley Farms Trail and ride the trail clockwise to the Bryan's Field Connector.

8.2 Turn left onto the Bryan's Field Connector.

8.6 Finish in the parking lot at the Possum Hill trailhead.

RIDE INFORMATION

Events/Attractions

White Clay Creek State Park, 750 Thompson Station Rd., Newark, DE; (302) 368-6900; destateparks.com/park/white-clay-creek, features extensive trails for hiking and mountain biking.

Restrooms

Start/end: There is a portable toilet at the Possum Hill trailhead.
Mile 2.7: There is a portable toilet at the Nine Foot Road trailhead.

Maps

Delorme Pennsylvania Atlas & Gazetteer: Page 85, G5

Crossing Delaware Ride

Cross-state rides are very common bicycle events in many states. Some of them can measure hundreds of miles. Delaware, however, is a very small state so this ride will take you all the way across the state of Delaware in a single day. Twice. At just over 30 miles it is a nice ride anybody should be able to enjoy.

Start: Battery Park, Delaware City, DE

Length: 33.3 miles round-trip

Approximate riding time: 2.5 hours

Best bike: Road bike

Terrain and trail surface: The terrain is paved and mostly flat. The main climbs are on the bridges over the Chesapeake and Delaware Canal.

Traffic and hazards: The roads are mostly quiet. There are brief segments on busy highways with paved shoulders or bike lanes.

Getting there: Drive south on I-95 past Wilmington, DE, and take exit 5A to DE 141 South. Continue on DE 141 until it ends at DE 273, and go straight through the intersection and continue until the street ends in a T intersection at DE 9. Turn right and follow DE 9 to Delaware City. Turn left at the stoplight onto Clinton Street and follow Clinton Street until it ends at Battery Park. GPS: N39 34.767 / W75 35.257

THE RIDE

The small state of Delaware has a lot to offer bicyclists. The roads are mostly flat and there are a lot of quiet roads to explore. This ride will take you across the state into Maryland and back all in just over 30 miles. Along the way you will see some of the parks and wildlife areas along the canal that crosses the state. To start the ride leave Battery Park in Delaware City and ride west on Clinton Street. Continue on Clinton Street across DE 9 and out the west side of town. Ride on this road until the road ends in a T intersection at US 13 (a four-lane highway). Cross the highway carefully to get to the paved shoulder on the other side, and turn left onto the paved shoulder. When the highway crosses the Chesapeake and Delaware Canal on the St. Georges bridge, the highway will narrow to one lane, and there will be a dedicated bike lane on the outside of the bridge. There is an exit ramp before you get to the bridge, so be careful. The Chesapeake and Delaware Canal connects Chesapeake Bay with the Delaware River and has been an important route of commerce since it was finished in 1829.

When you get to the other side of the bridge, take the first exit ramp at the base of the bridge. The ramp circles back 180 degrees and ends at Lorewood Grove Road. Turn left onto this road and bike 4.8 miles to Summit, where the road ends in a T intersection. Turn left at the T intersection, and bike 0.6 mile to US 301/DE 896, which is another four-lane highway. Turn right and bike on the shoulder until you reach the stoplight at Bethel Church Road. Carefully make your way into the left-turn lane and turn left at the stoplight. Ride 1 more mile, and then turn right at the roundabout to stay on Bethel Church Road. From this point, simply ride 1.8 more miles, and you will reach the Maryland border and complete your first crossing of Delaware. You can choose to turn around at this

View of the canal from Chesapeake City

point, or you can ride 2 more miles to Chesapeake City, MD, and stop at a cafe or restaurant to celebrate.

When you are done in Chesapeake City, simply leave town the same way that you came in (on 2nd Street, which becomes Bethel Church Road). When you get back to the roundabout, turn left and continue back to US 301/DE 896. Turn left at the stoplight and recross the canal at the Summit Bridge. At the base of the bridge on the other side of the canal, there will be another stop-light at DE 71. Turn right at this light. DE 71 turns back and circles around the south side of Lums Pond State Park before heading north. Lums Pond State Park is built around the largest freshwater lake in Delaware and is a great place to do some boating, fishing, hiking, or camping. They also have some nice mountain bike trails.

Bike Shops

Performance Bicycle, 1267 Churchmans Rd., Center Pointe Plaza, Newark, DE; (302) 266-8330 Performance Bicycle is a chain store that specializes in discount bikes, parts, and accessories. Performance Bicycle also provides repair services for all makes. From Delaware City, drive north DE 9 to Hamburg Road (about 5 miles), and then drive west to DE 1 (1 mile farther). Drive 5.0 miles north on DE 1 to the Churchmans Road exit, turn right onto Churchmans Road, and drive 0.6 mile. Performance Bicycle is in the Center Pointe Plaza shopping center on the right.

Continue on DE 71 until you cross a set of train tracks, and then turn hard right onto Kirkwood St. Georges Road. This is a very tricky intersection because the train tracks are at a bad angle, and the turn doubles back on itself, so be careful.

Continue on Kirkwood St. Georges Road for 2.7 miles. When you reach the St. Georges (US 13) bridge again, turn right onto Main Street and continue 2 blocks to Delaware Street. Turn left onto Delaware Street and ride 0.7 mile to the stop sign at Cox Neck Road. Turn right onto Cox Neck Road, which will take you directly back to Delaware City.

MILES AND DIRECTIONS

0.0 Start at Battery Park, Delaware City, DE; head southwest on Clinton Street.

4.0 Turn left onto the paved shoulder on US 13 and cross the bridge over the canal.

5.4 Exit right onto Lorewood Grove Road (the turn is at the base of the bridge).

10.2 Turn left onto Old Summit Bridge Road.

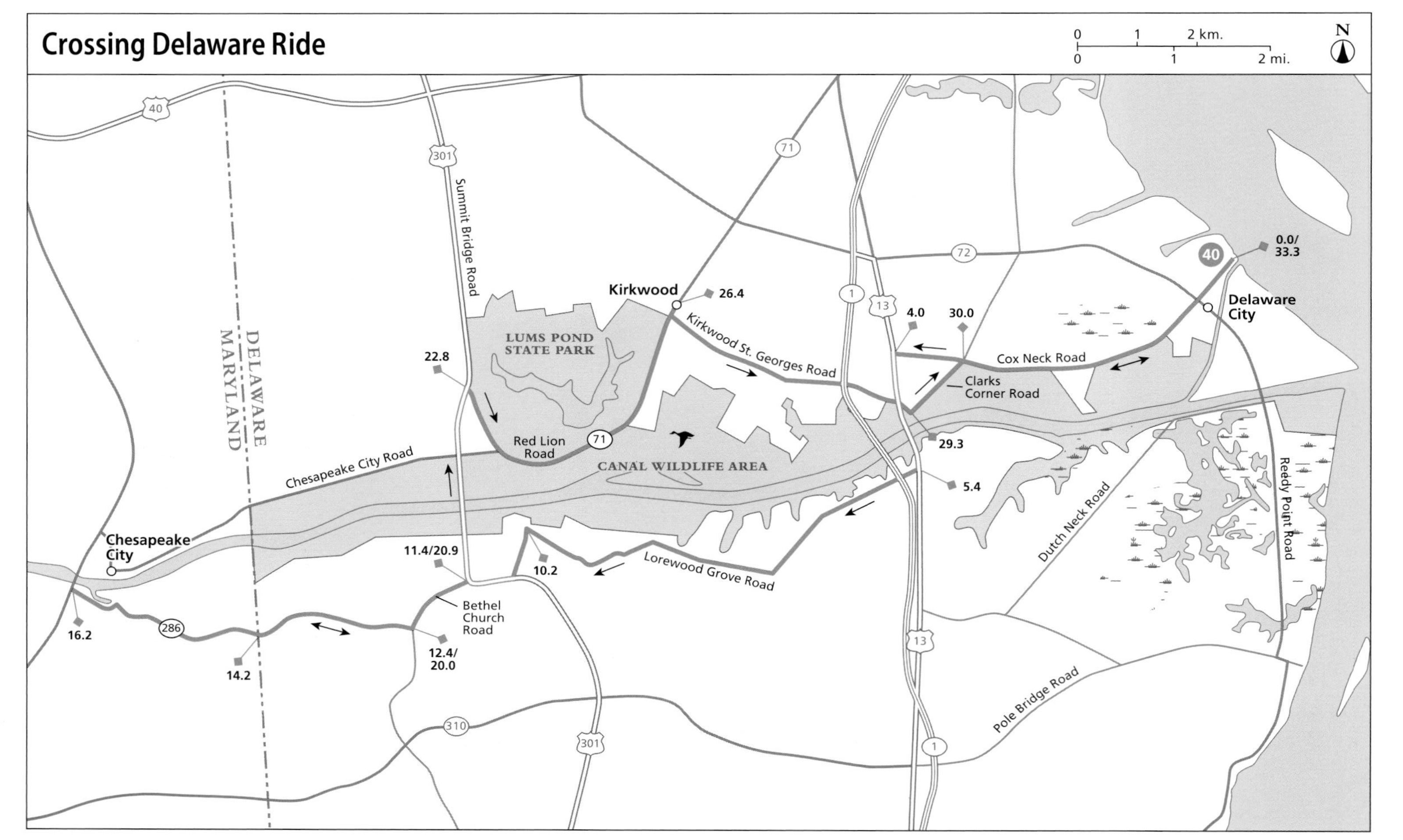
Crossing Delaware Ride
0 1 2 km.
0 1 2 mi.
N
Summit Bridge Road
Kirkwood
26.4
Kirkwood St. Georges Road
4.0
30.0
Cox Neck Road
Clarks
Corner Road
0.0/
33.3
Delaware
City
LUMS POND
STATE PARK
22.8
Red Lion
Road
CANAL WILDLIFE AREA
29.3
5.4
Dutch Neck Road
Reedy Point Road
DELAWARE
MARYLAND
Chesapeake City Road
Chesapeake
City
11.4/20.9
10.2
Lorewood Grove Road
Bethel
Church
Road
16.2
14.2
12.4/
20.0
Pole Bridge Road
40
301
71
72
1
13
286
310

10.8 Turn right onto US 301/DE 896 North.

11.4 Turn left onto Bethel Church Road.

12.4 Turn right at roundabout to stay on Bethel Church Road

14.2 Continue past the border into Maryland.

16.2 You reach the intersection of 2nd Street and George Street in Chesapeake City, MD. Turn around and head back the way that you came.

20.0 Turn left at roundabout to stay on Bethel Church Road.

20.9 Turn left onto US 301/DE 896 North and cross the bridge over the canal.

22.8 Turn right onto DE 71 North.

26.4 Sharp right onto Kirkwood St. Georges Road immediately after the train tracks.

The starting point at Delaware City

29.1 Turn right onto Main Street.

29.3 Turn left onto Delaware Street.

30.0 Turn right onto Cox Neck Road.

33.3 Finish at Battery Park, Delaware City, DE.

Fort on Pea Patch

After the Revolutionary War, the Federal government rebuilt Fort Mifflin on Mud Island, just downriver from Philadelphia, to defend the port and ensure that Philadelphia could never again be taken from the sea. As time passed, however, the US Army saw the need for a fort that was much farther downstream from Philadelphia, so that the invaders could be held at bay while reinforcements arrived. For this purpose, the federal government acquired Pea Patch Island in the Delaware River and built a star-shaped fort on it. A fire damaged this fort in 1831, and two years later, the remainder of the fort was torn down.

It took until 1848 for the Army to start construction on a new fort, and it took until 1859 to complete the new Fort Delaware, but when they were done, the end result was the largest fort in the United States at that time. Two million bricks were used to construct the interior of the fort, and the exterior was constructed from hard gneiss and granite rock.

The fort's eventual main use was to house Confederate prisoners of war during the Civil War. Its location on an island made it the ideal place for a prison. Barracks and hospital buildings were therefore built outside the fort, and Confederate prisoners were transferred to the fort's grounds. Prisoners from the Battle of Gettysburg were sent straight to Pea Patch Island. By August 1863, the prison population swelled to 11,000 prisoners. Over the course of the war, 33,000 prisoners spent at least some time in the prison on Pea Patch Island. Of those prisoners, 2,500 prisoners died, mainly from illness. Half of the deaths took place during a smallpox epidemic in 1863. One hundred nine Union soldiers and 40 civilians also died on the island during the war.

The Civil War also revealed that steam-powered ships could run past standard masonry forts with acceptable levels of damage, and that ships could punch holes in the walls from a distance with powerful rifled cannon. Soon after the Civil War, construction stopped on forts like Fort Delaware in favor of earthen fortifications, which could be repaired simply by dumping dirt into the shellholes. The completion of Fort Delaware therefore marked the end of an era in fort construction.

RIDE INFORMATION

Events/Attractions

Fort Delaware State Park, 45 Clinton St., Delaware City, DE; (302) 834-7941; destateparks.com/park/fort-delaware, features its namesake fort on Pea Patch Island in the Delaware River, with historical exhibits and reenactors in Civil War costume. Access is by ferry only. The ferry runs in the spring and summer, and on a limited basis in the fall.

The St. Georges Bridge has a clearance of 133 feet over the Chesapeake and Delaware Canal, making the bridge one of the tallest "hills" in Delaware south of I-95.

Lums Pond State Park, 1068 Howell School Rd., Bear, DE; (302) 368-6989; destateparks.com/park/lums-pond, features the largest freshwater pond in Delaware, a campground that's open year-round, and an extensive network of trails for hiking, horseback riding, and mountain biking.

Restrooms

Start/end: The Fort Delaware State Park ferry terminal has toilets and water.
Mile 16.2: Chesapeake City, MD, has a number of businesses with toilets.
Mile 24.3: Lums Pond Campground has toilets and water.

Maps

Delorme Maryland Delaware Atlas & Gazetteer: Page 79

Rides at a Glance

3–20 MILES

30. Cooper River Park Ride: 3.7 miles
2. Falls Bridge: 8 miles
39. White Clay Creek State Park: 8.6 miles
20. Tyler State Park: 8.9 miles
15. Valley Forge Ride: 9.4 miles
11. John Heinz Ride: 9.5 miles
32. Wharton State Forest: 9.8 miles
8. Fairmount Park: 10 miles
3. Forbidden Drive: 10 miles
4. Battleship *New Jersey:* 10.1 miles
1. Center City Tour: 10.2 miles
27. Devon Ramble: 10.9 miles
9. Airport Loop: 12.6 miles
31. Brendan Byrne State Forest: 12.8 miles
14. Cobbs Creek Ride: 13.6 miles
17. Washington Crossing Ride: 15.1 miles
7. Bryn Athyn Cathedral: 16.1 miles
36. Smith's Bridge: 16.6 miles
25. Perkiomen Trail Ride: 18.3 miles
5. The Manayunk Wall: 19 miles
10. Pennypack Park: 19.2 miles

20–30 MILES

37. Newark Ramble: 20.3 miles
29. Brandywine South: 21 miles
24. Farm to Farm Ride: 22.6 miles
26. Ridley Creek State Park: 23.1 miles
22. Green Lane: 25.2 miles
28. Longwood Gardens: 25.2 miles
16. Fort Washington: 25.4 miles
12. Center City Connector: 26.5 miles
6. Schuylkill River Trail Ride: 26.5 miles
21. D&R Canal Towpath Trail: 27 miles

34. Batsto Village: 27.8 miles
19. Lake Nockamixon: 29.4 miles
38. Blackbird Loop: 29.6 miles

30–40 MILES

33. Nixon's General Store Ride: 30.7 miles
23. Bucks County Covered Bridges: 33.1 miles
40. Crossing Delaware Ride: 33.3 miles
18. Doylestown: 33.9 miles

40 MILES AND UP

13. Ambler Ramble: 45.1 miles
35. Philadelphia to Atlantic City: 63.2 miles

Bicycling Resources

There are a lot of good places to find information about biking. This section contains a brief list of the best ones to help you find more information about biking in and around Philadelphia.

WEBSITES

There are many good websites where you can find information about biking. Here are a few of our favorites.

The Bicycle Coalition of Greater Philadelphia (bicyclecoalition.org) is a nonprofit bicycle advocacy group that works to promote and improve bicycling in Philadelphia and the surrounding counties as well as South Jersey and Delaware. This site has a lot of information about bike safety, safe bike routes, information about important bike legislation, bike education, and much more. The Bicycle Coalition also hosts an annual bike event called Bike Philly, which is the city's biggest bicycle event.

PennDOT's Bike Safe Website (dot.state.pa.us/bike/web/index.htm) contains information about bicycle safety, laws, and a nice tour section that contains bicycle routes throughout the state.

NJ Bike Map (njbikemap.com) should be your first stop if you plan on riding a bike in or near New Jersey. This site contains over 190 detailed street-level maps of New Jersey and surrounding states. These maps have a great color-coded system that shows the best and most scenic roads to ride on as well as where to park, get food, camp and much more.

Montgomery County Trails (trails.montcopa.org/trails) contains information about all the great trails in Montgomery County, including the Perkiomen, Schuylkill, and others.

Pennsylvania State Park Web Site (dcnr.state.pa.us/stateparks) contains information about all of the state parks in Pennsylvania, including information about biking in the various parks.

Delaware Bicycle Council (deldot.gov/information/community_programs_and_services/bike/index.shtml) was formed by the state of Delaware to create policies and facilities to promote biking and improve the biking infrastructure in the state. This site contains a wealth of information about biking in the state, including detailed bike maps for each county.

Map My Ride (mapmyride.com) is a great site to search for bike routes or create and share your own.

Bike Kinetix (bikekinetix.com) is a good resource to find mountain bike trails in the northeast.

BICYCLE CLUBS

Joining a bike club is the best way to learn the best roads and places to ride and meet like-minded people. Novice riders will especially benefit from joining a club and learning valuable bike handling skills from experienced riders. Most bicycle clubs publish a list each month of rides of various lengths and difficulties so you can usually find a ride that fits your ability. The Philadelphia area has a lot of great bicycle clubs; some more popular ones are listed below.

Bicycle Club of Philadelphia (BCP) (phillybikeclub.org) is a great club that offers a wide variety of rides of all abilities each month in and around Philadelphia. They also are very active in the community and work with the Bicycle Coalition of Greater Philadelphia to help promote and improve bicycling in Philadelphia. If you regularly ride in Philadelphia, you should check out this club.

Suburban Cyclists Unlimited (suburbancyclists.org/quad.htm) is a group of recreational cyclists who ride the areas of Montgomery and Bucks Counties. They also host two great events each year: the Quad County Metric and the Lake Nockamixon Century Ride.

Central Bucks Bicycle Club (cbbikeclub.org) is based in Bucks County and is an active group of recreational cyclists that offers a variety of rides each month and hosts the popular Covered Bridge Ride each fall.

South Jersey Wheelmen (sjwheelmen.org), a South Jersey club based in the Vineland area, offers rides in Cumberland, Gloucester, and Salem Counties in New Jersey and hosts a number of events including the Jersey Devil Century.

White Clay Bicycle Club (whiteclaybicycleclub.org) is based in northern Delaware and offers a wide variety of rides in Delaware, Pennsylvania, Maryland, and New Jersey. They also host a number of great events each year, including the Shorefire Century.

ORGANIZED RIDES

Part of the fun of riding a bicycle is participating in the many events and organized rides in your area. These are great opportunities to get out in mass with many other cyclists on tried-and-true routes with great support and amenities. Some of these rides are also for a good cause so besides having a good time you will be supporting a good charity. Below is a small sampling of the many events in and around Philadelphia.

Bike Philly (bikephilly.org) is the second Sunday in September and is a ride through the streets of Philadelphia. There is a 10- and 20-mile loop through closed, car-free streets and a longer 35-mile loop on shared roads.

Scenic Schuylkill Century (phillybikeclub.org) is the day before Bike Philly and is run by the Bicycle Club of Philadelphia (BCP). This event has rides of 25, 40, 65, or 100 miles through Philadelphia and Montgomery County.

Covered Bridge Ride (cbbikeclub.org), held in early October, is run by the Central Bucks Bicycle Club and features 20-, 30-, 33-, 50-, or 63-mile rides through the roads of Bucks County and includes visits to some of the covered bridges.

Quad County Metric (suburbancyclists.org/quadcounty.asp), put on by the Suburban Cyclists Unlimited, is usually the second weekend in May and starts from Green Lane Park in Montgomery County. The event features rides of 21, 31, 45, 53, 68, and 76 miles on scenic, low-traffic back roads.

Lake Nockamixion (suburbancyclists.org), in the end of August, is put on by the Suburban Cyclists Unlimited and starts in Doylestown. It has rides of 25, 50, 75, 100, and 107 miles through the quiet roads of Bucks County.

Shorefire Century (whiteclaybicycleclub.org), an event of the White Clay Bicycle Club, at the end of August, starts in Middletown, DE, and features rides of 35, 65, or 100 miles on flat-to-gently-rolling terrain in central Delaware and Maryland's Eastern Shore.

Jersey Devil Century (sjwheelmen.org/jersey_devil_century.htm): This South Jersey Wheelmen event starts at Parvin State Park, Centerton, NJ, and features rides of 25, 50, 75, or 100 miles on the flat terrain of the New Jersey farmlands.

Greater Philadelphia Tour de Cure offers easy 3- and 12-mile rides as well as longer 35-mile and 63-mile rides. It's a fun event that supports the American Diabetes Association, which helps to prevent and cure diabetes.

Ride of Silence is an international event ride organized by various bicycle clubs to honor those who have been killed or injured while on a bike. This is a free, silent, slow-paced ride, usually held during National Bike Month. In Philadelphia the ride is held on the third Wednesday of May and starts from the base of the Art Museum steps.

Gran Fondo Colnago Philadelphia. A Gran Fondo is a luxury biking event geared toward the performance-oriented bikers who enjoy challenging rides and competing against others. This is not really a race, but all cyclists are usually timed and prizes are awarded in different categories. This is an expensive event but the rides, support, and food are first class.

Covered Bridge Metric Century is a beautiful mid-August ride through Lancaster County and through some covered bridges organized by the Lancaster Bicycle Club (lancasterbikeclub.org).

American Cancer Society Bike-a-Thon is a well-organized and -attended charity ride held in mid-July. The ride starts at Independence Mall and heads over the Ben Franklin Bridge into New Jersey for a 60-mile-plus ride to Buena, NJ. Short ride options are also available.

Index

About the Authors

Tom Hammell has liked riding a bike as long as he can remember. As an avid bike rider and ride leader he enjoys exploring the roads of the tri-state area with his friends. You can follow his adventures on his blog at frisket.blogspot.com.

Tom Hammell

Mark Ploegstra is an avid cyclist who has crossed many states by bicycle. He sometimes loads his bike with a week's camping gear, and sometimes with just enough to go across town. No matter how much he carries, though, he always enjoys life best from the seat of a bicycle.

Mark Ploegstra